Towards Inclusive Learning in Higher Education

This authoritative overview brings together current thinking about disability and academic pedagogy in higher education and explores how developing good practice for disabled students is good practice for all students. It demonstrates how inclusive provision can be achieved through innovative thinking about practice to ensure an equality of opportunity, and not necessarily just through significant expenditure or time. Including international contributions, topics covered include:

- transition and access into higher education
- current barriers to inclusive education
- communication and information technology
- employability and work placements
- examination and assessment
- quality assurance and benchmark descriptors

Drawing on existing good practice across the higher education sector, *Towards Inclusive Learning in Higher Education* provides a valuable source of practical information and established interventions for all practitioners who teach and support in higher education institutions.

Mike Adams is Assistant Director for Delivery and Learning at the Disability Rights Commission. He was previously Director of the National Disability Team, which provided consultancy services to higher education institutions in England and Northern Ireland. He has a wealth of experience in learning and teaching related issues, has produced a wide range of papers for conferences and has been published in refereed journals both in the UK and abroad.

Sally Brown is Professor of Higher Education Diversity and Pro-Vice-Chancellor at Leeds Metropolitan University with responsibility for assessment, learning and teaching. She is also a visiting Professor at the Robert Gordon University. She was for five years Director of Membership Services for the Institute for Learning and Teaching and has published widely on teaching, learning, and particularly assessment.

Towards Inclusive Learning in Higher Education

Developing curricula for disabled students

Edited by Mike Adams and
Sally Brown

Routledge
Taylor & Francis Group

LONDON AND NEW YORK

First published 2006 by Routledge
2 Park Square, Milton Park, Abingdon, Oxon, OX14 4RN

Simultaneously published in the USA and Canada
by Routledge
270 Madison Ave, New York, NY 10016

Routledge is an imprint of the Taylor & Francis Group, an informa business

Typeset in Times New Roman by
Keystroke, Jacaranda Lodge, Wolverhampton
Printed and bound in Great Britain by
TJ International Ltd, Padstow, Cornwall

British Library Cataloguing in Publication Data
A catalogue record for this book is available from the British Library

Library of Congress Cataloging in Publication Data
A catalog record for this book has been requested

ISBN10: 0–415–36528–7 (hbk)
ISBN10: 0–415–36529–5 (pbk)
ISBN10: 0–203–08862–X (ebk)

ISBN13: 978–0–415–36528–4 (hbk)
ISBN13: 978–0–415–36529–1 (pbk)
ISBN13: 978–0–203–08862–3 (ebk)

This book is dedicated to my mum and dad whose love, support and determination always made sure my potential was maximised. To my wife, Amanda, who has shared in the journey of producing this book, and as editorial assistant has worked to ensure that quality and deadlines have been met. To Mary, my personal assistant at the time the book was conceived, for all her support in ensuring administrative arrangements were in place. And to Sally Brown, my co-author for all her guidance, support and committed enthusiasm in making the production of this book such a positive experience.

Mike Adams

Contents

List of illustrations

Figures

Tables

Contributors

Mike Adams is Assistant Director of Delivery and Learning at the Disability Rights Commission. He was previously the Director of the National Disability Team, which provided consultancy services to higher education institutions in England and Northern Ireland. Mike has a wealth of experience in issues concerned with learning and teaching and has produced a range of papers for conferences and publication in refereed journals, both in the UK and abroad.

Victoria Boyd is a Learning Technologist. Victoria is a member of the Learning Technologies Team at the University of Durham and is an officer on the ALERT project.

Andrew Bradley is a Lecturer in Events Management and Sports Tourism at the University of Gloucestershire. His research interests are in the increasing importance of events as a mechanism of place marketing and the integration of sport and tourism. His pedagogic publications relate to the learning experiences of disabled students, the understanding that undergraduates in the field of geography have of their discipline, and student learning styles.

Sally Brown is Professor of Higher Education Diversity in Learning and Teaching at Leeds Metropolitan University and a visiting professor at the University of Hertfordshire, the Robert Gordon University and at Buckinghamshire Chilterns University College. She publishes widely and undertakes consultancy on issues of policy and practice in higher education teaching, learning and particularly assessment in the UK and internationally.

Helen Carlisle is the Project Manager for Academic Standards and Benchmark Descriptors: Developing Strategies for Inclusivity at the University of Worcester. Helen has been responsible for the day-to-day management of the project since its inception in January 2003. She has a degree in library and information science and 10 years' experience of working in information management.

Val Chapman was author and director of the project, 'Academic Standards and Benchmark Descriptors: Developing Strategies for Inclusivity' at the

University of Worcester. Her work in the area of Equal Opportunities in Higher Education in the UK was recognised in 2004 by the award of a National Teaching Fellowship and, more recently, by the designation of the Equal Opportunities Centre at University College Worcester as a Centre of Excellence in Learning Teaching (one of 16 HEI partners forming 'LearnHigher').

Val Farrar is a Project Officer at the University of Newcastle upon Tyne. Val has coordinated two projects in disability issues in higher education. She has worked as a teacher, adviser and researcher for 30 years, mainly in further, community and higher education with students with learning difficulties and disabled students.

Benedict Fell is a Research Assistant within the Faculty of Health and Social Care at the University of Hull. Benedict is a qualified social worker with experience of working in the fields of mental health and care management. His research interests include disability issues, adult social care and social work education.

Todd Fernie is a Recruitment Support/Disability Awareness Development Officer at Auckland University of Technology, New Zealand. His role in the university is to create awareness among teaching and non-teaching staff of the rights and issues pertaining to people with impairment. Todd works from a 'Social Model' and 'Economic Model' foundation, in conjunction with 'Social Role Valorization' principles.

Mary Fuller is Professor of Education at the University of Gloucestershire and Director of ESRC TLRP project 'Enhancing the Quality and Outcomes of Disabled Students' Learning in Higher Education'. Her research and teaching interests are in social justice and inclusivity in educational settings. She has authored more than 40 research-based publications on equalities and inclusion in school and higher education, from projects on disability, gender and 'race'.

Tim Hall is a Senior Lecturer in Geography at the University of Gloucestershire. He is author of *Urban Geography* (2001) and *Everyday Geography* (forthcoming) and co-editor of a number of volumes on the city. His pedagogic publications include 'Fieldwork and disabled students: discourses of exclusion and inclusion' (with Mick Healey and Margaret Harrison) (*Transactions of the Institute of British Geographers*, 2002) which was the winner of the *Journal of Geography in Higher Education* Biennial Award in 2004. He is also a member of the Geography Discipline Network Inclusive Curriculum Project team.

Tracey Hall is a Senior Research Scientist and Instructional Designer at the Center for Applied Special Technology (CAST), Wakefield, MA, specializing in alternative assessment and instructional design grounded in effective teaching practices. Tracey served as Director of Curriculum for the US National Center on Accessing the General Curriculum (1999–2004), led by CAST. Before joining CAST, Tracey was an Assistant Professor at Pennsylvania State University in the Department of Educational and School Psychology and Special Education, where she co-directed a federally funded Model Demonstration project, 'Reading and Intensive Learning Strategies (RAILS): A Model of Early Reading Instruction with Progress Monitoring'. She has been a special education teacher and administrator in public schools in Oregon. More recently, she has provided consultation at national and international levels.

Mick Healey is Professor of Geography at the University of Gloucestershire; Director of Geography Discipline Network; Co-Director of ESRC TLRP project 'Enhancing the Quality and Outcomes of Disabled Students' Learning in Higher Education'; Director of the Centre for Active Learning in Geography, Environment and Related Disciplines; and Senior Adviser to the Higher Education Academy Subject Centre for Geography, Earth and Environmental Sciences. In the past 10 years, Mick has given over 180 conference papers and educational presentations worldwide and has published over 80 books, articles, chapters and guides on teaching and learning in higher education, including linking research and teaching, active learning and disability.

Marcus Henning is a Senior Lecturer at Auckland University of Technology, New Zealand. He is a registered psychologist and teacher. He has been involved in university-related research projects associated with neuropsychology, learning disabilities and medical education.

Sarah Holland is the Researcher for the National Disability Team, Chelmsford, Essex, where she is responsible for gathering information to support members of the NDT and staff within the higher education sector. She has experience in quantitative and qualitative research methodologies and in the design and management of research projects. Sarah is a science graduate and holds a PhD in biology.

Alan Hurst is a Professor in the Department of Education and Social Sciences at the University of Central Lancashire. Alan is also a trustee of Skill: National Bureau for Students with Disabilities and chairs its Higher Education Working Party. He has published books and articles and been invited to lecture and lead workshops on disability in higher education in many countries.

Tony Koppi is an Associate Professor and Director of the Educational Development and Technology Centre (EDTeC) University of New South Wales, Australia. The Centre is concerned with supporting teaching staff in the use of all forms of educational technologies to enhance the student learning experience. Previously he was a research scientist with the Australian Government and a lecturer and thus is aware of the needs and circumstances of teaching staff in a research-intensive university.

Judith Mole is Director of Direct Learn Services Ltd. Judith is a consultant in d/Deafness and disability issues. She has worked as an interpreter, lecturer and support service manager and now writes on support issues for deaf students.

Barbara Newland is a Senior Lecturer in Educational Development based at Bournemouth University. Barbara has over 12 years' experience of supporting the effective use of e-learning. Prior to joining Bournemouth University in 2003, Barbara was the Learning Technology Team Leader at the University of Durham, where she was responsible for developing the university's e-learning strategy including the implementation of Blackboard.

Bethan O'Neil has worked with CADISE, the Consortium of Arts and Design Institutions in Southern England since its inception in 1999, first, as its Co-ordinator, and latterly in the role of Executive Director. Previously she held curriculum posts in both further and higher education, working closely on inclusivity issues, both in terms of promoting wider access and partnerships and in learner enhancement.

Melanie Parker is Project Coordinator on the SPACE (Staff–Student Partnership for Assessment Change and Evaluation) Project at the University of Plymouth and has contributed to journal articles and written various conference papers. Melanie is currently studying for a Doctorate in Education through the University of Sheffield, which is concerned with educational inclusion in post-modernity.

Juliette Pavey is a Learning Technologist. Juliette is a member of the Learning Technologies Team at the University of Durham. Her role is to encourage, support and develop e-learning throughout the university.

Diane Peacock is a freelance Art and Design Educational Adviser at Wolverhampton University, project developer and teacher. Diane worked in FE and HE art and design education for 30 years before becoming a freelance adviser in 2003. She is particularly interested in creativity, student support and the 'language' of learning.

Elaine Pearson is Director of the Special Needs Computing Research Unit at the University of Teesside and Principal Lecturer in the School of Computing. Elaine has a PhD in multimedia programmes for the development and assessment of language in children with special needs. Her particular research expertise is currently in the field of accessibility and online learning, with wider research interests in all aspects of inclusive computing. She publishes and presents papers nationally and internationally on accessibility issues and is a member of the conference review committees for EDMEDIA and ALT and a referee for a number of journals including *ALT-J* and *IJEL*.

David Sloan is Project Lead at the Digital Media Access Group, Division of Applied Computing, based at the University of Dundee. David has been involved in the area of accessibility and usability of information and commu-nication technology for disabled people since 1999. He has advised many clients in the commercial, public and higher education sectors on accessible web and software design, and has also been involved in a number of academic research projects investigating accessibility and usability issues applied to technology, including the HEFCE-funded Skills for Access project.

Skip Stahl is Director of Technical Assistance at the Center for Applied Special Technology (CAST), Wakefield, MA, and is Project Director for the National Instructional Materials Accessibility Standard (NIMAS) Development Center, a cooperative agreement between CAST and the United States Department of Education, Office of Special Education Programs. Skip has extensive experience providing leadership in the application of Universal Design to instructional practice in both K–12 and in postsecondary settings. Skip directs CAST's Universal Learning Center, an initiative implementing the transformation of textbooks into specialized accessible formats for students with print disabilities. Skip is the author of over 20 articles published in peer-reviewed, popular, and trade publications, and contributes a regular technology column to *Counterpoint*, a publication of the National Association of Directors of Special Education (U.S.). He is a consultant for a number of national elementary, secondary, and higher education initiatives focused on Universal Design for Learning.

Sarah Stone is the Project Coordinator of the Skills for Access project and is based at the Learning Development and Media Unit at the University of Sheffield. She works closely with the production teams based in Sheffield and Dundee and coordinates the activities of the project. She recently graduated with a Master's degree in Human Communication and Computing which is where she first became interested in accessible and usable design of digital media.

John Stratford is Director of the Learning Development and Media Unit and is based at the University of Sheffield. John has spent most of his career in media production for education and training, and his unit at the University of Sheffield produces a wide range of high quality multimedia and e-learning materials. His approach to accessibility is as a practitioner looking to ensure multimedia empowers learning for the largest numbers of people with the minimum of compromise.

Anne Tynan is Director of DIVERSE – the UK Veterinary Medicine Disability project, based at the Royal Veterinary College, University of London. Anne has worked on disability-related projects at the University of Glasgow, the London Science Museum and the University of London, acting also as an adviser to the British Office of the Deputy Prime Minister, 2000–2003. She has an international reputation as a writer on disability issues including a book on attitudes to disability (1997), three major reports for the veterinary and medical sectors (2001–2004), and numerous articles and conference papers.

Judith Waterfield is Head of Disability Assist Services at the University of Plymouth and is involved in supporting strategic planning, review and practice for inclusivity. Judith has contributed to chapters, articles and editorials for journals, books and conference papers. She has also been Project Manager on five HEFCE Projects related to Special Initiative Funding and Widening Participation and has recently been awarded a National Teaching Fellowship (NTF) to look at Universal Design in learning, teaching and assessment.

Bob West Since the mid-1980s, Bob has worked to support the aspirations of disabled people in further and higher education in the UK, specifically in the fields of assessing learning support needs and staff development. His recent involvement has centred on creating guidance and audit tools for higher education academic staff to help establish legislative compliance in the sector. He is currently working on proposals to encourage inclusive assessment practices for the broadest cohort of students, including those who are disabled.

Kate Wilson is currently Director of Ashford Excellence Cluster. Kate has worked as a practitioner, teacher and manager within specialist creative arts HEIs and more recently in primary and secondary schools. Her management roles have focused on multi-disciplinary practice, on teaching and learning and on progression, access, inclusion and diversity. Much of her work has been done in the context of collaborative partnerships, including the CADISE consortium.

Jane Wray is a Research Fellow within the Faculty of Health and Social Care at the University of Hull. Jane has worked in the field of higher education research for 10 years and has undertaken a range of projects including working with disabled people and their families, with children with challenging behaviour, advocacy, social inclusion and discrimination. She has worked as the Disability Officer at the University of Hull and was the PEdDS project manager.

Foreword

A few years ago we featured on *In Touch*, Radio 4's programme for visually impaired people, the case of a blind mature student who was experiencing considerable difficulties on her drama course. Some of them concerned the usual problems of getting the right equipment, and persuading tutors to give her information in an accessible form, but by far the greatest problem for her was the difficulty of getting staff to treat her as the responsible adult she was. It was typified for her in a phrase used when she went on to explain some of the problems she was facing to her tutor. 'So, who looks after you, then?' he asked.

This was a woman who was bringing up a family, running a home, and fitting in a full-time university course at the same time, and it illustrates perfectly the mindset that I hope this book will help to eradicate. Legislation such as Part 4 of the Disability Discrimination Act (2005) places responsibilities on higher education institutions to ensure that disabled students are neither deliberately or negligently put at a disadvantage, but they cannot on their own ensure that staff regard disabled people as equals, who might occasionally need to have things done in a different way.

You would perhaps expect centres where the brightest minds in the country are gathered to be full of people who wouldn't find this idea too difficult to grasp, but I'm afraid my own experience as a disabled student 40 years ago confirmed for me the unoriginal perception that having a keen academic mind was no absolute guarantee of common sense. Forty years on, we are much more dedicated to the idea of inclusion, as Lady Warnock, chair of the committee which originally espoused the idea of integration in our schools in the 1970s, has pointed out as she agonises over some of the problems her well-meant policy has encountered. People find difficulty with a concept which asks them to treat disabled people equally, while still maintaining the extra adaptations that a physical or a sensory loss is bound to involve. I cannot be equal without Braille; Tani Grey-Thompson cannot be equal without ramps; a deaf student cannot be equal without signers and interpreters; and none of us can be equal if academic and support staff don't understand that 'inclusion' means far more than just being in the same lecture room as everyone else: it means being able to take part fully in the life of the institution; joining the societies, enjoying the social life, and being treated with informed respect. This book is an attempt to give all those connected with the teaching and learning of disabled students in higher education both a theoretical and practical understanding of how to make this approach towards an equality of opportunity a reality. It's long overdue, and I commend it to you.

Peter White
BBC Disability Affairs Correspondent
July 2005

Introduction

Mike Adams and Sally Brown

In many developed countries there have been major developments in higher education to improve provision for disabled students. One of the key catalysts for this change in emphasis has been the emergence of government policies to widen participation in higher education generally, which have focused attention on a need to actively consider access for 'non-traditional' groups of students. These policies have led to a significant improvement in both the quality and quantity of services offered to disabled people (Adams and Brown 2000).

In England, this commitment to widening access was reflected by the introduction of specific disability funding programmes by the Higher Education Funding Council for England (HEFCE 1994). The original focus concentrated on two traditional areas of activity. First, the funding was used to improve the physical state of institutions which included the installation of lifts, ramps and adaptations to halls of residences to enable disabled students to live on campus. Second, the funding was used to develop the organisational infrastructure of institutions to support disabled students on a daily basis. The role of the Disability Officer was established to coordinate students' support needs and ensure appropriate equipment and levels of personal care were provided. At this time, the locus of disability support was firmly located in student welfare departments, although its wider impact did raise awareness across those funded institutions (Parker 1998).

Similar funding programmes were also being established in other countries. In Scotland, funding was provided to all of the 18 higher education institutions (HEIs) within the sector at that time to support the development of a disability adviser. In Australia, a series of pump-priming initiatives were introduced to heighten awareness of the issues so that equality of opportunity in all aspects of an institution's activities must explicitly include that for disabled people (DEET 1990). Tough targets, in terms of recruiting disabled students, were set and institutions were expected to identify and implement a range of strategies to address identified barriers to participation. This policy was later superseded by the introduction of the Australian Disability Act 1992 which imposed a duty on HEIs to make adjustments to ensure that disabled people were not discriminated against in applying to, or succeeding in, higher education.

The situation in the United States was somewhat different. The Americans with Disabilities Act 1990 had built significantly on earlier legislation (Rehabilitation Act 1973) by extending Section 504, which prohibited discrimination on the grounds of disability by HEIs in receipt of financial grants from the federal state (West *et al.* 1993). Section 504 had been specifically related to the accessibility of academic programmes only, meaning that institutions were not required to establish a totally barrier-free environment as long as they did not significantly hinder participation on academic courses. Following the 1990 legislation, however, resources were much more evenly spread between funding innovative programmes to address access to the curricula, and employing disability advisers and improving physical access to the campus; this focus on teaching and learning inevitably involved the active participation of academic staff who engaged greater numbers of disabled people to accept places at their institution. Further details on developments in the United States are explored in Chapter 6 by Stahl and Hall.

Although disabled students still remain under-represented in higher education, direct policies and activities are starting to have an impact. For example, in the UK, 5.4 per cent of all UK undergraduate students in higher education (121,085 students) self-assessed themselves as having an impairment in 2003–4 (NDT 2005). In Australia, 3.0 per cent of non-overseas students declared an impairment in 2000 (Fraser and Sanders 2005) and 6.0 per cent of undergraduate students in the United States are recorded as having an impairment (DO-IT no date). These figures are increasing, it appears, largely because improved support services, stimulated by legislation and quality assurance codes of practice, are encouraging more disabled students to enter higher education and declare their impairments. However, the statistics underestimate actual numbers as many students, particularly those with mental health difficulties and various unseen impairments, choose not to declare. In the UK, 41 per cent of disabled students in higher education in 2003–4 have dyslexia and 20 per cent have an unseen impairment (such as epilepsy, diabetes and asthma) with no other category accounting for more than 10 per cent (except 'other impairments' – 12 per cent) (NDT 2005).

Although there is no published evidence, there is clearly a causal link between the increase in student numbers and the significant developments taken to improve services within higher education institutions. However, there have been ongoing issues regarding the differences between the concepts of 'access' and 'participation'. Institutions, particularly in the UK, sought to improve their physical environment yet continued to disadvantage students by restricting access to, and participation within, the broader curricula delivered in those buildings.

The impact of anti-discrimination legislation in the UK

In the UK, a focus on the participation of learning and teaching issues was stimulated by the introduction of anti-discrimination legislation. In the original Disability Discrimination Act 1995, education provision was omitted and only later amended through the Special Educational Needs and Disability Act (SENDA) 2001. In ways similar to the Australian experience, education providers are now required to ensure reasonable measures are undertaken to avoid discrimination and that reasonable adjustments are made (DRC 2002).

This need to ensure reasonable adjustments is an important shift in emphasis. Hitherto, the implicit institutional stance regarding disabled students (and indeed all students) had been that they should 'fit in' to the traditional education model offered (Porter 1994). The discriminatory nature of this approach is power- fully outlined in Chapter 10 by Mole and Peacock in terms of deaf students having to integrate into traditional styles of learning. Although the onus of instigating litigation is placed on the disabled person, HEIs are still required to prove they have not discriminated and/or failed to make reasonable adjustments. The new Disability Discrimination Act 2005 will further require HEIs to be proactive in their provision for disabled students. Compliance notices can be issued by external agencies rather than solely the individual involved which should enhance opportunities to ensure due consideration to the delivery of equitable services is given (DDA 2005).

As part of the preparation for SENDA, Directors of the English and Scottish Disability Teams visited higher education providers in Australia (including the equivalent of the UK funding councils) to identify the impact of anti- discrimination legislation and the lessons learned from their experience to inform policies and strategies for the UK. The methods of meeting the needs of disabled students were remarkably similar in each country in so far as 'disability liaison officers' were primarily responsible as the locus for all support. Most legal cases which had ended up in court related to issues concerning teaching and learning. As with the UK experience, there appeared to be a disengagement in actively addressing disability issues by the academic community.

A report was produced (Adams and Brown 2001) which recommended that any future funding programmes should specifically address learning and teaching and require the participation of academic staff. In addition, the HEFCE commissioned a mapping exercise to identify existing resources and materials for the learning and teaching of disabled students (French 2002). This study identified a dearth of resources particularly related to individual subject-specific level issues, materials based directly on the views and experiences of disabled students, and resources related to work placements, e-learning and study abroad.

The HEFCE funding programme

The current HEFCE funding programme supports 24 projects which have a direct remit to 'develop, promote and transfer activity which will help institutions across the sector to develop and enhance learning and teaching provision for disabled students' (HEFCE 2002). Each project engages the active involvement of aca- demic staff, disability practitioners and disabled students themselves, who best know their own impairments and how they are likely to impact on their study.

It is recognised that this partnership approach is imperative, if innovative solutions are to be found to enable disabled students to fully engage in the curriculum. Conversely, the active involvement of academic staff is fundamental if inclusive practices are to be sustained.

Inclusive practice

The issue of moving towards inclusive practice is the primary focus of this book. In a landmark report, John Tomlinson (FEFC 1996) stressed that inclusive learning is an educational idea fundamental to good teaching and learning practice. For most higher education institutions, this will require a significant cultural shift, from seeing disabled students as 'outsiders coming in', to an institution which openly embraces 'all comers'.

As a starting point, this shift will require institutions to view all disabled students and staff equally, and view difference as a positive contribution to the lifeblood of an institution, rather than as problems which need to be overcome. An innovative attitude towards identifying the key issues and how these challenges might be incorporated into the day-to-day operation of the institution is required. Specifically, new ways of approaching access to the curriculum will need to be considered with a focus on achievement, rather than the inherent 'deficit model' which is more concerned with what cannot be undertaken. A flexible approach to learning, teaching and assessment needs to be seen as the norm, rather than as an exception for the few. This debate is not about the dilution of academic standards but a recognition of difference, and the creation of a rigorous framework that reflects that position. A recurrent theme throughout all of the chapters is that good practice for disabled students is generally good practice for all students.

Structure of the book

The editors, as Director of the National Disability Team, with a remit for improving provision for disabled students in higher education, and a Professor of Higher Education Diversity in Learning and Teaching, originally conceived the idea for this book as a way of stimulating discussion and leaving an indelible legacy for the academic community. We chose to include chapters by a number of staff involved in HEFCE-funded disability projects as well as including chapters commissioned more widely from the international community, to reflect the broader perspective of disability in higher education. In some cases the chapters represent 'work in progress' while others are more advanced in their analysis, but all are informed by wider issues concerned with the development of an inclusive curriculum.

The book is intended to be read either as a complete volume or as a dip-in resource for those with particular or specialist interests. For this reason readers may encounter some overlap between chapters, particularly in relation to legislative matters and the HEFCE funding programme. To facilitate browsing, we will outline the content of the chapters that follow.

The first group of chapters explore some strategic issues in relation to inclusive practice in higher education. In Chapter 1, Mike Adams and Sarah Holland explore issues that impact on disabled students considering higher education. In reviewing the education journey they identify a range of barriers disabled students confront, which influence the decision-making process in determining whether higher education is an option. An account of the experiences of a disabled student illustrates how difficulties all students can incur can unintentionally be exacerbated for disabled students by staff and institutions if these barriers are not directly addressed. In the second half of the chapter, the authors propose a range of actions and interventions that higher education institutions can make to raise aspirations and facilitate this transition.

In Chapter 2, Todd Fernie and Marcus Henning provide a New Zealand perspective on how academic providers world-wide view disability and the disabled student. The authors explore the social and historical discourses that have impacted, directly and indirectly, on teaching and learning environments for disabled students. They conclude by offering some pragmatic ideas about how the future higher education landscape needs to develop to further ensure inclusive provision for disabled people.

In Chapter 3, Mick Healey, Andrew Bradley, Mary Fuller and Tim Hall make use of systematic surveys undertaken at the University of Gloucestershire and other HEIs to find out what disabled students themselves have to say about their experiences on entry to higher education. They also utilise a substantial survey to contrast the experience of a large sample of disabled and non-disabled students studying in the same institution. The authors have extensive experience of working on disability matters in the UK and internationally, and draw on this experience to reflect on and analyse the outputs of their work.

Chapter 4 by Val Chapman and Helen Carlisle provides an overview of work undertaken reviewing how the HEFCE's Quality Assurance Agency Subject Benchmarking exercise impacted on the experiences of disabled students. The project examined the use and perception of Benchmark Statements by staff in HEIs and the extent to which they promoted inclusive practice. The chapter is enlivened by an interspersed commentary by one of the authors acting as a participant observer working within a higher education institution. While the experiences are UK-based, there is a great deal of learning that is transferable to wider contexts internationally about how national regulatory frameworks impact (for better or worse) on higher education practice.

For staff to engage fully with inclusive flexible learning approaches, they need effective and relevant support in the design and development of materials. In Chapter 5, Elaine Pearson and Tony Koppi, using as a basis for their writing a bi-national project they undertook in the UK and Australia, discuss the design rationale that underpins their staff development activities. They also describe their evaluation approach which aimed to discover whether staff received appropriate, targeted and timely training in accessibility to ensure inclusive practices were adopted across the board.

Chapter 6 by Tracey Hall and Skip Stahl provides a US perspective on how the education framework of Universal Design for Learning can be infused within higher education practice. Examples of universal designed goals are considered to reflect the needs of students with a broad range of impairments. The chapter culminates with a treatise about the effective use of alternative assessment strategies to track the progress of, and inform future curriculum innovations for, all students.

Chapter 7 by Judith Waterfield, Bob West and Melanie Parker is entitled 'Supporting inclusive practice: developing an assessment toolkit'. Fair assessment arrangements are often high on the lists of concerns about inclusive practice raised by academic staff. Here the authors outline the benefits of developing alternative assessment practices to avoid the use of *ad hoc* arrangements which treat disabled students as 'special cases'. Instead they argue for an inclusive approach to assessment design, and as a result of an action research project, they provide some useful tools for others wishing to emulate their approach.

The next pair of chapters offer perspectives on particular issues for two cognate subject areas. Chapter 8 by Bethan O'Neil and Kate Wilson is entitled 'Learning, teaching and disabled students: challenging traditional models of support'. Based on the work of a consortium of specialist institutions, the chapter highlights the complexity and challenges facing smaller institutions as they mainstream disability matters at both subject and institutional level. Drawing on real case studies, the authors identify a range of learning outcomes to inform both future policy and practice.

Anne Tynan asks in Chapter 9 the extent to which Vetinerary and Medical Schools can be made accessible to disabled people. Traditionally the issue of admission of disabled students onto courses such as these has been highly contentious, with worries expressed about the cost of training for students who may not ultimately be able to practise in their chosen professions. Once the issue of omnicompetence has been tackled, however, and limited licensing has been considered, the author shows how an inclusive approach can be taken. She suggests that the principal barriers are in relation to the ways in which admissions staff view disabled applicants, rather than the students' inherent capability.

Looking next at a particular area of disability, in Chapter 10, 'Language issues for deaf students in higher education', Judith Mole and Diane Peacock illustrate some of the communication and linguistic difficulties facing deaf people entering higher education and show how the system consistently fails to provide appropriate support. They offer some advice to HEIs and individuals on principles of good practice and provide practical pointers for the future.

Two chapters follow on how we can best use information technologies to support inclusive practice. In Chapter 11, David Sloan, Sarah Stone and John Stratford outline ways in which multimedia elements within e-learning resources can enhance the learning experiences of disabled students to ensure that the resources are accessible. The authors argue against the trend among some multimedia designers and academic staff to shy away from engaging fully with e-learning out of misplaced fear that inclusivity issues make it all just too difficult to handle. They advocate the approach used in the Skills for Access Project, which has taken a collaborative attitude to maximising the accessibility of multimedia and they offer some pointers to sensible decision-making at the design stage of multimedia learning materials.

In Chapter 12, Barbara Newland, Victoria Boyd and Juliette Pavey take the topic further by describing how learning can be enabled and enhanced using Virtual Learning Environments (VLEs) and how this can then be used to support effective and enjoyable learning by disabled students. They argue that blended learning can provide opportunities to combine flexibility and inclusivity, as well as breaking down some of the physical barriers to learning that disabled students can experience. The authors conclude by providing practical guidance on effective implementation.

Looking at ways to ensure that inclusive practice does not become ghettoised into the domain of disability specialists, Chapter 13 by Alan Hurst is based on a disability project to produce a handbook that non-disability specialists can use in their training and continuing professional development programmes, working alongside disability services staff to develop HE practitioners' understanding of good inclusive practice. The author describes how, following feedback and evaluation, he observed colleagues organising and delivering sessions. Subsequent critical reflection was used to fine tune the handbook, which is now available via the Internet.

In Chapter 14, Benedict Fell and Jane Wray consider how best to ensure that disabled students are well prepared to undertake placements as part of their HE study. Additionally, they offer suggestions about reasonable adjustments that may need to be made so that disabled students can demonstrate their competence and gain maximum benefit from their placements. The authors offer practical advice on effective planning, communication and negotiation between the involved parties prior to the placement to ensure that the experience is successful all round for both students and placement providers. A semi-fictionalised case study is used to illustrate the key points.

Most work to date on disabled students in higher education has focused on the undergraduate experience. However, the issue of disabled post-graduates is considered here by Val Farrar in Chapter 15, entitled 'Equal to the task: disability issues in postgraduate research study'. The steadily rising proportion of disabled students at undergraduate level is beginning to be reflected in the numbers of disabled students registering for higher degrees. In a project based at the University of Newcastle upon Tyne, the author and colleagues worked with disabled research students to identify and address issues particular to them. They questioned disabled researchers from a wide range of universities and academic disciplines about their experiences from pre-entry through to transition to employment. The outcomes of this work provide some valuable prompts for HEIs wanting to address the needs of disabled postgraduates.

In the Conclusion, the authors and editors provide a manifesto for main-streaming inclusive practice in higher education. It brings together the collective wisdom of the contributors to this volume who argue for a cohesive, humane and systematic approach to inclusive practice in higher education. Much has been achieved to date, as the contributing authors can testify, particularly through the work of the National Disability Team which has coordinated, supported and guided many of the initiatives outlined here. But there is no room for complacency. Legislation internationally has meant that in many countries inclusive practice is no longer an option that HEIs can choose to ignore. It is incumbent upon practitioners to ensure that it becomes a reality. We hope that this book will help them to do so.

References and further reading

Adams, M. and Brown, S. (2000) 'The times they are a changing: developing disability provision in UK higher education', paper presented at Pathways 4 conference, Canberra, Australia, 6–8 Dec. Available at: http://www.canberra.edu.au/pathways/papers/adams.pdf (accessed 07/2005).

Adams, M. and Brown, S. (2001) 'Disability and higher education: the Australian experience – report to the funding councils'. Available at: http://www.natdisteam.ac.uk/documents/AUSTRALIA%20REPORT%20for%20wider%20dissemination.doc (accessed 07/2005).

Department of Employment, Education and Training (DEET) (1990) *A Fair Chance for All.* Available at: http://www.dest.gov.au/nbeet/publications/pdf/90_06.pdf (accessed 03/2005).

Disability Discrimination Act (2005) Available at: www.opsi.gov.uk/acts/acts2005/200 50013.htm (accessed 07/2005).

Disability Rights Commission (DRC) (2002) *Code of Practice: Post-16 Education and Related Services, Part 1.* London: DRC. Available at: http://www.drc-gb.org/pub licationsandreports/pubseducation.asp (accessed 07/2005).

DO-IT (n.d.) The Faculty Room, Statistics, University of Washington, Seattle. Available at: http://www.washington.edu/doit/Faculty/Rights/Background/statistics. html (accessed 05/2005).

Fraser, K. and Sanders, E. (2005) 'Educating university teachers about students who have a disability: participation and access', in K. Fraser (ed.) *Educational Development and Leadership in Higher Education: Developing an Effective Institutional Strategy.* London: RoutledgeFalmer.

French, D. (2002) *Mapping Resources Related to the Teaching and Learning of Disabled Students.* Bristol: HEFCE.

Further Education Funding Council (FEFC) (1996) *Inclusive Learning.* London: HMSO.

Higher Education Funding Council for England (1994) *Special Initiative to Encourage Widening Participation for Students with Special Needs.* Bristol: HEFCE.

Higher Education Funding Council for England (HEFCE) (2002) *02/21 Improving Provision for Disabled Students: HEFCE Strategy and Invitation to Bid for Funds 2003/05.* Bristol: HEFCE. Available at: http://www.hefce.ac.uk/pubs/hefce/2002/02%5 F21.htm (accessed 07/2005).

National Disability Team (NDT) (2005) *Statistics on Course*. Available at: http://www. natdisteam.ac.uk/resources_statistics_oncourse.html (accessed 07/2005).

Parker, V. (1998) 'Promoting inclusive learning in higher education for students with disabilities in the United Kingdom', *Journal on Post Secondary Education and disability*, 13, Summer: 6–9.

Porter, J. (1994) 'Disability in higher education: from person-based to interaction-based', *Journal on Excellence in College Teaching*, 5: 69–75.

West, M., Kregel, J., Getzel, E., Zhu, M., Ipsen, S. and Martin, E. (1993) 'Beyond Section 504: satisfaction and empowerment of students with disabilities in higher education', *Exceptional Children*, 59(5): 456–467.

Chapter 1

Improving access to higher education for disabled people

Mike Adams and Sarah Holland

Introduction

The previous educational experiences of all students will play a major part in their decision to enter higher education (HE); after all, it is at one end of the educational supply chain. However, for disabled people there may be additional, often complex, decisions that can shape their educational path. This chapter will discuss these additional decisions by highlighting the main barriers to HE participation that currently exist for disabled people and how these barriers can impact on the choices disabled people make. We examine the journey for disabled people to, and into, HE rather than focusing on students' on-course experiences (which are addressed by other authors within this book). We will also highlight a range of interventions and models of good practice to assist practitioners to improve support, and increase opportunities for disabled people into HE.

The story of Matthew, a recent entrant into a British higher education institution (HEI), has been included in this chapter to reinforce the 'lived experience' of these issues. We hope that sharing Matthew's experiences will demonstrate that the HE sector still needs to take further steps to improve provision for disabled people.

The higher education context

The case for improving access to HE for disabled people is compelling. In the UK, a National Audit Office report (2002) suggested that an 18-year-old with a disability is 40 per cent less likely to enter HE than an 18-year-old without a disability. Moreover, a report from the Disability Rights Commission (2003) found that 30 per cent of young disabled people who did not go on to post-16 education felt they were prevented from doing so for a reason related to their disability.

These figures are a concern because we know that HE can improve the employment opportunities of disabled people. For example, an analysis of the Spring 2004 Labour Force Survey (DRC 2004) showed that the difference in employment rate between non-disabled and disabled people with a degree or equivalent is 15 per cent (89.7 per cent for non-disabled people compared to 74.9 per cent for disabled people). However, the differential is 23 per cent for those with GCE A Levels or equivalent (82.2 per cent for non-disabled people compared to 59.6 per cent for disabled people) and 39 per cent for those without qualifications (63.1 per cent for non-disabled people compared to 24.6 per cent for disabled people). In terms of full-time employment, an Association of Graduate Careers Advisory Services (AGCAS) report (2004) showed that 48.4 per cent disabled graduates are in full-time work compared to 54.6 per cent for non-disabled graduates (a difference of 6 per cent). In terms of being unemployed, the differential is less than 3 percentage points. These research findings challenge the assertion that all disabled people are much less likely to gain equivalent employment than their peers.

Encouragingly, we know that the number of disabled students studying at UK HEIs is growing and that students are disclosing a diverse range of impairments. For example, the number of recorded students on UK HEI programmes who declared a disability rose from 86,250 in 2000/01 to 121,080 in 2003/4 (HESA student record 2000/1, 2003/4). This represents an increase from 4.33 per cent of the total student population to 5.39 per cent.

The funding initiatives and focused disability programmes described in the Introduction have clearly contributed to the increase in both the quality and quantity of services now offered in many HEIs (Adams and Brown 2000). However, significant improvements are still required to ensure that all disabled people who are able to benefit from a HE experience have equivalent opportunities to their peers.

Matthew's story

Matthew's tale highlights the inequalities and practical difficulties that disabled people can meet when planning to enter HE. Matthew is currently in his first year in a HEI and has just received a distinction for his first piece of coursework. However, it is the combination of his own determination, support from key staff and good fortune that has enabled him to reach his current position.

Matthew originally attended a specialist school for disabled children and was one of the highest achieving pupils in his class. He had always been interested in travel and had wanted to pursue a career which would involve travel and maybe even the opportunity to work abroad. His school curriculum had been limited, however, he was motivated and given opportunities to pursue his varied interests. Matthew's teachers were very supportive and had encouraged him to think about HE.

Matthew's parents had been much more apprehensive; they felt he should have lowered his ambitions and were concerned he would be disappointed if HE study wasn't possible. In preparation for Matthew leaving school, they had been talking to a careers adviser about opportunities in a local sheltered employment venture which had recently been established.

However, at 16, Matthew had been determined to continue his education and attended a mainstream college while living at a residential college for disabled people nearby. He studied Geography, Maths and Business Studies and felt he had to work much harder than his fellow students to keep up with the workload. Additional support, including one-to-one tutorials and study skills sessions, was made available. Matthew's overall experience was an enjoyable one although his biggest frustration was that, living at a residential college, he had been limited in the level of social activities he could take part in. He felt denied the social opportunities his peers were experiencing and was determined this would not be repeated once he started HE.

Despite the perceived lack of support from his family Matthew had contacted a number of HEIs he knew had a good reputation for supporting disabled people. Identifying those who had been positive to his initial call about the level of support he might expect, he was then able to cross-reference those institutions which also offered courses in Geography and Business Studies, the subjects he was particularly interested in studying further. This unconventional method provided the basis for his choice of HEIs on his admissions form. Matthew's final choice of course was a BA in Environment and Business.

Identifying the barriers to higher education

Reflecting on Matthew's journey to HE, it is clear that disabled people do face additional barriers and challenges as they strive to continue their education. Subsequent chapters of this book address some of the issues that may be encountered. Barriers may be structural, organisational, behavioural and attitudinal but all are underpinned by a society that, despite the introduction of anti-discrimination legislation in many countries, still does not fully embrace the inclusion of disabled people.

In determining whether a disabled person progresses to HE, there appear to be two key factors that can influence the journey (NDT 2004). The first is whether there is a belief in the individual's ability to undertake HE study (i.e. HE aspiration); the second is having timely access to the full educational experience, as students move through educational silos (i.e. a trouble-free transition). We believe that positive aspiration and smooth transitions throughout the educational journey (i.e. through school, further education and HE) are key to promoting and preparing disabled people for HE study.

Aspiration raising

A guidance document from the English funding council (HEFCE 2003) highlights the importance of raising the aspirations of non-traditional student groups at an increasingly early age, if positive choices about entering higher education are to be considered. Within this guidance, disabled people are identified as a key target group where specific action is required.

Anecdotal feedback as part of a National Disability Team (NDT)-led research study (2004) suggests that some disabled people tend to focus on shorter-term goals, usually linked to their impairment, rather than viewing longer-term aspirations as a priority. If this position is widely held (and there is no concrete evidence that suggests either way), it would have a major impact on how such funding programmes would need to approach aspiration raising with disabled people to ensure the student's educational potential is maximised.

A range of individuals play a role in raising the educational aspirations of disabled people, for example, parents, teachers, career advisers and friends are all highly influential in determining aspirations. However, the evidence presented below suggests that additional work is required to provide these key individuals with information about the opportunities and practical support that now exist for disabled people in HE.

> Matthew knew that his parents did not support his decision to enter HE. This was not for reasons of control but a fear of the unknown; concern about what support would be provided and how he would cope in the 'big bad world' where hitherto he had been surrounded by a loving and understanding family, friends and staff who knew about his disability.

Powell (2003) asserts that, although parents are often experts on their child and the impact of their impairment, they are not so familiar with the complexities of the educational system and therefore tend to take a default position which is usually risk-adverse and often entrenched. This observation is a concern, as it suggests that parents can inadvertently reinforce a viewpoint that non-academic issues take priority for disabled people. However, it is also important to acknowledge that invariably, those same parents will have single-handedly fought for the rights of their child throughout their educational journey. Therefore, it is essential that appropriate and timely information is provided to parents in order that they can take an active and informed role in raising the aspirations of their children.

The school system and individual teachers also play an important role in raising academic aspirations. Although Matthew clearly had supportive teachers who recognised and encouraged him to achieve his potential, there is evidence to suggest that some disabled people do not receive the level of education that would enable them to consider further study within a HE environment. Leung (1992) observed that disabled adults in the United States were four times more likely than non-disabled adults to have only a ninth-grade education (equivalent to a 15-year-old in the UK). In the UK, the differential is not so significant but disabled people are still less likely to attain a general level of education. For example, an analysis of the Spring 2004 Labour Force Survey (DRC 2004) indicates that 18.5 per cent of disabled people have GSCEs as their highest qualification, compared to 22.2 per cent of non-disabled peers.

Sameshima (1999), in a study of deaf students in New Zealand, found that students had progressed to HE in spite of the schooling they had received. Two key factors contributed to these difficulties. First, there was a lack of deaf role models whom students could aspire to emulate; most HEI literature and information did not provide case studies of disabled people and their achievements. Second, and of more concern, the teachers in primary and secondary schools failed to motivate students to realise their potential. These low expectations were reflected in the narrow range of academic options the students felt were available to them.

In addition to the role that individuals can play in making HE an attractive choice, the learning environment may also shape the educational aspirations of disabled people. In the UK, there is currently a highly political debate about the merits of teaching at compulsory level in mainstream versus specialist schools. It is beyond the scope of this chapter to address this complex issue; however, the evidence suggests that education providers tend to be moving in the direction of integrating disabled people into mainstream schools, albeit at differing rates of change.

It may be questioned what effect this shift will have on the educational aspirations of disabled people. Slee (1993), in his school-based research, identified three distinct groups of disabled people who were reflected in the school system. First, there were those children who had always been taught in a specialist school and therefore had received a particular education experience. The second group of disabled children were predominantly those with less severe impairments, who had been educated in mainstream schools with little, or no, additional resources or support. The final group were defined as 'integration children'. These children attended mainstream schools but required significant resources, usually including one-to-one teaching assistants to participate in the activities of the school. Such resources were provided by local education authorities who needed to 'label' these students to administer the required level of support. Slee identified that, in most cases, children within the latter group felt extremely isolated and struggled to attain a level of achievement which maximised their potential. Interestingly, Polat et al. (2001) contend that disabled people, regardless of whether they attend mainstream or specialist schooling, feel set apart from non-disabled peers and experience a sense of isolation in terms of building friendships and instigating general social interaction.

How best to maximise potential is a key issue, but this tends to be a point of contention and solutions can compete with political and ideological imperatives.

Indeed, it is impossible to know whether Matthew's aspirations would have been as high, or higher, if he had studied in a mainstream school or become an 'integrated child'.

Transition

A smooth transition between school and further education and then on to HE can aid students in their journey to higher study. A literature review, undertaken by the NDT (2004), identified a range of barriers that can hinder the transition of disabled people from further education to higher education. A number of the barriers identified were relevant to all students, for example, some students had difficulty adjusting to living away from family and friends. However, many of these issues were more complex for disabled students, for example, not only were disabled students adjusting to living away from home, if the individual had previously received personal support from family members, or had devloped relationships with personal assistants to meet their needs, they would be additionally adjusting to a new support structure.

Often transition barriers relate to difficulties disabled students can have when adapting to the differing learning styles of school, further education and HE study. For example, students may be required to use new software packages and other Information Technology to engage appropriately with the different styles of learning required. The need to ensure this software is compatible with a disabled student's existing assistive technology is not always straightforward and can again lead to delays.

However, it is not just access to equipment that can hamper learning. For example, for people with particular impairments, such those who are deaf, the difficulties of adapting to different learning styles can be compounded by the lack of qualified sign language interpreters (Sameshima 1999). In Chapter 10 of this book, Mole and Peacock highlight the real difficulties this situation can present for deaf students when trying to access a HE system in which students feel they are made to integrate within traditional models of learning, rather than a system which automatically makes reasonable adjustments to accommodate the needs of the individual student.

A successful education experience is not simply about academic study but also the development of social skills and achieving independence. For example, for a large proportion of all students, attending a HEI provider represents the first experience of leaving home. Adapting to this different academic experience was discussed by Oosterhoorn (2005) in a survey with disabled students in Scotland. Oosterhoorn found evidence that additional pre-course and ongoing bridging support assisted the transition process for students. This bridging support included the acquisition of academic skills but also extended to wider independent and social skills in dealing with a new, and often quite different, lifestyle. The link to wider social skills is often a crucial issue for disabled students. A survey of young disabled people undertaken by Hirst and Baldwin (1994) found that, compared to the general population, between 30 per cent and 40 per cent of disabled people had greater difficulty (than non-disabled peers) in attaining a degree of independent life. More recent research (e.g. Morris 2001; Hendley and Pascall 2002; DRC 2003) reinforces this position.

Differing funding methodologies in each educational silo can also make the transition challenging for some disabled people. For example, within the UK, further education colleges receive additional financial support to provide the necessary provision for disabled people, whereas in the HE sector the majority of additional funding is directed to the individual disabled person to purchase the required support. Furthermore, this might be the first time that the disabled person has needed to take responsibility for organising their equipment and personal support arrangements. The locus for coordinating this support is not always clear. Anecdotal evidence would suggest this can often lead to feelings of isolation and marginalisation and result in individuals starting their course without the necessary equipment or support required to access the curriculum on the same level as their peers.

In many ways, the barriers to both aspiration and transition that are outlined above stem from an education model that changes at each stage in the educational journey and invariably requires individuals to integrate, rather than adapting to their individual needs. Given this 'deficit model', the next section of this chapter highlights some existing practice and interventions that can smooth the journey to HE for disabled people.

Key interventions and strategies

All education sectors must take responsibility for helping to improve access to HE. In many ways this could be perceived as a difficult task for the HE sector. At one end of the education supply chain, it might be argued that by the time individual HE providers are involved, disabled people's decisions and pathways have already been set.

Despite increased admission into HE being highly contingent on the quality and transitions of people's experiences through the school and college systems, there are effective interventions that HE providers can employ to engage those disabled people who would benefit from HE study. Table 1.1 suggests some of the key issues for disabled students considering HE, and the direct interventions that can address these issues. Table 1.1 is adapted from the NDT report (2004) and from the authors' own research in preparing this chapter.

The interventions given in Table 1.1 are based on existing practice within the UK HE sector and have been chosen to demonstrate that improved access to HE requires a whole-institution approach. We further argue that these interventions are highly transferable internationally. To support HEIs' strategies for implementing these interventions we have identified the lead individual/s responsible for facilitating action. This is an indicative rather than prescriptive list and therefore will vary depending on context. However, it does reinforce the argument that the

Table 1.1 Student considerations and HEI interventions

Key considerations for disabled students	Suggested interventions undertaken by HEIs	Suggested lead individuals responsible for coordinating intervention
A named key contact to coordinate the transition process	Appoint and train a member of staff to undertake this coordination role	HEI management/disability support services
	Contact the student on application to discuss individual support needs and to outline what the institution can and cannot provide	Admissions tutors/course leaders
A detailed knowledge of the resources/support available from the HE provider	Produce a comprehensive guide of available resources and support	Disability support services
	Dedicate an area on the corporate website focused on disability issues	IT management/marketing
A detailed understanding of funding entitlements and personal rights	Liaise with relevant external bodies to ensure students receive information in a timely manner	Admissions tutors/course leaders/personal tutors
	Provide a summary of entitlements, including disability benefits on the corporate website	IT management/disability support services
An understanding and knowledge of the differences between the culture of post-compulsory (post-16) education, including the different learning and teaching styles	Ensure all students have an opportunity to visit the HE provider and discuss their needs before and/or during the application process	Admissions tutors/course leaders
	Consider running taster session days and pre-HEI/college bridging sessions on transition	Admissions tutors/course leaders/widening participation coordinators
	Conduct outreach work with FE colleges and schools (e.g. coordinate visits to and from HE for staff/students)	Admissions tutors/course leaders/widening participation coordinators
Access to additional study skills support if/when required	Develop and advertise a programme of study skills which is ongoing for the duration of a student's course	Course developers/learning support units

continued

Table 1.1 continued

Key considerations for disabled students	Suggested interventions undertaken by HEIs	Suggested lead individuals responsible for coordinating intervention
Access to additional study skills support if/when required (continued)	Enable access to one-to-one tuition when required	All learning and teaching staff
	Consider building in additional study skills support for all students, particularly in the first term/semester	Admissions tutors/course leaders
A level of independence equivalent to their non-disabled peers	Ensure disabled students are integral to all decisions concerning the individual's support, accommodation and curriculum arrangements	Disability support services/accommodation office
	Provide accessible accommodation and facilities that are integrated within general institution facilities	HEI estate management
An accessible physical environment	Undertake a physical audit and prioritise a programme of works, within the HEI's strategic plan	HEI estate management/HEI senior management
	Ensure all new buildings comply with, or surpass, regulations for accessibility	HEI estate management
	Provide an honest assessment of the current physical environment so that individual students, with varying impairments, can make informed decisions about their choice of HEI	Admissions tutors/course leaders/website managers/HEI estate management/marketing
An accessible curriculum	Undertake an audit of the non-built environment to examine the accessibility of the institutional policies, procedures and practice	HEI management/course leaders/disability support services

A level of reassurance that individual adjustments to the curriculum will be considered	Clearly identify and state the key learning objectives of each course so students understand what is required before they undertake the HE programme	Admissions tutors/course leaders/course developers
	Provide disability awareness training for all staff (e.g. provide positive communication training for all front line staff)	Educational development/staff development teams
	Develop a policy on the process of enabling individual adjustments, and provide academic staff with the necessary training to support good practice	HEI senior managers/quality enhancement unit
	Develop case studies of existing practice to promote the HEI's commitment to embracing all students' needs	Disability support services
	Provide students with regular opportunities to disclose a disability	All teaching/support service staff
	Develop a policy that clearly tells staff what they should do when a student discloses a disability	HEI senior managers/quality enhancement unit
	Use the outcomes of any audits to develop a detailed strategy to improve inclusive learning and teaching practice, thereby reducing the level of individual adjustments necessary	HEI senior managers/quality enhancement unit
Access to enabling technology and equipment on campus	Ensure that accessibility issues are considered and appropriate measures implemented when developing an IT strategy	IT management
	Provide enabling software on existing PCs and other equipment where necessary	IT management
	Provide training for technicians on accessibility so individual adjustments can be accommodated where possible	IT management/staff development teams

involvement of a wide range of staff from across the institution is required. Specifically, it also demonstrates that the delivery of an inclusive curriculum will necessitate an understanding of the issues and engagement of solutions by academic staff. This must not be in isolation but in consultation with disability practitioners and the disabled person themselves, as they know best their impairment and how it is likely to impact on their study.

Given the whole-institutional responsibility for inclusive practice, there is also a need to identify key individuals to work with the disabled person and other stakeholders. This is not to reduce the autonomy of the disabled person but merely acknowledges that HE can be both a complex and challenging environment and that contact with key individuals can ensure timely solutions are found to any issues raised.

There are other, less direct interventions that all education providers can undertake to improve access to HE for disabled people. A recent UK government report (DWP 2004) suggested a majority of barriers confronted by disabled people are created by a lack of joint working between and across organisations. This includes social care departments and local education authorities with responsibility for funding personal care and academic-related support respectively.

A model of partnership and mutual collaboration has been adopted in Australia, where Regional Disability Liaison Officers (RDLOs) have responsibility for coordinating disability-related issues across individual states. The focus is on facilitating support to both education institutions (schools, colleges and HEIs) and to individual disabled people. The RDLOs' remit is to raise aspirations, facilitate outreach activities and support the transition process across education sectors. By working with institutions and disabled people they provide a level of consistency as well as being a conduit to all stakeholders (NDT 2004).

Evidence of joint thinking and partnership working between national bodies, HEIs and advocates for disabled students is beginning to emerge in the UK. For example, the HE sector is increasingly playing a central role in raising the overall aspirations of disabled people to consider HE as a feasible option from a young age. In England, the Aimhigher programme (HEFCE 2003) provides outreach and aspiration-raising activities to traditionally under-represented groups participating in education (funding is directly provided to the school, college and HEI sectors). This partnership initiative is starting to develop a range of resources, activities and models of practice to address some of the barriers identified in this chapter. Moreover, there is the additional benefit of a growing number of practitioners developing their knowledge and understanding about disability, which hitherto had been the sole preserve of disability specialists.

Conclusion

This chapter has argued that raising aspirations and improving the transition process is key to improving the number and experiences of disabled people entering HE. Some of the existing barriers confronted by disabled people are structural, others political, while others can be reduced by tackling attitudes and disabling behaviours.

We acknowledge that many of the barriers identified are not unique to disabled students. For example, improving motivation to study; thinking about future options; leaving home for the first time; adapting to different learning styles; and achieving a greater level of independence are issues for all students. However, for disabled people, these issues can be more complex, take longer to achieve, and may be counter to what others think could, and should, be achieved. It is imperative therefore that the HE sector should continue to use its influence to raise the aspirations of disabled people, and work with other organisations to enhance the transition process.

As demonstrated in this chapter and the remaining chapters in this book, there is already internationally a wealth of good practice that the HE sector can draw upon. This existing knowledge and understanding need to be better harnessed by the HE sector to ensure they becomes part of everyday policy and practice.

In addition to implementing some of the interventions suggested in this chapter, HE providers are also encouraged to undertake research to provide a sound evidence base to inform future interventions. This should focus on the impact of existing activities but also include greater opportunities for the student voice to be heard. There is a growing literature based on the experiences of disabled people (Borland and James 1999; Sameshima 1999; Oosterhoorn 2005) but further research is required to ascertain both actual and perceived barriers confronted by disabled people. In addition to informing practice within HE, the findings should further inform social care and education sector policies which support disabled people to maximise their abilities.

The HE sector can play a key role in creating an environment where higher learning becomes a right, not a constant battle, thus ensuring that equality of opportunity is achieved.

Acknowledgements

The authors wish to thank Carol Wilson from the National Disability Team and Jenni Dyer from Skill for their work as key contributors to the Scoping Study Report, on which many of the ideas and discussion points for this chapter are based.

References and further reading

Adams, M. and Brown, S. (2000) 'The times they are a changing: developing disability provision in UK higher education', paper presented at Pathways 4 conference, Canberra, Australia, 6–8 Dec. Available at: http://www.canberra.edu.au/pathways/papers/adams. pdf (accessed 07/2005).

Association of Graduate Careers Advisory Services (AGCAS) Report (2004) *What Happens Next? A Report on the First Destinations of 2003 Graduates with Disabilities*. Available at: http://www.natdisteam.ac.uk/resources.php?id=909 (accessed 06/2005).

Borland, J. and James, S. (1999) 'The learning experience of students with disabilities in higher education: a case study of a UK university', *Disability and Society*, 14: 85–101.

Department of Employment, Education and Training (DEET) (1990) *A Fair Chance for All* Canberra, Australia. Available at: http://www.dest.gov.au/nbeet/publications/pdf/90_06.pdf (accessed 03/2005).

Department of Work and Pensions (DWP) (2004) *Making the Transition: Addressing Barriers in Services for Disabled People*. Research report 204. London: DWP.

Disability Rights Commission (2003) *Young Disabled People: A Survey of the Views and Experiences of Young Disabled People in Great Britain, Conducted by NOP for the DRC*. London: DRC.

Disability Rights Commission (2004) *Disability Briefing 2004*. Available at: http://www.drc.org.uk/uploaded_files/documents/10_666_Disability%20Briefing%20Dec%202004.doc (accessed 07/2005).

Hendley, N. and Pascall, G. (2002) *Disability and Transition to Adulthood: Achieving Independent Living*. *Brighton*: Pavilion Publishing for the Joseph Rowntree Foundation.

Higher Education Funding Council for England (2003) *Aimhigher: National Activity – Invitation to Bid*, Circular letter number 07/2004. Available at: http://www.hefce.ac.uk/pubs/circlets/2004/c107_04/ (accessed 07/2005).

Higher Education Statistics Agency (HESA) *HESA Student Record 2000/1 and 2003/4*. personal communication, July 2004.

Hirst, M. and Baldwin, S. (1994) *Unequal Opportunities: Growing up Disabled*. London: HMSO.

Holland, S. and Wilson, C. (2004) 'Transition from FE to HE: challenges for disabled people?', *Inclusion*, 3: 24–27. Available at: http://www.inclusion.ac.uk/ (accessed 03/2005).

Leung, P. (1992) 'Keynote address', *Australian Disability Review*, 2: 3–13.

Morris, J. (2001) 'Social exclusion and young disabled people with high levels of support needs', *Critical Social Policy*, 21(2): 161–183.

National Audit Office (2002) *Widening Participation in Higher Education in England*. London: National Audit Office.

National Disability Team (2004) *Aspiration Raising and Transition of Disabled Student from Further Education to Higher Education: Final Report*. Available at: http://www.natdisteam.ac.uk/documents/Aspiration%20raising%20report%20(final)%2021%20july.pdf (accessed 03/2005).

Oosterhoorn, B. (2005) 'Transitions Project: The experience of disabled students making transition between institutions to begin or continue their higher education', *Skill Journal*, Spring edition: 1–4.

Polat, F., Afroditi, K., Boyle, W.F. and Nelson, N. (2001) *Post-16 Transitions of Pupils with Special Educational Needs*, DfES Research Report RR315. London: DfES.

Powell, S. (2003) *Special Teaching in Higher Education: Successful Strategies for Access and Inclusion*. London: Kogan Page.

Sameshima, S. (1999) *Perceptions of Deaf Students in Universities and Polytechnics: WEBB Accessibility Project*. Available at: http://www.bath.ac.uk/learning-support/webb/sameshim.htm#findings (accessed 03/2005).

Slee, R. (1993) *Is There a Desk with My Name on It? The Politics of Integration*. London: Falmer Press.

Chapter 2

From a disabling world to a new vision

Todd Fernie and Marcus Henning

In recent times higher education providers have attempted to offer structures to improve the learning of disabled students. There are numerous examples from tertiary providers world-wide that acknowledge a change in the way the academic community views disability and the disabled student. Many of these changes are continuing to evolve and we advocate lifelong refinement and affirmative action in terms of promoting a more inclusive learning environment.

This chapter will begin by briefly highlighting how traditional social and historical conditioning, with a particular focus on stereotyping, creates discourses which have impacted, directly and indirectly, on the teaching and learning environment for disabled students. This will be followed by a more pragmatic exchange of ideas in terms of existing practices, and how the future higher education landscape needs to evolve to further ensure inclusive provision for disabled people. Implications will focus on responsibilities for disabled students and academic staff, and a range of interventions will be presented with the aim of better enabling the disabled student.

Traditional social and historical conditioning and the development of discourse

This section will explore some of the ideas that have been presented regarding the traditional social and historical conditioning related to the concept of disability. One key aspect has been Wolfensberger's (1972) framework of different stereotypes used by society to define and describe the disabled person. In general, stereotypes are learned from family members, friends and the mass media, and through social conditioning this leads people to make a pre-cognitive decision about certain groups of people. In almost all cases, stereotypes are exposed as being far too simplistic and incorrect. Moreover, they have the harmful effect of creating a self-fulfilling prophecy, in which being perceived as inferior leads the target of the prejudice to act that way.

Stereotypes can be expressed in different ways. At one end of the spectrum, the disabled person is perceived as a 'threat' to society; the individual is seen as being deviant or troublesome. Often the disabled person is seen as an 'object of ridicule', a position traditionally reinforced through cultural imagery found in, for example, film and literature. On a different level, the disabled person is seen as the 'eternal child' and this can be illustrated by the use of diminutive naming, e.g. the use of Tommy rather than Tom. The tendency then is to expect the adult to behave like Tommy the boy and not Tom the man. Historically, it has been common to adopt a medicalised approach to the disabled person, which is closely aligned to the individual being viewed as an 'object of pity' or as being 'sick'. In the latter case the person is said to require treatment through various forms of 'therapy', which are given to the 'patient' by a wide range of personnel from the medical and/or professional fraternity.

Stereotypes are closely linked to role expectations in that human beings respond to how they are treated. This truism has important implications for disabled people which have often been ignored. If people are expected to develop and achieve, they generally will, and similarly negative expectations often reinforce failure. Studies of teachers' expectations about students have illustrated the powerful effect of attitudes. Therefore, disabled people need to be supported to live lives where they can play positive roles as friends, neighbours, lovers, parents, brothers, sisters, students, teachers, home owners, rate payers, workers, volunteers, instead of the role of eternal child, dependent person, special student, trainee and recipient. Disabled people have a contribution to make to society and need the expectation that they can fulfil valued roles.

The philosophical and psychological implication of these stereotypes is that before and after they are used there is a tremendous sense of social devaluation. When devaluing stereotypes change into discriminatory behaviour, this process is known as 'disablism'. Wolfensberger (1972) started by emphasising culturally normative means and practices, but later shifted his focus to the impact of discrimination on disabled people and the need to concentrate attention on achieving socially valued roles. He follows labelling and social reaction theory in explaining how people with learning difficulties find themselves locked into a spiral of devaluation. What he terms 'social role valorisation' is defined as the creation, support, and defence of valued social roles for people who risk devaluation including 'socially valued life conditions' (Wolfensberger and Thomas 1983). These ideas do not challenge the legitimacy of the professional role in the lives of disabled people, but guarantees its continued authority. The whole focus of this approach is on 'normalising' disabled people rather than challenging the concept of normality itself.

Towards a social model of disability

An alternative and much more progressive way of viewing disability is as 'the disadvantage or restriction of activity caused by a contemporary social organisation which takes no or little account of people who have physical impairments and thus excludes them from participation in the mainstream of social activities' (Union of the Physically Impaired Against Segregation 1976). Disability is represented in terms of social barriers. The reality of impairment is not denied, but rather the emphasis is on how society goes out of its way to render people with impairments dependent and unable to engage in many social and economic activities.

Abberley (1987) used social theory to represent some of the most sophisticated discussion of understanding disability as a form of social oppression. He draws on comparable work on sexism and racism while identifying what was specific about the situation and experiences of disabled people. In his account, oppression is an all-inclusive concept, which is located in hierarchical social relations and divisions.

However, Abberley also argues that the biological element in disabled people's oppression – impairment – is far more real than its counterparts for women and black people, in this case, gender and skin colour. Indeed, for many disabled people 'the biological difference . . . is itself a part of the oppression' (Abberley 1987). Impairment, by definition, is functionally limiting, whereas gender and race are not. A social oppression theory of disability must address the socially constructed difference and the very real impact of function.

The socio-political model articulates a very different definition and analysis of disability (including its causes and positive policy responses). The Social Model of Disability has its origins in campaigns by disabled people against discrimination, isolation and dependency; the Social Model or Social Barrier approach is sociological and environmental by nature. Oliver (1990, 1996) suggests that theorising disability should not be seen as an attempt to deal with the personal restrictions of impairment, but rather to confront the environmental and social barriers that constitute disability. The minority group route may then accord disabled people's demands a degree of political legitimacy they do not have at present, but without eradicating the causes of their disablement (Liggett 1988). Such an approach is based on an explicit recognition that discriminatory attitudes, rather than functional impairments, lie at the heart of disability.

Future higher educational landscape: inclusive provision

The social model of disability is underpinned by the concept of inclusion, with seamless access to all areas of independent living, including education and employment. Within higher education, the authors recognise that to promote inclusive provision will require a multi-level partnership between students, the academic teaching staff community, higher education administration, and the government. However, the following suggestions will specifically focus on the issues related to the partnership between students and academic teaching staff in a higher education context. In this way the notions of the past conditioning practice in terms of 'medicalising' disability, and thus creating limited conditioned scenarios, become obsolete and the way ahead is seen as synchronised teamwork. This future direction promotes self-advocacy and self-determination which inevitably leads to a greater sense of student empowerment (Owens *et al.* 1996; Eaton and Coull 1998a, 1998b; Layton and Lock 2003).

One key tenet of higher education is that students have a responsibility to self-determine their own passage of study, which will develop a sense of empowerment and reduce the likelihood of the development of learned helplessness (the Australian National University 1995; Eaton and Coull 1998a, 1998b; Sylvestro 2001). It has been shown that disabled students' sense of self-advocacy can be enhanced through development of self-awareness, and communication and goal identification skills (Layton and Lock 2003).

Self-advocacy and self-determination inculcate a sense of partnership between academic staff and students, in which each group are responsible for their respective roles, ensuring students succeed in maximising their academic potential. The Australian National University (1995) has identified two major issues for disabled students to explore on entry into a tertiary provider. First, students need to be familiar with the services being offered by the tertiary provider and, second, they also need to develop good study habits; the relevance of these issues are transferable to all students, not just those who are disabled.

In familiarising themselves with services in the university, students need to know what the provider can offer. In New Zealand and Australia, many universities and polytechnics have a disability office and a learning support centre (e.g. the Australian National University 1995; Auckland University of Technology 2004a, 2004b) and this is consistent with the provisions available in British higher education providers (University of Wales Institute 2000). The disability offices usually administer and manage pastoral and academic provisions such as exam accommodations (Auckland University of Technology n.d.). In addition, general learning support centres are specifically designed to support the delivery of academic and study skill development (Auckland University of Technology 2004b).

Disabled students and disability offices need to work together to ensure that appropriate support services are put in place in a timely manner. For example, in New Zealand, different support activities are made available to individual disabled students contingent on need and impairment (Royal New Zealand Foundation for the Blind 2001).

In terms of developing good study habits, students can continue the notion of lifelong learning and as such can implement straightforward strategies to ensure that they can better adapt to the learning environment (the Australian National University 1995). The strategies suggested by the Australian National University include understanding course objectives, requirements, expectations and assignment criteria (Eales 1995).

Students can also use efficient learning strategies, such as taping lectures, ensuring key reading is undertaken prior to the lecture and even positioning themselves in the correct location in the lecture theatre, such as sitting at the front of the lecture to receive optimal information, e.g. for people who lip-read (the Australian National University 1995). Moreover, students need to be aware of innovative techniques designed to help students who have challenges with learning such as process mnemonics (Manalo *et al.* 2000) or different ways of learning (Eales 1995). Finally, for assignments, students need to ensure that they understand what is required and use the student learning centres if they require further guidance and clarity (Auckland University of Technology 2004b). Each student is, in effect, a unique case and the requirements of each student need to be considered by educators.

Academic staff in tertiary education

Good teaching principles are relevant to all students world-wide. In terms of the disabled student, often the areas that impact on the notion of inclusion are the beliefs held by academic staff and their teaching repertoire (Stanovich and Jordan 2000). Strong leadership and collaboration between staff are also often seen as contributing factors towards ensuring that inclusion is effective (Mamlin 1999), and it is widely agreed that teaching staff play a major role in ensuring optimal inclusion (Garnett 1998). In terms of developing inclusion in the teaching environment, higher education professional development educators can view academic staff education in terms of six categories: social, philosophical and legal issues; educational service delivery trends; attitudes; educational interventions; personnel preparation; and research (Putnam *et al.* 1995).

In creating the philosophy of inclusion, academic teachers could reflect on the way they teach in the academic environment that is shaped through critical reflection on issues related to the six categories. Research, in particular, informs praxis, and the use of diverse research methodologies such as the Delphi technique (a technique that incorporates and collates information from experts in the field) can inform the quality of this praxis (ibid. 1995). On the social side of the teaching environment, academics need to be aware of the negative stigmas often attributed to disabled students resulting in greater levels of isolation, loneliness and social controversy (Pavri and Luftig 2000), as this adversely impacts this target group. Academic teachers need to use teaching methods that are inclusive by encouraging student engagement from diverse backgrounds, resulting in greater awareness of diverse cultural differences and the richness associated with such diversity. When breaking down stigmas and stereotypes, staff and non-disabled students need to be well informed and guided to attitudes of acceptance of the notion of difference, and the positive aspects of difference. This process could be incorporated implicitly into curriculum structures, as well explicitly through informed lectures and other media sources such as the student newspaper and radio.

Furthermore, like all students, those who are disabled require explicit communication of objectives, requirements and directives. At the practical end of the teaching spectrum, academic teaching staff need to consider how to develop and disseminate course information, lectures, assignments and examinations (the Australian National University, 1995). This is in line with the notion of promoting a least restrictive teaching environment (Kuehne 1999).

Consequently, there needs to be a move towards more creative ways in presenting course information to students. A diverse repertoire of teaching behaviours and skills, producing information in different ways, can be useful for students who appear to learn differently from mainstream thinking (Stanovich and Jordan 2000). Moreover, academic staff need to provide clear course outlines, book lists, readings, and assignment details before the start of the course. In addition, academic staff should provide clear administrative information both verbally and in writing. There also needs to be easy access to staff by clarifying when they are available to see students (the Australian National University 1995). Academic staff, where appropriate, also need to engage with students about how their impairment might impact on learning and the teaching adjustments that would be most effective (Al-Mahmood *et al.* 2002). Within each individual's impairment are also unique factors that need to be recognised and acknowledged in terms of developing the least restrictive environment for the student in question and promoting the inclusive environment.

Lectures can be presented in imaginative and diverse ways to accommodate different learning styles, and could be made available on audio or videotape or DVD/CD (the Australian National University 1995; Massey University 1999). For further information on the use of multimedia, see Chapter 11 by Sloan, Stone and Stratford. Academic teaching staff could ensure that they provide outlines of lecture content, preferably before the start of the lecture. Language needs to be carefully considered and instructions need to be clear, specific and free of jargon (Massey University 1999). Academics could also set aside a time close to the finish of the lecture so that students have time to talk to them. Finally, any written handouts of overheads used also need to be made readily available. This practice is, of course, a part of best teaching practice and will benefit all students, and although many of the ideas presented here have an Australian origin, the principles outlined here are applicable to educators worldwide.

In addition, some students prefer small group sessions or tutorials. This allows for time and settings so that students can ask specific questions to focus discussion (the Australian National University 1995). Students need to be supported and encouraged to develop greater collaboration with academic teaching staff to ensure that they meet their workloads; consideration of extra tuition could be considered an optional strategy if existing teaching regimes are not meeting the needs of the student (Massey University 1999).

When setting assignments, teaching staff should be aware that students benefit from having a clear idea regarding the objectives of each assignment; again, this practice will benefit all students. In developing this notion of clarity, assignments need to have unambiguous guidelines of what is to be expected. Teaching staff could also provide examples of satisfactory and unsatisfactory work. When working with students, this feedback needs to be done in a sensitive manner, and compassionate consideration of reasonable and fair assignment extensions needs to be put in place (the Australian National University 1995). Assessments need to be flexible in terms of assignment deadlines and the consideration of resubmission (Massey University 1999).

In developing and designing examinations, there are diverse and inspiring methods of appraising students in terms of their knowledge, skills and ability. There should be consideration of alternative testing formats, e.g. oral presentations, computer simulations and photographic essays. There could be alternative methods of responding to exams, e.g. taping or typing responses or via computer simulations. The use of exam accommodations is commonplace and can include provision for distraction-free rooms, extra time and reader/writers. There are also creative ways of preparing examination scripts such as using different coloured sheets, larger fonts, and clearer formats. Clear questions and consideration of oral examinations and computer responding are aspects of tests construction that could be employed (Massey University 1999). Teaching staff could also be available to clarify any question related to the examination before the start of every examination. Moreover, examination markers could focus on content in written answers rather than spelling, grammar and presentation (the Australian National University 1995). A further exploration of alternative assessment practice is provided in Chapter 7 by Waterfield, West and Parker.

Conclusion

In answering the title 'From a disabling world to a new vision', this chapter has essentially been divided into two parts. The first part aimed to create a theoretical backdrop to disability, by developing an argument that transforming past and some existing teaching practices will benefit disabled students, and will in fact probably be useful for all students. The second aspect of the chapter has focused on the pragmatic end of the statement, by transcending theory into practice so that the new vision can become a reality.

Post-modern theory promotes the notion of empowerment and self-advocacy and the need to consider the environment in terms of policies and physical adjustment. Consequently, the notion of partnership between the major players – students and teachers – is highlighted, with the acknowledgement that other parties are involved in this educative process such as administrators and governing bodies. This chapter thus advances the idea of collaboration for the greater good of higher education and all those who engage in it.

Acknowledgements

The authors would like to express their appreciation to Diana Murray for providing us with the opportunity to write this chapter, and to Mitchell Hutchings and John Lambert for their invaluable feedback.

References and further reading

Abberley, P. (1987) 'The concept of oppression and the development of a social theory of disability', *Disability, Handicap and Society*, 2(1): 5–19.

Al-Mahmood, R., McLean, P., Powell, E. and Ryan, J. (2002) 'Towards success in tertiary study'. Available at: http://www.services.unimelb.edu.au/ellp/publications/towards. html (accessed 05/2005).

Auckland University of Technology. (2004a) 'Disability Resource Office'. Available at: http://www.aut.ac.nz/student_services/disability/ (accessed 05/2005).

Auckland University of Technology (2004b) *Te Tari Awhina: The Learning Development Centre*. Available at: http://www.aut.ac.nz/student_services/te_tari_awhina/ (accessed 05/2005).

Auckland University of Technology (n.d.) *Exam Procedures*. Auckland: Disability Resource Office.

Chopra, D. (1991) 'What is the true nature of reality? The basics of quantum healing'. Available at: http://www.ascendedmasters.ac/reality.html (accessed 05/2005).

Eales, C. (1995) *Going up? Help for Tertiary Students with Learning Disabilities*. Sydney: University of New South Wales.

Eaton, H. and Coull, L. (1998a) *Transitions to Postsecondary Learning: Self-advocacy Handbook*. Vancouver, BC: Eaton Coull Learning Group, Ltd.

Eaton, H. and Coull, L. (1998b) *Transitions to Postsecondary Learning: Student Work Guide*. Vancouver, BC: Eaton Coull Learning Group, Ltd.

Garnett, K. (1998) 'Thinking about inclusion and learning disabilities: a teacher's guide'. Available at: http://www.ldonline.org//pdf/dld_ecologies.pdf (accessed 05/2005).

Kuehne, C. C. (1999) 'Least restrictive environment: how do we prepare both our special educators and our general educators to comply with the provision?' Available at: http://www.ldonline.org/ld_indepth/legal_legislative/complying_with_provision.html (accessed 05/2005).

Layton, C. A. and Lock, R. H. (2003) 'Reasoning and self-advocacy for postsecondary students with learning disabilities', *Learning Disabilities*, 12(2): 49–56.

Liggett, H. (1988) 'Stars are not born: an interactive approach to the politics of disability', *Disability, Handicap and Society*, 3(3): 263–275.

Mamlin, N. (1999) 'Despite best intentions: when inclusion fails', *The Journal of Special Education*, 33(1): 36–49.

Manalo, E., Bunnell, J. K. and Stillman, J. A. (2000) 'The use of process mnemonics in teaching students with mathematics learning disabilities', *Learning Disability Quarterly*, 23(2): 137–156.

Massey University (1999) *Flex-ability: Information for Lecturers on How to Provide a Non-Disabling Learning Environment*. Palmerston North, New Zealand: Disability Services.

National Institute on Disability and Rehabilitation Research (2000) 'The four paradigms of disability', Aavailable at: http://www.rehabinfo.net/pmandr/resource%20guide/ disabilityresources/disabilityparadigms.htm (accessed 05/2005).

Oliver, M. (1990) *The Politics of Disablement*. London: Macmillan.

Oliver, M. (1996) *Understanding Disability: From Theory to Practice*. London: Macmillan.

Owens, T. J., Mortimer, J. T. and Finch, M. D. (1996) 'Self-determination as a source of self-esteem in adolescence', *Social Force*, 74: 1377–1404.

Pavri, S. and Luftig, R. L. (2000) 'The social face of inclusive education: are students with learning disabilities really included in the classroom?', *Preventing School Failure*, 45: 8–14.

Putnam, J. W., Spiegel, A. N. and Bruininks, R. H. (1995) 'Future directions in education and inclusion of students with disabilities: a Delphi investigation', *Exceptional Children*, 61(6): 553–577.

Royal New Zealand Foundation for the Blind (2001) *Tertiary Study Information Pack for Blind and Sight Impaired Students and Tertiary Institution Staff*. Auckland: ENABLE/ Accessible Format Production.

Stanovich, P. and Jordan, A. (2000) 'Effective teaching as effective intervention', *Learning Disabilities*, 10(4): 235–238.

Sylvestro, D. P. (2001) 'Breaking down the walls of learned helplessness', paper presented at the LDA Conference, 10 February, New York.

Teymur , N. (1982) *Environmental Discourse*. Oxford: Blackwell.

The Australian National University (1995) 'Students with learning disabilities: a guide for staff and students', Available at: http://www.anu.edu.au/disabilities/swld.html (accessed 05/2005).

ThinkExist (2004) 'ThinkExist.com Quotations', Available at: http://en.thinkexist.com/ quotation/the_ancestor_of_every_action_is_a_thought/223822.html (accessed 05/2005).

Union of the Physically Impaired Against Segregation (1976) *Fundamental Principles of Disability*. London: Author.

University of Wales Institute (2000) *Information for Students with Disabilities*. Cardiff: UWIC.

Wolfensberger, W. (1972) *The Principle of Normalization in Human Services*. Toronto: National Institute of Mental Retardation.

Wolfensberger, W. and Thomas, S. (1983) *PASSING: Program Analysis of Service Systems Implementation of Normalization Goals*, 2nd edn. Toronto: National Institute of Mental Retardation.

Chapter 3

Listening to students

The experiences of disabled students of learning at university

Mick Healey, Andrew Bradley, Mary Fuller and Tim Hall

Introduction

There has been growing international interest in supporting the learning of disabled students in higher education, stimulated in part by legislation, such as the Americans with Disabilities Act of 1990 in the United States, the Commonwealth Disability Discrimination Act (1992) in Australia, and the Disability Discrimination Acts of 1995 and 2005 in the UK (Doyle and Robson 2002; Tinklin *et al.* 2004; Fraser and Sanders 2005; DO-IT n.d.a.). However, what the students themselves have to say about their experiences has not been sought in any systematic way. This chapter explores the barriers to learning faced by disabled students in higher education. It is illustrated by selected findings from three of the few systematic surveys to be undertaken on the topic, in each of which at least two of the authors have been involved. It also includes some initial findings from, as far as we can ascertain, the first ever survey to contrast the experience of a large sample of disabled and non-disabled students studying in the same institution. We draw on our experiences of presenting this material in several workshops and conferences in different countries.the UK, the United States, Austria and Australia. The responses at these events of disability advisers, learning support staff, educational developers, and academic staff from a wide range of disciplines have influenced this chapter.

Most interest in investigating the learning needs of disabled students in HEIs and the way they can be supported comes from staff in the disability advisory services and sometimes staff in learning and teaching centres (Stefani and Matthew 2002). It is unusual for this work to be led, as in the studies reported here, by a group of academic staff. HEIs are beginning to recognise that these issues 'cannot remain closed within a student services arena but must become part of the mainstream learning and teaching debate' (Adams 2002: 8). This viewpoint is reinforced by the legislation in the UK which puts a duty on universities and colleges to make reasonable adjustments in advance for the needs of disabled students and to produce disability equality statements. The implication is that all staff, academic and support, have a responsibility to provide a learning environment in which disabled students are not disadvantaged.

Context

Even though the enactment of various disability laws has contributed to the increasing enrolment of disabled students in higher educational institutions, Paul (2000: 209) suggests that 'these students constantly face various barriers in their educational environment' (italics added). Surprisingly little research has examined the nature of these barriers (Baron *et al.* 1996). A decade ago, Hurst (1996) pointed out that what has been missing from previous studies is the lived experience of disabled students. Despite the publication in recent years of guides to support university and college staff teaching disabled students (Teachability 2000; Gravestock and Healey 2001; Doyle and Robson 2002), little research has been initiated in response to Hurst's call. A few studies have undertaken in-depth investigations of the experience of higher education of small groups of disabled students, between 6 and 22 participants (Baron *et al.* 1996; Borland and James 1999; Hall and Tinklin 1999; Holloway 2001). With the exception of one study, which examined 56 students in eight HEIs (Riddell *et al.* 2002), none has systematically analysed a large sample of disabled students' experience of learning in higher education. UK research on disabled students' experiences in higher education has only recently come to include studies which focus exclusively on teaching, learning and assessment (Hall *et al.* 2002; Freewood and Spriggs 2003; Healey 2003; Fuller *et al.* 2004a, 2004b).

Listening to the experiences of disabled students themselves has the advantage of letting individuals express their 'lived experience' of being a student in higher education and enables the physical (Jayram and Scullion 2000) and hidden (Gaze 2000) barriers that they encounter to be highlighted. However, we recognise that there are also potential disadvantages to building policies solely on the experience of individuals as this can depoliticise the discourse and encourage individualised, piecemeal responses. On the other hand, we would argue that the findings from our research emphasise the variety of experience and the need for provision which is flexible. Our research evidence from students talking about their own learning needs and about strategies which are more or less successful in meeting them contradicts the view that there is a clear and straightforward relationship between impairment, barriers to learning and appropriate adjustment.

Our emphasis on identifying the barriers faced by disabled students places this research within the social model of disability as against the medical model. However, we support recent modifications to the social model which emphasise the reality of the lived experience of disabled people, and we are sympathetic to calls to construct a more adequate social theory of disability which recognises that everyone is impaired (Shakespeare and Watson 2002; Healey *et al.* 2006).

Survey aims and methods

The broad aim of three of the surveys reported here was to identify and evaluate disabled students' experience of teaching, learning and assessment. The fourth focused on these issues for non-disabled students. The purpose of the surveys was to shed light on the nature of the barriers disabled students face in learning in higher education and the extent to which these differ from difficulties that non-disabled students experience. In the UK 5.4 per cent of all undergraduate UK students in higher education (121,085 students) self-assessed themselves as having a disability in 2003/4 (NDT 2005).

Two of the studies of disabled students are complete, with some of the results already published (Fuller *et al.* 2004a, 2004b; Hall and Healey 2004; Hills and Healey 2006). The third, a large-scale longitudinal study funded by ESRC, is only part-way through the data collection stage. Three of the surveys were undertaken in the same institution at different dates: two surveys (the Institutional Survey 1) in 2001 and ESRC (Survey 2) in 2004 contacted every undergraduate student in the institution who had declared an impairment. Survey 1 asked disabled students to identify learning and assessment barriers, while Survey 2 examined the teaching, learning and assessment experiences of the students. Another Institutional Survey (Survey 3, also in 2004) asked the same questions of a 10 per cent sample of non-disabled students. The Geography, Earth and Environmental Sciences (GEES) Survey (Survey 4) used a modified version of the questionnaire from Survey 1 and was distributed in 2003 to all disabled students studying geography, earth and environmental sciences and closely related subjects in six different universities. In all cases, the questionnaire survey was only one of several methods used to elicit the experiences of the disabled students, including one-to-one and group interviews, case studies, and observations. This chapter assesses and compares a selection of the findings from the four questionnaire surveys.

The case study higher education institution (HEI) is an institution teaching mainly vocational subjects, with approximately 7,000 undergraduates spread across four campuses. The HEI has twice the national average percentage of disabled students (10 per cent). There is a cross-institution modular scheme in which the majority of students take two subjects in a major–minor or joint combination. The survey of disabled students in the GEES set of disciplines was undertaken in six English universities.

Altogether, over 800 responses were received from the four surveys. There were 173 completed questionnaires from the first survey in the HEI, a response rate of 29 per cent; while 548 responses resulted from the second and third surveys (276 disabled and 272 non-disabled students, each with a response rate of 40 per cent). The fourth GEES survey received 80 completed questionnaires, a response of 32 per cent.

Main findings

The experiences of disabled students are varied. Box 3.1 gives some feedback from Survey 1. Some encounter significant barriers, others are not aware of any; some find the support they receive highly praiseworthy, others find it does not meet their needs. Between 9 per cent and 15 per cent of disabled students in the institutional and GEES surveys said they chose their institution or their field of study in light of their disability.

Box 3.1 Experiences of three disabled students in one institution

I didn't actually know what my disability was when I came here. It was actually because of the university that I found out I was dyslexic and since then I can't praise them enough for the help I have actually received.

(Sport, dyslexia)

The hearing [*sic*] is just terrible and the lecturers know this, the ones that we had, but if it was a visiting lecturer they wouldn't know. They tend to show slides because the projector is in the middle of the room so they're standing behind it and they're not speaking to you, they're speaking to the screen.

(Art, deaf/hearing impaired)

At the beginning of some of my modules, I think one of the lecturers did say, 'If there are any problems, please tell me about them.' I still didn't take that opportunity! I think that would be helpful. If they put us at ease as well, and made them approachable about our disability.

(Environment, unseen disability)

(*Source*: Institutional Survey 1)

Perhaps most surprisingly, less than half of the respondents, and in many cases less than 25 per cent, identified disability-related barriers in terms of most of the modes of teaching that they experienced. Only 19 per cent of GEES students recognised barriers related to residential or non-residential fieldwork. The two exceptions were lectures, where close to 50 per cent of respondents in both the Institutional and GEES Surveys identified barriers, and independent fieldwork (e.g. undertaking a dissertation) where 43 per cent of GEES disabled students acknowledged barriers (Table 3.1). The reasons for this were explored in the GEES Survey (Boxes 3.2 and 3.3). The nature of the difficulties the students identified varied but included issues involving attendance, note taking, participation, confidence, concentration, and the longer time it takes them to complete tasks.

Table 3.1 Barriers related to modes of teaching

Disability-related barriers	HEI (%)	GEES (%)
Lectures	44	54
Laboratories/practicals		25
Other on campus classes	22	29
Fieldwork – residential		19
Fieldwork – non-residential		19
Fieldwork – independent		43
Off-campus sessions	21	
Using IT facilities	17	17

Source: Institutional Survey 1 and GEES Survey

Box 3.2 Responses from students who indicated that they had faced barriers which have impacted on their learning experience in lectures

The three-hour lectures could pose a problem if no break was given as it's important for me to eat to avoid hypos and if they clash with lunch/dinner times, this can be awkward.

(Diabetes)

In Geography, there are not so many slides and notes on the intranet as in sport. This means I have to take more notes and I find this difficult when I am trying to concentrate on what is being said.

(Dyslexia)

My assimilation of knowledge is made more difficult by my having to take medication which slows the process down; so many more hours than would usually be expected are taken at study within the laboratories and trying to recall data within lectures.

(Mental health difficulty and spondylosis)

Couldn't get to some distant lectures for a while – missed out on vital information.

(Wheelchair user/mobility difficulty – broken leg)

(*Source*: GEES Survey)

Box 3.3 Responses from students who indicated that their experience of independent fieldwork has been affected by their impairment

I found it difficult to get started on the dissertation and I felt that extra support from a tutor helped as well as a disability tutor.

(Dyslexia)

Takes me longer than others to carry out the research for this, should have asked about an extension.

(Dyslexia)

I'm not confident doing this sort of thing because of my disability.

(Dyslexia)

Dissertation research was very hard and in large quantities. This made me base my dissertation on physical work so that I didn't have to read as much.

(Dyslexia)

Concentration for long periods of time can be a problem. If I work for days on end, I find by the end I'm not taking in as much as I would have at the beginning.

(Dyslexia)

Yes, I feel my epilepsy holds me back, as on days I am not feeling well, [it] affects my work considerably. In general, the seizures do affect my long-term concentration and I take a long time to do work.

(Unseen disability – epilepsy)

I was feeling constant headache, dizziness and tiredness throughout the time I was doing research for my dissertation, up to now I still feel the same way.

(Unseen disability)

(*Source*: GEES Survey)

Barriers were rather more prevalent when it comes to assessment, especially among the GEES students. About a third of the disabled students in the institutional survey identified barriers with examinations and coursework, while this rose to almost two-thirds among the GEES students. Relatively fewer students acknowledged difficulties with multiple-choice tests and oral presentations (Table 3.2). Again, the reasons for the difficulties were explored in the GEES Survey. The nature of the difficulties covered a wide range of factors including concentration, tiredness, misreading, structuring, and the length of time taken (Box 3.4).

Table 3.2 Barriers related to modes of assessment

Disability-related barriers	HEI (%)	GEES (%)
Examinations	30	
Written examinations		62
Multiple choice/other exams		45
Coursework	34	63
Oral presentations	12	37

Source: Institutional Survey 1 and GEES Survey

Box 3.4 Responses from students who have faced barriers related to their impairment which have affected their experience of different types of assessment

Written exams – I get pain, even though [I'm] given longer. Hard to concentrate.

(Complex, multiple disability)

Written exams and course work – hard to concentrate because I suffer from tinnitus and am easily distracted; oral presentations – speech problems sometimes.

(Deaf/hearing impairment)

Written exams – have worried about having a hypo in an exam and I'm a little shy about telling the examiners so I must let them know about my condition beforehand. Also high blood sugars can affect performance and revision can lead to tiredness.

(Diabetes)

Written exams – short-term memory loss affected my ability to answer exam questions effectively but extra time does help. Written course work – structuring an essay can be tricky as ideas can end up being scattered and not following well, as well as language. Oral presentation – I felt that dyslexia affects my ability to explain clearly orally.

(Dyslexia)

I always read the questions wrong in written exams. Multiple choice is better but I get confused quickly when I try to read fast. I am really bad at course work. Luckily my course is mainly portfolios. Good at oral presentations but sometimes misspell on OHPs then everyone sees.

(Dyslexia)

I am often told my written work doesn't do credit to my understanding of the subject. I am continually frustrated by my inability to convey my understanding and views of a subject whenever written work is involved.

(Dyslexia)

I am much better doing a multiple choice exam than a written exam as it is difficult for me to explain the knowledge of a subject I know in essays but I would be quite confident in a multiple choice exam because I would know the information in order to be able to answer the question and would not have to worry about language structuring and spelling and grammar. I hate oral presentations because it is very difficult for me to converse my ideas out aloud and this is not to do with confidence but speech problems.

(Dyslexia)

My disability does not affect me orally. However, in written exams I need the use of a scribe, which is very difficult, as I lose my train of thought. Other exams, I write myself, and if they are multiple choice I don't have too many problems, but short answer tests tend to be more difficult. In course work, it takes me a lot longer to write stuff up. I have also had problems in getting deadline extensions.

(Other disability – arthritis)

(*Source*: GEES Survey)

Difficulties with assignments and different modes of teaching are not, of course, restricted to disabled students. Indeed, similar statements to those found in Tables 3.1 and 3.2 regarding difficulties faced in learning are often heard from non-disabled students. However, it was expected that the extent and nature of the difficulties would be more severe for the disabled students, because of anecdotal evidence of the barriers that they face. The initial findings from the second and third institutional surveys generally bear this out. Table 3.3 identifies six learning experiences where the percentage of disabled students acknowledging a difficulty with a learning experience exceeded the percentage of non-disabled students by 10 or more percentage points. These include difficulties taking notes, problems with literacy and the amount of time taken reading and completing assignments. Surprisingly, there were three areas in which fewer disabled students identified difficulties compared with non-disabled students. These were in knowing the

Table 3.3 Selected learning experiences of disabled and non-disabled students in one
university

Agree/Strongly agree	% disabled students (n=276)	% non-disabled students (n=272)
Areas in which disabled students have greater difficulty (10 per cent + point difference)		
I have had difficulty in taking notes	55	24
I have had difficulty due to the time given to read material not being realistic	45	32
I have had difficulties with the amount of time I require to complete assignments	55	39
I have had physical difficulties with writing	25	5
I have had difficulties with lecturers not understanding my circumstances	29	11
I have had difficulty with literacy skills	54	17
Areas in which non-disabled students have greater difficulty (5 per cent+ point difference)		
It's easy to know the standard of work expected	51	43
I have had difficulties with participation in group work	19	29
I have had difficulties with oral presentations	28	33

Source: Institutional Surveys 2 and 3

standard of work expected, participation in group work, and undertaking oral
presentations. It is possible that these differences reflect the relative significance
of the difficulties that disabled students face and not that the extent of the difficulty
is in reality any less than for non-disabled students.

Conclusion

This chapter has presented selected findings from three of the largest surveys of
the teaching and learning experiences of disabled students in higher education and
the first every survey asking identical questions about the learning experiences
of non-disabled students. Although the focus has been on the barriers that they
face, many examples of good practices were also revealed by the surveys. With
the exception of lectures, over half of the disabled students and often as many as
three-quarters have not experienced any disability-related barriers with teaching
and learning. However, up to two-thirds of GEES students identified barriers with
a variety of assessments.

Although the surveys found that in many cases only a minority of disabled
students faced barriers in teaching, learning and assessment, for those who did,

their impact was serious. These findings suggest that using a catch-all category 'disabled students' is problematic and that devising generic policies to support their teaching, learning and assessment may not always meet the specific needs of individuals. This emphasises the importance of individual discussion with disabled students, rather than assuming that an impairment indicates the teaching or assessment adjustment that is required:

> Unless we recognise the unevenness of understanding of disabled students' needs and willingness and ability to accommodate to those needs it would be easy to think that legislation will in itself create, or have created, a higher education environment that can accommodate the educational needs of disabled students.
>
> (Fuller *et al*. 2004a: 316)

In terms of learning needs, it is invidious to treat disabled students as a separate category; rather, they fall along a continuum of learner differences and share similar challenges and difficulties that all students face in higher education (Hall *et al*. 2002); sometimes the barriers are more severe for them, but sometimes not. Arguably, in the long run, the main beneficiaries of disability legislation and the need to make suitable adjustments in advance are the *non-disabled* students, because many of the adjustments, such as well-prepared handouts, instructions given in writing as well as verbally, notes put online, and variety and flexibility in forms of assessment, are simply good teaching and learning practices which benefit all students.

> One unintended consequence of this [disability] legislation is that as departments and institutions introduce more flexible learning and alternative ways of assessment for disabled students, demand is likely to rise for giving greater flexibility for all students. Disability legislation may prove to be a Trojan horse and in a decade, the learning experiences of all students may be the subject of greater negotiation.
>
> (Healey 2003: 26)

The surveys discussed here show that there is a vital need to continue to seek out, listen to, and act upon the views of disabled students in our attempts to make higher education thoroughly inclusive. However, more radically, given the overlap identified here in the learning experiences of students labelled as 'disabled' and 'non-disabled', would be to start from the basis that everyone is impaired. As Shakespeare and Watson (2002: 27) conclude: 'We believe that the claim that everyone is impaired, not just 'disabled people', is a far-reaching and important insight into human experience, with major implications for medical and social intervention in the twenty-first century.'

Acknowledgements

The Institutional Survey (Survey 1) (2001) of disabled students was funded by University of Gloucestershire's Scholarship of Learning and Teaching Fund and SCOPE. The ESRC Survey (Survey 2) (2004) 'Enhancing the Quality and Outcomes of Disabled Students' Learning in Higher Education' was funded by the ESRC Teaching and Learning Research Programme, ESRC award RES-139-25-0135. The Institutional Survey (Survey 3) (2004) of non-disabled students was funded by the University of Gloucestershire's Teaching Quality Enhancement Fund. The GEES Survey (Survey 4) (2003) was undertaken as part of the Geography Discipline Network's Inclusive Curriculum Project funded by HEFCE's Improving Provisions for disabled students' Funding Programme.

References and further reading

Adams, M. (2002) 'Learning, teaching and disability: the need for a new approach', *Planet Special Issue*, 3: 7–10.

Baron, S., Phillips, R. and Stalker, K. (1996) 'Barriers to training for disabled social work students', *Disability and Society*, 11: 361–377.

Borland, J. and James, S. (1999) 'The learning experience of students with disabilities in higher education: a case study of a UK university', *Disability and Society*, 14: 85–101.

DO-IT (Disabilities, Opportunities, Internetworking, and Technology) (n.d.a.) The Faculty Room, University of Washington, Seattle. Available at: http://www.washington.edu/doit/Faculty/Strategies/

DO-IT (n.d.b.) The Faculty Room, Statistics, University of Washington, Seattle: Available at: http://www.washington.edu/doit/Faculty/Rights/Background/statistics.html

Doyle, C. and Robson, K. (2002) *Accessible Curricula: Good Practice for All*. Cardiff: University of Wales Institute Cardiff Press. Available at: www.techdis.ac.uk/pdf/curricula.pdf

Fraser, K. and Sanders, E. (2005) 'Educating university teachers about students who have a disability: participation and access', in K. Fraser (ed.) *Educational Development and Leadership in Higher Education: Developing an Effective Institutional Strategy*. London: RoutledgeFalmer, pp. 129–155.

Freewood, M. and Spriggs, L. (2003) 'Striving for genuine inclusion: academic assessment and disabled students', in C. Rust (ed.) *Improving Student Learning Theory and Practice: 10 Years On*. Oxford: The Oxford Centre for Staff and Learning Development, Oxford Brookes University, pp. 353–362.

Fuller, M., Bradley, A. and Healey, M. (2004a) 'Incorporating disabled students within an inclusive higher education environment', *Disability and Society*, 19: 455–468.

Fuller, M., Healey, M., Bradley, A. and Hall, T. (2004b) 'Barriers to learning: a systematic study of the experience of disabled students in one university', *Studies in Higher Education*, 29(3): 303–318.

Gaze, H. (2000) 'Break down the barriers to disabled students, nursing schools urged', *Nursing Times*, 96(15): 7.

Gravestock, P. and Healey, M. (eds) (2001) *Providing Learning Support for Disabled Students Undertaking Fieldwork and Related Activities: A Set of Six Guides*.

Cheltenham: Geography Discipline Network, University of Gloucestershire. Available at: http://www/glos.ac.uk/gdn/disabil/index.htm

Hall, J. and Tinklin, T. (1998) *Students First: The Experiences of Disabled Students in Higher Education*. Report No. 85. Edinburgh: Scottish Council for Research in Education. Available at: http://www.scre.ac.uk/resreport/rr85/index.html

Hall, T. and Healey, M. with other members of the GDN ICP Project Team (2004) *The Experience of Learning at University by Disabled Students in Geography, Earth and Environmental Sciences and Related Disciplines: A Report on the Geography Discipline Network (GDN) Inclusive Curriculum Project (ICP) Student Survey*. Cheltenham: University of Gloucestershire, Geography Discipline Network. Available at: http://www.glos.ac.uk/gdn/icp/survey.htm

Hall, T., Healey, M. and Harrison, M. (2002) 'Fieldwork and disabled students: discourses of exclusion and inclusion', *Transactions of the Institute of British Geographers* NS, 2: 213–231.

Healey, M. (2003) 'Trojan horse is good bet for all: strategies to improve flexibility for disabled students could benefit everyone', *The Times Higher Education Supplement*, 19 September.

Healey, M., Jenkins, A. and Leach, J. (2006) *Issues in Developing an Inclusive Curriculum: Examples from Geography, Earth and Environmental Sciences*. Cheltenham: University of Gloucestershire, Geography Discipline Network. Available at: http://www.glos.ac.uk/gdn/icp (forthcoming).

Hills, M. and Healey, M. (eds) (2006) *Inclusive Curriculum Project: A Set of Ten Guides*. Cheltenham: University of Gloucestershire, Geography Discipline Network. Available at http://www.glos.ac.uk/gdn/icp.

Holloway, S. (2001) 'The experience of higher education from the perspective of disabled students', *Disability and Society*, 16: 597–615.

Hurst, A. (1996) 'Reflecting on researching disability and higher education', in L. Barton (ed.) *Disability and Society: Emerging Issues and Insights*. London: Longman.

Jayram, R. and Scullion, P. (2000) 'Access to all areas', *Nursing Management*, 7(1): 17–19.

NDT (National Disability Team) (2005) 'Statistics on course'. Available at: http://www.natdisteam.ac.uk/resources_statistics_oncourse.html

Paul, S. (2000) 'Students with disabilities in higher education: a review of the literature', *College Student Journal*, 34: 200–210.

Riddell, S., Wilson, A. and Tinklin, T. (2002) 'Disability and the wider access agenda: supporting disabled students in different institutional contexts', *Widening Participation and Lifelong Learning*, 4(3): 12–26.

Shakespeare, T. and Watson, N. (2002) 'The social model of disability: an outdated ideology?', *Research in Social Science and Disability*, 2: 9–28.

Stefani, L. and Matthew, R. G. S. (2002) 'The difficulties of defining development: a case study', *International Journal for Academic Development*, 7(1): 41–50.

Teachability (2000) *Creating an Accessible Curriculum for Students with Disabilities*. Glasgow: University of Strathclyde. Available at: http://www.teachability.strath.ac.uk/

Tinklin, T., Riddell, S. and Wilson, A. (2004) 'Policy and provision for disabled students in higher education in Scotland and England: the current state of play', *Studies in Higher Education*, 29(5): 637–657.

Chapter 4

Academic standards and benchmark descriptors

Val Chapman and Helen Carlisle

Introduction

From January 2003 to December 2004, the Equal Opportunities Centre at University College Worcester (UCW) was responsible for the management of a Higher Education Funding Council for England-funded disability project, *Academic Standards and Benchmark Descriptors: Developing Strategies for Inclusivity* (HEFCE 2002). The project explored the quality agenda and its impact on the experiences of disabled students. Within the framework of the Quality Assurance Agency's Benchmark programme (Jackson 2002: 139–151), the project examined the use and perception of Subject Benchmark Statements by the academic community, and their potential for supporting inclusive practice. This chapter explains the background, process and outcomes of this project and the description is supplemented by the 'voice' (boxes) of Dr Val Chapman, project leader, as a participant observer working from University College Worcester. These interjections provide a live commentary on our discussion of the funded project.

Background

UCW has an academic history that spans more than five decades. It was first established as an emergency Teacher Training College in 1947 to provide newly qualified teachers to a greatly depleted profession. Over the years the range of courses offered has been greatly extended. UCW now has over 8,000 students undertaking a wide range of academic, professional and vocational programmes at undergraduate and postgraduate level both full-time and part-time. It works closely with schools and Further Education colleges throughout Herefordshire and Worcestershire and has developed a significant strategic partnership with the University of Birmingham.

My career progression in Higher Education is fairly unusual, and it was precisely this particularity that led to my interest in the work that forms the basis of the project. After six years of teaching at UCW, I was promoted to the position of Head of the Equal Opportunities (EO) Centre, and shortly afterwards also became employed by the UK's Quality Assurance Agency (UK QAA) as a subject reviewer. On taking up my new post in the EO Centre, I discovered very quickly that academic qualifications, enthusiasm, passionate commitment to equal opportunities and diversity, and a developing expertise in the field were not enough to achieve the range and/or rate of progress at UCW that I would have liked. While Equal Opportunities was very well supported by senior management and championed by the Principal, resources for the development of the service were limited. It was in discovering the possibilities offered by project funding that I found a way to achieve dramatic improvements to provision.

Finding the key to enter the 'secret garden' of funding was not easy. It involved time, energy, substantial research, and much hard work, frequently during vacation time since project submission deadlines seem always to fall during these periods; but the rewards were well worth the effort invested.

Given that institutions are normally in competition for project funding and therefore loath to share their secrets of successful bidding, it is also worth mentioning that I benefited from the very helpful training on bid writing provided by the HEFCE's eQuip Team, the first national disability co-ordination team in England. The eQuip team has since been superseded by the National Disability Team (NDT) who provide a coordination service to support current HEFCE/DELNI funded projects. They provide a focal point of information about funded projects, play a central role in the dissemination of project outcomes and work closely with other national teams and organisations to provide information and advice about disability-related developments in higher education.

Following that training, the EO Centre at UCW developed a strong track record in successful bid writing and managing funded projects (nine to date) and, as a direct consequence of these projects, UCW now has a comprehensive and highly valued Disability Service, and the recruitment of disabled students has been substantially enhanced, significantly exceeding the national average.

As UCW entered the new millennium, a colleague from the Learning and Teaching Centre at UCW was engaged in research and development of personal development profiling, and intended to pilot the use of the Student Qualities Profile (SQP) within UCW. Anticipating that some dyslexic students might need some additional support and/or guidance in completing these new profiling documents, I invited the colleague to meet me and the EO team to discuss the implications of the SQP for disabled students. In preparing for this staff development event, I checked through the SQP and was immediately struck by the fact that some students supported by the EO Centre would find some of the key skills listed in the document extremely difficult, if not impossible, to achieve for reasons directly related to their impairments. For example, some deaf or autistic students might find difficulty with group work and, certainly, many dyslexic students would have difficulty with writing skills. This observation prompted me, wearing my UK QAA subject reviewer hat, to recognise that Subject Benchmark Statements also might contain learning outcomes that could be challenging for disabled students. A quick check of a random sample confirmed my concern and the idea for another funding bid was born.

In order to help those unfamiliar with the UK Quality Assurance system to understand the relevance of Subject Benchmark Statements to the project, we provide here some indication here of their origin and *raison d'être*. Since 2000, the UK QAA has been developing an infrastructure to strengthen, elaborate, and make more comprehensive the purposes and outcomes of higher education in the United Kingdom (Wright and Williams 2001). This has largely been in response to the Dearing Report (1997) and the Widening Participation agenda, and constitutes an attempt to maintain broadly comparable academic standards across the whole of higher education.

As part of this agenda, the UK QAA, working with subject groups of academics from a wide range of disciplines, introduced a collection of Subject Benchmark Statements in two phases. Phase 1 subjects were launched in April 2000, and included 33 subjects, of which 11 were specifically related to healthcare disciplines. Phase 2 subjects were introduced in March 2002 and included 26 subjects. Since then, many additional subject areas have expressed an interest in creating their own benchmark statements and on 24 November 2004, the UK QAA launched the 'Recognition Scheme' to facilitate this, and also published guidelines and arrangements for the review of existing statements (QAA 2004).

Subject Benchmark Statements, for those unfamiliar with them, can be described as authoritative documents, written by representatives of the academic communities and published by the UK QAA. They act as one of a set of reference points for designing and reviewing higher education programmes of study by describing the characteristics of particular subjects, outlining the attributes and capabilities that graduates in those subjects might demonstrate, and representing the general expectations about the standard of honours degrees in the subject area.

The benchmark information provides an external source of reference that, while recognising diversity and variety in higher education provision, informs the process of designing programmes of study.

Since assessment is also integral to the design of programmes and the delivery of learning and teaching, it was not unrealistic that I originally assumed a relationship between benchmark information and the criteria for assessment as well . . . though this proved to be not quite the case, as is explained later in this chapter. In preparing the project bid, I was pleased to read that the UK QAA expected that the infrastructural activities should encourage, or 'induce' academics into mapping and interrogating their own tacit practices and underlying assumptions. I believed that UCW's proposed collaboration with the UK QAA to consider the infrastructure (and persuade academic staff to consider ways in which their subjects could be made more inclusive) seemed supportive of the true spirit of the Dearing recommendations. The project's proposed activity also coincided with the implementation of the DDA (2002) Part 4 and I anticipated this would prove an opportune time to work with the UK QAA to encourage academic communities to address the precepts of good practice relating to disability in the UK QAA's own Code of Practice (QAA 1999).

The main aim of our project was to act as a catalyst for change, and help promote a more inclusive approach to student engagement and achievement through the vehicle of Subject Benchmark Statements. It was felt that this approach went to the very heart of a subject's planning, delivery and assessment, and it was hoped that the project would extend the underlying concept of 'graduateness', as evidenced by subject benchmark descriptors, to include disabled people. The project director, together with the Assistant Director, UK QAA, who is project manager for all the UK QAA's benchmarking work, selected 10 subjects for inclusion in the pilot that constituted a representative cross sample of subject areas. These were:

Computing	Music
Dance, Drama and Performance	Nursing
English	Physiotherapy
Hospitality, Leisure, Sport and Tourism	Social Work
Maths, Stats and OR	Veterinary Science

In order to achieve the project's aim, first of all, it was intended to produce a framework for the review of Subject Benchmark Statements against principles of inclusion (piloted with the sample of ten subject areas) and, second, to identify reasonable adjustments that should be made by academic teams to enable disabled students to achieve those learning outcomes embedded in the benchmark descriptors identified as problematic. This information would be further supplemented by the inclusion of subject-specific case studies and embedded web links to other relevant sources of advice and guidance.

The project activities were facilitated through the establishment of a project team which had a composite range of appropriate expertise in the areas of academic standards and Subject Benchmarking, disability, project management, Information Technology (IT), and quality assurance (Figure 4.1). This management structure was particularly effective for a number of reasons, not least the spread of the relevant expertise. First, the involvement of the Assistant Director, UK QAA, was critical since he was the gatekeeper to the UK QAA, giving a very clear steer of the organisation's perception of the role and value of Subject Benchmark Statements; he also facilitated access to the Chairs of Benchmarking teams. Second, while the project manager and project director interacted on a routine basis, the monthly meetings of the Executive Group were a key factor in the successful review and development of the project's activities. Third, an external evaluator was employed from the outset of the project. He attended all Steering Group meetings, most Executive Group meetings, and also participated in each consultation with the Chairs of the Benchmarking teams. His contribution as a critical friend at each meeting ensured that assumptions were tested, lines of inquiry completed, and decisions appropriately questioned. Once the conceptual framework of the online resource had been agreed, the team was further supplemented by the employment of an Information Technology (IT) web designer to construct the site following the brief developed by the Executive Group.

Project outcomes

The core achievement of the project was the development of the SCIPS (Strategies for Creating Inclusive Programmes of Study) website. The SCIPS resource has been made available for academic staff to consult during the interpretation of

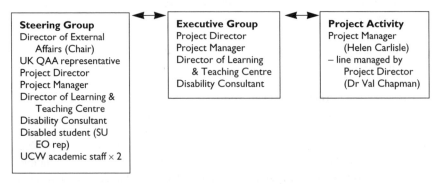

Figure 4.1 Project management structure

Subject Benchmark Statements when creating programme or course specifications. It helps academic staff identify potential challenges to the achievement of learning activities/outcomes for students with certain impairments or degree of difficulty. The potential challenges are cross-referenced with recommended adjustments to practice so that academic staff can enable disabled students to meet the learning outcomes as described in the Subject Benchmark Statements.

The project built upon previous research within the field, most notably: Teachability, the DEMOS Project (Online Materials for Staff Disability Awareness), SWANDS (South West Academic Network for Disability Support), COWORK: Widening Access for Disabled Students, and TechDIS. Key to the successful development of the resource was consultation with a variety of interested parties. As well as consulting former Chairs of Benchmarking teams, feedback from key stakeholders was gained during presentations at a variety of conferences. These included academic staff (Institute of Learning and Teaching, now part of the Higher Education Academy); staff developers (Staff and Educational Development Association); disability professionals in the UK, in particular, E.A. Draffan of TechDis (Skill: National Bureau for Students with Disabilities conferences, n = 2), and disability professionals overseas (4th International Disability Conference, Innsbruck). TechDis (http://www.techdis.ac.uk), the leading educational advisory service, works across the UK, in the fields of accessibility and inclusion. It aims to enhance provision for disabled students and staff in higher, further and specialist education and adult and community learning, through the use of technology. Skill: National Bureau for Students with Disabilities (http://www.skill.org) is a national charity promoting opportunities for all disabled young people and adults in post-16 education, training and employment across the UK.

In order to develop the on-line resource, SCIPS, the project team listed the learning outcomes from all Subject Benchmark Statements in the sample of ten, and these were compiled into a list for ease of comparison. In completing this process, it became apparent that the Benchmarking Teams had interpreted the guidance issued by the UK QAA for the benchmarking exercise quite differently. Some teams had identified generic learning outcomes for proficiency in the subject using somewhat loosely defined terminology, for example, 'develop an argument' (Hospitality, Leisure, Sport and Tourism) and some were expressed more explicitly: 'the ability to present sustained and persuasive written and oral arguments cogently and coherently' (English).

It was also interesting to note that what was categorised as a 'generic' graduate skill in one discipline was considered a 'core' graduate skill in another. For example, 'effective written communication' is generally considered to be a generic graduate skill in all disciplines, but for graduates of English Language and Literature programmes, this outcome was considered core to the discipline. This notion of what is absolutely core to different disciplines raises an interesting topic for discussion among subject communities, not least in deciding what alternative methods might be legitimately used to teach and/or assess disabled students in order for them to achieve the desired learning outcomes. To illustrate, if good writing skills are defined within the Subject Benchmark Statement as a generic skill, a reasonable adjustment to practice for those whose impairment make this difficult might be the employment of a proof reader, voice recognition software and/or the use of a spellchecker for either coursework or examinations. However, for some courses in some subject areas, the vehicle, written skills, is as important as the content of the student's work and proficiency in both may comprise key learning outcomes of the course. Following the introduction of the UK Disability Discrimination Act Part 4, subject teams will need to consider and distinguish the core features of their disciplines in order to define clearly – and defend – the standards of a prescribed kind they wish to adhere to.

Another important consideration for the teams in compiling the Subject Benchmark Statements was whether or not students graduating from programmes of study within their discipline might be expecting to gain professional accreditation within an appropriate specialist field at the end of the course. This was of particular relevance to health subjects. Examples of subjects included in this pilot included Nursing, Physiotherapy, Social Work and Veterinary Science and Social Work (see also Chapter 9 of this volume). For these subjects, the learning outcomes, as defined within the Subject Benchmark Statements, are almost wholly aligned to the learning objectives prescribed by the professional body for graduates gaining professional status and fitness to practice. In these statements, the project team observed a much more prescribed approach whereby the learning outcome itself is much more specific, and attention is also paid to how the outcome might be achieved and demonstrated. This is especially true of learning outcomes that have a practical nature, for example, 'handle and restrain animals safely and humanely whilst ensuring personal safety and that of others in the vicinity' (Veterinary Science).

In developing an understanding of the different processes and procedures adopted by each of the Benchmark Teams when constructing their statements, it became evident that, for many of the teams, achieving a consensus about what best represented standards of achievement in their discipline had been a hard-fought battle. The project team very quickly became aware that the statements were not available for revision, further, they were conscious that some academic communities would regard any review of the statements (no matter how altruistic in purpose) as criticism. It was therefore imperative to the success of the project that the SCIPS resource identified potentially problematic learning outcomes embedded in the Subject Benchmark Statement, *as published*.

The SCIPS resource provides a breakdown of the Subject Benchmark Statements for the ten subjects selected in order to highlight where there might be learning activities and/or learning outcomes, written into each statement, that could be potentially challenging for some students directly related to their impairments. This also provides a useful framework with more generalized utility beyond the UK. For each possible challenge identified, a number of strategies are offered to overcome it through recommended adjustments to teaching and learning practices to make them more inclusive. Subject-specific case studies are also provided as well as links to further resources. To offer multiple access routes into the substantial bank of information contained within the resource, users are invited to browse by key skill, subject area, disability, or potential challenge to the achievement of learning. Key skills are generic to all statements and might include those such as, 'develop written arguments', 'planning and time management', or 'develop effective IT skills'.

The project team recognised that many academic staff have little confidence in matters relating to supporting disabled students and operate on the assumption that particular impairments equate to standardised sets of difficulties in learning. It was judged that academic staff, with a limited understanding of the associated needs of students with particular impairments, might be unlikely to find their way through to the relevant information unless clearly signposted. In other words, the team understood that a facility to search SCIPS by impairment (using UCAS codes for disabilities) might prove helpful, and so this has been included.

However, this raised a clear tension between the needs of academic staff and the project team's desire to promote the social rather than the medical model of disability. The team wished to emphasise that same medical conditions or impairments do not constitute the same life or learning experiences and/or needs. To this end, the SCIPS database focuses its search feature more on the use of issues, or 'potential challenges' to the achievement of learning. These are discrete areas where differences between students may pose challenges to academic staff in promoting effective learning. Such 'challenges' do not necessarily relate to specific impairments, and their use is intended to discourage academic staff from crude assumptions about the implications of particular disabilities. SCIPS therefore focuses on the provision of information about enabling learning environments rather than on students' impairments which perpetuates the medical model. If users search the database via the 'disability' route, they encounter general information regarding the disability, but are then directed to the more specific information contained within the 'potential challenges' pages of the resource.

The database is constructed in such a way that the user is required to move away from the medical model approach and, instead, it prompts the user to consider the potential challenges associated with learning, in order to access the strategies and case studies. Users can also take the subject route into the database, but again are directed towards subject-specific information relating to learning challenges in that discipline. The importance of this approach is that it recognises the continuum of ability and encourages the use of inclusive strategies for the delivery of the curriculum that benefit *all* students.

Evaluating the project

An external perspective on the project has been made possible by using the reports of the project's external evaluator to highlight both the strengths and the challenges experienced during the project. It is certainly worth emphasising that the employment of an external evaluator from the outset of the project with the dual role of critical friend and objective observer proved invaluable to the success of the project and the development of the SCIPS resource. The final paragraphs highlight the key factors contributing to the successful completion of the project.

The support of the UK QAA was essential to the credibility of the project and to the development of the project team's understanding of the Subject Benchmarking process and outcomes. The UK QAA also facilitated the meetings with the Chairs of the Subject Benchmarking teams.

My original project proposal held somewhat different conceptions of the Benchmarking process and its potential role in the project than proved to be the case. For example, the notion in the project application, that 'there is a clear relationship between benchmark information and the criteria for assessment', while true in some cases, turned out to be far from universal. It also became clear from our discussions with the Chairs of the Benchmarking teams that existing Subject Benchmark Statements were not available for redrafting, even where aspects were identified as problematic in relation to disabled students. On meeting Benchmarking Chairs for the first time, it became apparent that academic teams were unlikely to be receptive to any prescriptive recommendations regarding reasonable adjustments for disabled students. It was clear from our discussions that academic teams would be highly likely to resist what they would inevitably perceive as external impositions from non-subject specialists.

The Chairs of the Benchmarking teams' input was crucial to the success of this project since they modified early misconceptions of the form, the development and the authority of the Subject Statements. The Chairs stressed that Subject Benchmark Statements should be understood as negotiated outcomes, often involving the reconciliation of competing positions within disciplines. Some appear to have been the products of a willing consensus, others the results of compromise.

In drafting the project proposal I had (somewhat naïvely) thought that, where we could highlight barriers to participation posed within certain subject benchmark statements, the academic teams would have been prepared to modify these. Despite the new legislation highlighting the needs to make reasonable adjustments, this was clearly going to be problematic, and meant we had to revise my original intention to propose 'amendments' to the statements.

The chairs did the following:

*   emphasised that Subject Statements often cover a group of disciplines that are themselves only loosely related;
*   acknowledged that some Subject Statements are quite prescriptive in style, others more permissive, describing the range of options within which courses may be constructed.

> While unsurprised that the statements were not written to a template that either aimed to, or achieved, a uniform product, I was surprised by the very different perceptions of the benchmarks' perceived authority. In creating SCIPS we had to develop an on-line resource that recognised the different weight given to the sample of statements by the various academic communities while addressing the subject specific needs in relation to supporting disabled students.

The chairs were reluctant to see themselves as authoritative spokespeople or representatives able to talk on behalf of 'their' Benchmarking teams. They viewed their role simply as having been a facilitator in the production of the Benchmark Statements and were therefore generally disinclined to give an authoritative interpretation on the Benchmark Statements.

> In drafting the scripts for the website, we had agreed that some endorsement of the site by the participating Chairs might have been quite a helpful inclusion. However, it was evident that some were disinclined to assume any representative mantle of authority, possibly because of the difficulties experienced in gaining consensus in the benchmarks' development in the first place.

The chairs emphasised the difficulty for SCIPS to draw directly on Subject Benchmark Statements in anything other than their original language, arguing that only in this form do the Subject Benchmark Statements have legitimacy among the subject community; noting this, the project team ensured that links to the Subject Benchmark Statements in their intact original format were included for each subject.

> Again, given the substantial discussion and negotiation that contributed to the production of the Subject Benchmark Statements, some Chairs

were most anxious that the text and presentation of their statement, as finally agreed by the benchmarking team, should not be modified in any way. To accommodate this view, we included a hot link directly to each of the Subject Benchmark Statements on the relevant pages of the SCIPS website.

The Subject Benchmark Statements proved both useful and valid vehicles to inform academic staff regarding inclusion. They provided the project team with indications of areas where problems for disabled students might arise, but because they were formulated in ways that allow considerable autonomy to course teams in how they address inclusivity issues, SCIPS had to be developed in a format that was flexible enough to be useful across approaches that vary considerably.

SCIPS went live in 2005 and will continue to be updated with additional material and subject-specific case studies as these emerge from other HEFCE-funded projects and from Learning and Teaching Network subject centres. One of the remaining challenges for UCW will be to maintain and further extend the site developed in this pilot project in the hope that it will help teaching staff to understand and embrace inclusion.

References and further reading

Cowork (2002) 'Widening access for disabled students'. Available at: http://www.cowork. ac.uk/ (accessed 06/2005).

Dearing, R. (1997) *Higher Education in the Learning Society: Report of the National Committee of Enquiry into Higher Education*. London: HMSO.

Demos (2002) 'Online materials for staff disability awareness'. Available at: http://www. demos.ac.uk (accessed 06/2005).

Higher Education Funding Council for England (2002) *Improving Provision for Disabled Students: Strategy and invitation to bid for funds for 2003–05*. Bristol: HEFCE, 02/21.

Jackson, N. (ed.) (2002) 'Growing knowledge about subject benchmarking', *Quality Assurance in Education: UK QAA Subject Benchmarking*, 10(3): 139–151.

Quality Assurance Agency (1999) 'Section 3: Students with Disabilities', *Code of Practice for the Assurance of Academic Quality and Standards in Higher Education*. London: QCA.

Quality Assurance Agency (2004) 'Benchmarking', *Higher Quality*, 16, October.

SENDA (2001) *The Special Educational Needs and Disability Act*. London: The Stationery Office.

SWANDS (2002) 'SENDA Compliance in Higher Education: an audit and guidance tool for accessible practice within the framework of teaching and learning'. The University of Plymouth. Available at: http://www.plymouth.ac.uk/pages/view.asp?page=3243 (accessed 06/2005).

Teachability (2000) 'Creating an accessible curriculum for students with disabilities', The University of Strathclyde, Available at: http://www.teachability.strath.ac.uk/ (accessed 06/2005).

Wright, P. and Williams, P. (2001) 'How it all fits together: quality assurance and the standards infrastructure', *Higher Quality*, 9 November: 11–12.

Chapter 5

Supporting staff in developing inclusive online learning

Elaine Pearson and Tony Koppi

Introduction

This chapter focuses on the methods used to support academic staff in the design and development of inclusive flexible learning approaches. It discusses the design rationale underpinning the staff development activities, and includes an overview of the evaluation undertaken. We identify strategies for ensuring that staff receive appropriate, targeted and timely training in accessibility to ensure inclusive practices are adopted across an institution.

The Special Needs Computing Research Unit (SNCRU) at the University of Teesside (UoT) and the Educational Development and Technology Centre (EDTeC) at the University of New South Wales (UNSW), Sydney, Australia, have been working together for more than five years, researching ways of enhancing the learning experience for disabled students. The aim is to support staff in the development of inclusive flexible learning approaches. The approach we have adopted as a result of our research has been to provide staff development courses in different modes, suited to diverse cohorts and to a variety of contexts and time constraints.

The work was initially funded through a Leverhulme Fellowship which supported an evaluation of the accessibility of WebCT courses at UNSW. Analysis was undertaken both of the accessibility of the WebCT environment, and of the learning resources in the WebCT courses. We also surveyed academic staff on their understanding of the needs of disabled students with disabilities and interviewed disabled students themselves on their experiences and problems with online learning (Pearson and Koppi 2002).

As a result of the evaluation, 'Guidelines for Accessible Online Courses' (Pearson and Koppi 2001) was published to help support staff to address the accessibility issues identified. The Guidelines are in a format suited suitable for academic staff who is are not necessarily skilled in the use of technology and consists of hints, tips and practical advice. The user-friendly Guidelines are based on the relevant sections of the W3C (http://www.w3.org/WAI/) Web Accessibility Initiative (WAI) guidelines 1999, suitably interpreted for academics with references and links to the WAI guidelines where appropriate.

The Guidelines were well received although feedback identified the need for more practical support and therefore provided the rationale for the creation of staff development activities. Initially, an intensive (week-long) flexible online course for making developing accessible online courses was created specifically as part of an Innovative Teaching and Educational Technology (ITET) Fellowship scheme at UNSW. The course was also intended as an exemplary model for learning and teaching online from both a pedagogical and accessibility viewpoint.

Analysis of the evaluations from each of the four cohorts of fellows confirmed that the course was valuable, appropriate and timely. However, as few staff have the opportunity to undertake a week-long intensive course, it was refined and distilled (supported partially by a grant from the Higher Education Funding Council for England) to create a one-day staff development experience for anyone involved in the production, support or resource development for e-learning activities. This staff development programme has been adapted for several higher education institutions for staff with differing roles, and has been further adapted to mixed-mode with online activities followed by a face-to-face workshop aimed mainly at, though not exclusively, staff developers. The programmes differ in length, format and intensity but the emphasis for each is on activities, support and resources to help staff understand the issues, acquire the relevant skills, identify appropriate sources of support and empathise with the needs of disabled students.

The remainder of this chapter discusses the design rationale upon which the course is based, and includes an overview of the evaluation undertaken. We further identify strategies for appropriate support to ensure inclusive practices are adopted across an institution.

Barriers to student learning online

The introduction of e-learning can be beneficial to disabled students (Pearson 2001). Other authors (e.g. Grimaldi and Goette 1999; Ommerborn and Schuemer 2001), have also noted the benefits, particularly when physical access, classroom conditions and traditional learning and teaching methods are problematic. Buildings that lack suitable wheelchair access, teaching rooms without assistive technology (for example, induction loops for audio), paper-based handouts or board writing that is difficult to read, all limit the opportunities for disabled students to participate. The trend towards integration of e-learning with face-to-face learning and teaching methods give provides new opportunities for increased participation:

> A number of benefits for students related to the general use of technology in the classrooms have been reported. These include increased motivation, improvement in self-concept and mastery of basic skills, more student-centred learning and engagement in the learning process, and more active processing, resulting in higher-order thinking skills and better recall.
>
> (Stepp-Greany 2002)

However, if e-learning is not to further exclude this group, particular care needs to be taken in the design and development of learning materials and other resources. Disabled students experience a range of difficulties that may inhibit their ability to access e-learning. For example:

- students with sensory impairments may not be able to see or hear multimedia learning resources;
- students with cognitive and learning disabilities impairments may have problems with navigation, organisation, structure, use of colour or complex language;
- students with physical disabilities impairments may have difficulty navigating or interacting with the computer or using a mouse.

These difficulties have an impact on students' opportunities to take advantage of online learning. Course developers need to understand that students may be using assistive technology such as screen readers, alternative input devices or magnifiers, but also that resources need to be carefully designed and offered in alternative formats. Furthermore, the same difficulties may be experienced by other user groups, including students who are not fluent in the language of study and older students who may begin to experience physical, cognitive or sensory impairments. There may also be technical barriers arising both from older and newer technologies which impact on all students. Slow modems and hand-held wireless technologies such as personal digital assistants (PDA) can result in accessibility problems for all learners if the resources are not carefully designed. Effective access and a better learning experience for all students can be achieved with careful consideration for design and some basic practical skills based on knowledge of the way assistive technology is used to access web-based environments and the effect of differing impairments on the way students are able to experience online learning.

Design rationale

The accessibility programme is based on the rationale that in making developing accessible courses, staff are not just only catering for what may be a small minority of disabled learners, but that they are in fact making a more inclusive learning experience for all their students.

Academic and support staff have different varying needs to web developers in terms of the key skills they need to make their online learning resources accessible. They are less likely to be developing websites and instead are mainly placing documents, activities and learning supports within a virtual learning environment (VLE) such as WebCT or Blackboard.

Several versions of the accessibility course have been designed based on two models: the face-to-face one-day workshop; and the flexible online course which is more intensive and may take place over one or several weeks or even a whole semester. The activities in the single-day event are focused more primarily on the practical considerations while the longer course (like any other) is able to address theoretical issues and provides greater opportunities for discussion, research and reflection. The former may be more of an overview and has a more practical emphasis, and the latter allows for greater depth; both share similar outcomes.

The programme both for the workshop and for the online course is centred on five major themes that we identified as essential to support inclusive design. These themes involve the following:

- discussion of the issues relevant to accessibility of online learning for disabled people;
- legal and quality assurance requirements;
- the guidelines and protocols available to underpin accessible design;
- the assistive technologies used by disabled students and the implications of such tools in the design process;
- design issues particularly relating to commonly used document types in e-learning;
- checking tools and mechanisms that are available for the designer to check the accessibility of web pages.

Aims and outcomes

The aim of the accessibility programme is to enable staff to develop competence in the design of inclusive and accessible learning resources, to apply their knowledge in the development of their own projects and to encourage other staff to consider accessibility issues in e-learning resources. The long-term goal is for staff to accept and adopt accessibility principles and to develop accessible websites and learning materials as second nature. Familiarisation with the issues and practices is a necessary part of adopting new practices. The stated learning outcomes are as follows. At the end of the course you will be able to do the following:

1   Discuss the issues relevant to accessibility of online learning for with disabilities disabled people.
2   Appraise the use and application of assistive technologies.
3   Analyse barriers to accessibility in existing websites and online courses.
4   Formulate learner-centred design strategies for accessible online courseware.
5   Demonstrate skills in the use of relevant guidelines and accessibility checking mechanisms.
6   Apply skills in the design and development of accessible and inclusive online courseware relevant in individuals own area of activity.

The course is kept open to participants to enable them to re-visit and explore at their own pace, or utilise when the material is needed in their own online course design. The advantages of face-to-face interaction though cannot be denied. The time commitment is made and colleagues are there on hand for immediate discussion, however brief. Commitment to an online course can be problematic for busy people because it is too easy not to set the time aside (Forsyth 2001). A face-to-face workshop is provided to supplement the online component. The workshop gives the opportunity for participants to use and experience specialist software and assistive technologies.

Learning design

In the online component, participants need the same supports as would be provided for any course designed for students, and our philosophy was to apply a learning design based on educational theory and pedagogical principles that would provide an exemplar in inclusive design.

The design of the one-week course for the ITET Fellows was based on the cognitive apprenticeship model (Brandt *et al.* 1993) as detailed in Koppi and Pearson (2002). The cognitive apprenticeship model (Collins 1988) involves the use of modelling, coaching, reflecting on performance, articulation and application. Knowledge and skills are taught in contexts that reflect how the knowledge will be used in real-life situations.

The participants are introduced to the issues of accessibility through a video example of how an expert approaches the problem (modelling). This is followed by small group activities for participants to engage with the issues identified by the expert (coaching). These activities include research and an; the opportunity to experience and develop skills in each of the five themes of the course: the law, guidelines, designing accessible documents, assistive technology and checking mechanisms and group discussion (reflection). Each small group is given responsibility for investigating one theme in depth to share with the other participants (articulation). Finally, the participants evaluate an online learning environment by applying what they have learned from their activities and discussions (application).

The course has since been further adapted to a three-week online event to enable academics to participate in a less structured way and to support flexibility in terms of time, h allocation. However, the same course design principles are still applied.

Design features to support accessibility

One advantage of presenting the course online is that it provides the both an opportunity to demonstrate how accessibility can be incorporated into the learning design, and that it demonstrates. The online course was designed to follow accessibility principles as well as demonstrating sound pedagogical practices. The following list of design features are ones those that we believe meet these criteria and are based on our experience and analysis of websites and online courses. The interface features may vary slightly depending on the VLE used (WebCT or Blackboard) but the resources and supports are the same:

- The Home page has text and icon (with alt-tags) links to all the important elements of the course (WebCT only).
- High contrast text and background are used throughout, and no unnecessary graphics or icons are used.
- Tips for accessibility are given in a prominent position, e.g. for people using a screen reader, a suggestion to hide the left navigation bar which adds unnecessary complexity to the page.
- A link is provided to any downloads that may be necessary, e.g. Adobe Acrobat Reader to enable suitably formatted PDF documents to be read by a screen reader.
- The use of PDF has been avoided wherever possible because they can be difficult to make accessible to a screen reader, and alternative formats have been provided.
- A Welcome section provides tutor contact details, describes the course, its rationale, the activities, and invites feedback on/evaluation of the course.
- The aims, objectives and learning outcomes are prominent.
- A link to other parts of the course is provided wherever they are mentioned, and that link opens in a new window to enable easy return (closing the window).
- Links are provided directly to any particular discussion topic rather than just to the discussion area which would require further searching to find the specific relevant topic (WebCT only).
- A schedule is provided of tasks, their content, and an indication of how much time should be allocated to each task. This time allocation is a suggestion only, in that personal interests and different learning styles will result in different times being spent on the tasks.
- An orientation activity is provided for easing new online learners into the environment, and to enable course participants to meet each other and to comment on each other's interests. Practice is also provided in uploading a file to the VLE, with tutor contact details immediately to hand in case of difficulties.
- Each of the activities is developed as self-contained (to minimise searching other documents for relevant information) with introduction, task, reporting, discussion, all within the same area.
- All multimedia used include captioning (for audio files) and either subtitles or a text transcript (for video files).

An important principle for us as course designers and facilitators was to encourage participants to think not only about making resources accessible but also to consider alternative approaches in the use of online learning to maximise the benefits for all students.

Evaluation

Around 120 staff from the University of Teesside and other universities and colleges within the North-East of England, have taken part in the one-day workshops; seventy-five ITET Fellows have undertaken the mixed-mode one week course (or a variation of it) at the University of New South Wales, Sydney; a two-day programme for forty staff was held at Swinburne University, Melbourne; and a further forty participants from institutions across the UK are scheduled to take part in the mixed-mode course on a part-time basis over three weeks with a follow-up one-day workshop. The online component has been presented in both the WebCT and Blackboard learning environments.

A requirement for systematic evaluation will continues to grow as web-based learning environments proliferate (Owston 2000). For each context of its application, the accessibility programme has been evaluated to determine the extent to which it meets the learning outcomes of developing the learners' skills, awareness and understanding of accessible design, and its success in terms of the instructional design elements: its structure, support, and the quality and relevance of the activities. It was also important to evaluate whether the accessibility component had any lasting impact on attitudes and practice (Lockee *et al.* 2002). A combination of evaluation instruments was used (Table 5.1).

The aim was to capture relevant feedback during the course, perceptions of the participants as they experienced the process, immediate responses following the course and to determine whether the participants' experience had any lasting impact in practice (Patton 2002).

The particular methods used included an online discussion forum through which the participants could give feedback on aspects of the course during the module; a short paper-based evaluation at the end of the face-to-face workshops; an online survey that participants were encouraged to complete at the end of the module; and an email request to the first two cohorts six to twelve months after completion of the modules to determine whether there had been any lasting effect on attitude and practice.

Table 5.1 Methods used to evaluate the accessible course design module

Evaluation instrument	Timing of evaluation	Evaluation type
Feedback discussion forum	During accessibility module	Qualitative comments
Paper-based evaluation questionnaire	End of face-to-face workshops	Likert scaling and free text
Online survey questionnaire	End of module	Likert scaling and free text
Email survey	Six to twelve months after end of ITET Fellowship programme	Qualitative comments

The evaluation revealed that staff most appreciate the need to be inclusive when issues are presented to them in terms of the learners' perspective (Stodden *et al.* 2003). The evaluation also highlighted participants' need to learn some basic skills to get started in order to stimulate thinking about inclusive design and some practical support in they appreciate an understanding of the different checks that can be made to enhance accessibility.

The results from the evaluations of early versions of the online course and face-to-face workshops were used to inform the design of different subsequent versions of the course. The evaluation also reinforced both the importance of good pedagogical design and the need to provide all staff with continuing professional development opportunities to explore, study and discuss accessibility through a range of activities:

> I particularly enjoyed the tasks and what I learned.

> It was great to have the time to actually experience the material and begin to appreciate some of the access issues for specific groups in the student cohort.

It is was crucial to provide opportunities for participants to empathise with the experience of disabled students accessing e-learning and resources that help ensure support after the course has ended. A short course or workshop can only provide the stimulation and foundation for developing inclusive practices, so valid and interactive resources that staff can return to and explore further are important:

> The videos of the blind student and the practical work with assistive software are moving experiences for me personally.

> The resource material was excellent as it provided opportunities to access 'good' sources and useful links.

Another significant finding was that participants needed to learn workable strategies and understand that an incremental approach can be taken, otherwise the prospect of meeting the goal of full accessibility is can be too daunting:

> Also the materials and links provided this week have been really useful and I've learnt an awful lot from them – I've thought of accessibility as a huge, scary issue hitherto but I think this course is beginning to break it down for me and make me feel like I might be able to get a handle on it – really excellent.

The results of the course evaluations identified that while staff appreciate the flexibility of the online components, the face-to-face workshops with opportunities for personal support, discussion and practical experience are invaluable. Those staff who are sceptical about accessible practices or fear that they lack the technical skills, need to be motivated by understanding the disabled students' experience and by having access to relevant resources.

Key lessons learned

To support staff to consider inclusive practice requires influencing their own personal motivation, providing a broad range of practical skills and offering realistic expectations about what can be achieved in practice, particularly in the short term.

Viewing a student who is blind (live or as recorded video) navigating a VLE (WebCT), while he comments on the difficulties encountered or designs that are helpful, proved one of the most powerful and meaningful learning experiences for teaching staff. Also, the use of interactive computer activities (http://www. webaim.org/simulations/) that simulate the experience people with different disabilities impairments have when accessing the web helps staff appreciate the issues. It is important to note here that these activities do not simulate the disability impairment itself, rather the effect that this may have on a person's interactions with the computer. Engaging staff with the learner experience seems to provide motivation for engagement in making their own web materials accessible.

Resources used in the online course and the workshop provide ongoing support for staff if they are made readily available for future reference. The most important include easy-to-use guidelines, simulations, videos, discussion forums among participants, self-test quizzes, and links to other sources of support including websites, readings, support agencies and freely downloadable tools.

The need for reasonable adjustment to making accessible resources and online courses does not, however, necessarily mean wholesale re-design nor the a need for advanced technical skills. Having the ability to make small improvements gives staff who may be reluctant to make reasonable adjustments (Riddell *et al.* 2004) the confidence to take an incremental approach to inclusive practice (Riddell *et al.* 2004).

Other valued strategies within the workshops include hands-on practice with screen readers (such as Jaws), alternative input devices (including keyboard, touch screens, head-pointing devices), software for dyslexia and low vision, a wide range of automatic checking tools, and the opportunity to discuss experiences with fellow participants.

Conclusion

In the designing of the one-day staff development workshop, it proved difficult to condense and reduce the week-long activity programme. In the early workshops participants highlighted that this sometimes resulted in them feeling overwhelmed and even less confident about their ability to adopt inclusive practices. Following an appreciation of practical difficulties experienced by disabled students, the strategy agreed for the course development was to pare it down so that participants concentrated on practical skills such as making accessible PDF documents and PowerPoint presentations.

Once teaching staff understand the reasons why students have difficulties with accessing online materials, they readily engage with the hands-on activities. Participants are given practice in creating those documents that are most commonly used in VLEs: PowerPoint slides, Word documents and PDFs, all of which can be problematic for disabled students. Staff need the opportunity to reflect and then follow up with more specific training to meet their own particular needs. Initially many staff are concerned that there is just too much for them to know and be able to do. It is important to reassure staff that they are not expected to discard all their existing work (that isn't accessible) and that an incremental approach can be taken to introduce inclusive practices gradually and at a pace that suits their time and individual skills level.

Although activities have been evaluated through various methods and feedback has been positive, there is little evidence to confirm that staff have actually taken the issues on board in long-term practice. More research is required to identify the extent to which embedding has taken place and the further support that is required to enable staff to be continuously and consistently inclusive in their e-learning practices.

Many of the resources used within the course have been very well received and requested by staff to use independently. Informal feedback and our own research indicate that specially designed support resources would be helpful, including videos, simulations (that are appropriate to the educational context) and tools that support accessibility checking in various environments.

We believe the key to persuading staff to develop inclusive e-learning practices is by taking a pragmatic and incremental approach, to provide training which gives staff the skills to make immediate changes and to motivate staff by convincing them that inclusive practice means improving the learning experience for all students.

References and further reading

Brandt, B. L., Farmer, J.A. and Buckmaster, A. (1993) 'Cognitive apprenticeship approach to helping adults learn', in D. D. Flannery (ed.) *Applying Cognitive Learning Theory to Adult Learning*. San Francisco: Jossey-Bass, pp. 69–78.

Collins, A. (1988) *Cognitive Apprenticeship and Instructional Technology, Technical Report 6899*. Cambridge, MA: BBN Labs Inc.

Forsyth, R. (2001) 'Participation in online staff development: why is there a mismatch between intention and practice', paper presented at the Open and Distance Learning Association of Australia 15th Biennial Forum, 24–27 Sept., pp. 57–58.

Grimaldi, C. and Goette, T. (1999) 'The Internet and the independence of individuals with disabilities', *Internet Research: Electronic Networking Applications and Policy*, 9(4): 272–280.

Koppi, A. J. and Pearson, E. J. (2002) 'Design and development of a flexible online course for making accessible online courses', paper presented at AACE World Conference on Educational Multimedia (EDMEDIA2002), Denver, 24–29 June.

Lockee, B., Moore, M. and Burton, J. (2002) 'Measuring success: evaluation strategies for distance education', *Educause Quarterly* 1: 20–26.

Ommerborn, R. and Schuemer, R. (2001) 'Using computers in distance study: results of a survey amongst disabled distance students', FernUniversität – Gesamthochschule in Hagen, Zentrales Institut für Fernstudienforschung (ZIFF), Hagen, July 2001. Available at: http://www.fernuni-hagen.de/ZIFF/ommsch4.doc (accessed 04/2005).

Owston, R. D. (2000) 'Evaluating web-based learning environments: strategies and insights', *Cyber Psychology and Behavior*, 3(1): 79–87.

Patton, M. Q. (2002) *Qualitative Research and Evaluation Methods*, 3rd edn. London: Sage.

Pearson, E. J. (2001) 'Strategies for developing inclusive online courses', paper presented at WebCT Asia-Pacific Conference, Adelaide, Australia, 10 April.

Pearson, E. J. and Koppi, T. (2001) 'Guidelines for accessible online courses', internal publication, University of New South Wales. Available at: http://www.edtec.unsw.edu.au (accessed 05/2005).

Pearson, E. J. and Koppi, A. J. (2002) 'Inclusion and online learning opportunities: designing for accessibility', *Association for Learning Technology Journal*, 10, July.

Pearson, E. and Koppi, T. (2003) 'Developing inclusive practices: evaluation of a staff development course in accessibility', *Australian Journal of Educational Technology*, 19(3).

Riddell, S., Tinklin, T. and Wilson, A. (2004) *Disabled Students and Multiple Policy Innovations in Higher Education*, Final Report to the Economic and Social Research Council, Centre for Educational Sociology, Strathclyde Centre for Disability Research, University of Glasgow. Available at: http://www.ces.ed.ac.uk/Disability/publications.htm (accessed 11/05).

Stepp-Greany, J. (2002) 'Student perceptions on language learning in a technological environment: implications for the new millennium', *Language Learning and Technology*, 6(1): 165–180.

Stodden, R., Galloway, L. M. and Stodden, N. J. (2003) 'Secondary school curricula issues: impact on post-secondary students with disabilities', *Exceptional Children*, 70(1): 9–25. Available at: http://journals.sped.org/EC/Archive_Articles/VOLUME70 NUMBER1Fall2003_EC_Stodden%2070-1.pdf (accessed 04/2005).

Web Accessibility Initiative (WAI) http://www.w3.org/TR/WCAG10/ (accessed 04/2005).

WebAim simulations http://www.webaim.org/simulations/ (accessed 06/2005).

Chapter 6

Using Universal Design for Learning to expand access to higher education

Tracey Hall and Skip Stahl

At 9:48 a.m., dozens of first- and second-year students carrying overloaded backpacks begin to fill the cavernous lecture hall for Introduction to Psychology. Portable desks squeak into position as students prepare for listening, seeing, note-taking and learning. Physically and intellectually, these students exhibit great diversity. To the same course each will bring different learning needs, preferences, and backgrounds. Some students are well organized, with notebooks and laptop computers ready, while others scramble to find appropriate tools for class or to read the course text at the last moment. Most gather in pairs or groups to talk, and one can usually hear several languages. A few students arrive for class with assist dogs or in wheelchairs. Some of these students can take their own notes, but others will need to purchase lecture notes from the hired notetakers who sit at the front of the class.

As 10 o'clock approaches, so does the professor. Having taught the course for several years, the instructor is familiar with the large class size and diversity of students. She knows from past assignments and personal contact with students that about 8 per cent of the class is challenged by reading and 20 per cent of the students do not complete assigned readings. The professor is aware that, in the time and space constraints of a 50-minute large lecture hall course, no single presentation structure will satisfy the needs of all of her students. However, by working to serve the needs of those who are especially challenged in some way, the instructor knows she is most likely to help the widest range of students. Instructional tools available to her in the auditorium include a giant rotating chalkboard, an overhead projector, and a large white screen for the projection of overheads or slides. A microphone, originally installed to save professors' voices, may help students with some hearing impairments.

By 10:05, five minutes after class begins, the auditorium is packed with 350 students.

The postsecondary challenge – and the UDL response

In the United States, disabled students are graduating from high school at a steadily increasing rate and the percentage of these students choosing to enter postsecondary education has significantly increased in recent decades – from 3 per cent in 1978 to 19 per cent in 1996 (Blackorby and Wagner 1996). Despite these quantitative gains, disabled students continue to lag far behind their non-disabled classmates in academic attainment and persistence. Disabled students are far less likely to complete a degree or certificate program; for those who do, the process generally takes twice as long as it does for non-disabled students, a factor that negatively impacts the availability of financial aid, thus compounding the challenge (National Council on Disability 2003).

For those students who do persist to achieve a degree, the benefits are life-changing. Recent US census data indicate that disabled individuals are employed at a significantly lesser rate (49 per cent) than non-disabled individuals (79 per cent) (US Census Bureau 2000). However, when the employment rates of individuals with bachelor's degrees – disabled and non-disabled – are compared, the percentages are 67 per cent to 73 per cent respectively, indicating nearly equal employment potential for students attaining degrees (National Center for the Study of Postsecondary Educational Supports 2002). Since the impact of attaining a college degree is so significant in elevating the quality of life of disabled individuals, what factors in the educational process can be adjusted to increase the number of students who acquire degrees?

A 2003 report from the US National Council on Disability (NCD) identified three areas that each present unique challenges for disabled students seeking to become degree candidates: (1) preparation for; (2) transition to; and (3) progress in, postsecondary education.

1 *Preparation* – Two primary factors conspire to reduce a student's prepared-ness for postsecondary study: a lack of rigorous academic expectations and a lack of self-awareness/self-advocacy. Of these two factors, the latter can be rectified post hoc by teaching disabled students the advocacy skills they need; the former – a weak or ineffective secondary school curriculum – is far more debilitating and less easily remedied after-the-fact. There is a growing body of evidence that suggests that many disabled students receive a substandard secondary education for two reasons: immersion in a less rigorous curriculum combined with limited exposure to content-area instruction due to skill or strategy remediation (Stodden *et al.* 2003).

2 *Transition* – According to the NCD report, a major challenge facing disabled students in the USA in their transition from secondary to postsecondary institutions is unfamiliarity with the distinction between the individualized affirmative-action orientation of the Individuals with Disabilities Education

Act (IDEA), which applies to primary and secondary schools, and the more systemic civil rights orientation of the Americans with Disabilities Act (ADA) and Section 504 of the Rehabilitation Act. The former emphasizes corrective action and remediation, while the latter focuses exclusively on equal access to opportunity. Students unaware of this distinction often anticipate that in postsecondary settings they will be provided with the same suite of individualized supports afforded them in primary and secondary school, and, as a consequence, anticipate too much while simultaneously remaining unaware of accommodations to which they may be entitled.

3   *Progress* – In assessing the progress of disabled students in postsecondary settings, the NCD report identified two sub-areas of concern: (i) participation; and (ii) retention and persistence. Active participation in postsecondary education requires adequate background knowledge, communication strategies to express thoughts and ideas, and the capacity to actively engage in a culture of inquiry. A lack of preparedness or capacity in any of these areas can significantly decrease a student's chances of success. In fact, students who cannot attain a degree of success in each of these areas are unlikely to meet the fundamental requirements of a degree program, or maintain the concerted effort necessary to ensure progress. Successful persistence requires regular class or section attendance, regular assignment completion, effective problem-solving strategies, and the ability to access support and resources in a timely manner. These challenges are often magnified by a 'one size fits all' collection of curriculum materials and approaches to instruction.

We believe that a postsecondary curriculum developed within the context of Universal Design for Learning (UDL) can be both challenging and supportive of learning needs, while simultaneously providing students with access to rich and varied academic content and a heightened awareness of their own learning preferences. The core principles of UDL, discussed below, provide a series of guidelines and benchmarks for more effective and inclusive postsecondary instruction.

A universally-designed postsecondary experience will increase students' understanding of how accommodations – i.e. adjustments to the learning environment and its tasks – can significantly increase their potential for high achievement. Equal access to learning opportunity, including the provision of accessible, alternate-format instructional materials and assessments, is an essential key element of UDL. Also, a UDL approach expands the methods and resources available to postsecondary instructors, making them more capable of meeting the needs of diverse learners. Furthermore, the inherent accessibility and flexibility of UDL can increase the participation and persistence of disabled students in postsecondary settings, leading to increased retention in desired courses of study.

What is Universal Design for Learning?

Drawing on recent advances in neuroscience and new technologies, Universal Design for Learning is a framework to guide educators in maximizing learning opportunities for increasingly diverse student populations (Rose and Meyer 2002). Pioneered over the past 15 years by CAST (Center for Applied Special Technology), UDL reorients educational goals, materials, methods, and assessments to enable all learners to participate in the general curriculum, something a traditional print-based approach impedes. The increasing availability of powerful and flexible digital technologies makes it possible to create more flexible, or customized, learning environments for diverse learners.

Using data derived from recent research on how the learning brain functions, David Rose and Anne Meyer have identified three primary brain networks that play distinct but linked roles in learning: *recognition networks, strategic networks* and *affective networks*. Because each learner has unique brain processes that vary widely across these three networks, UDL employs three strategies that are analogous to the networks, offering *multiple means of representation, multiple means of expression* and *multiple means of engagement* (see Figure 6.1) (Rose and Meyer 2002: 10–39).

Recognition networks allow us to gather facts and information. They guide the collection, categorization, and identification of the stimuli that we perceive. Because of differences in individual recognition networks, each learner processes some types of media better than other types. Delivering course content using *multiple means of representation*, including a variety of formats, will provide diverse learners with the opportunity to acquire the information and knowledge necessary to succeed in class.

Strategic networks aid us in planning and performing tasks, essentially choosing a strategy for all of our actions. Differences in strategic networks mean that the tools students prefer to express their knowledge will vary greatly. Offering students *multiple means of expression* enables them to most effectively demonstrate what they have learned.

Affective networks determine our engagement, motivation, interest, and emotional connection with activities, tasks, or materials. Providing *multiple means of engagement* is necessary to motivate learners with widely varying affective networks, and thus varying interests. While students often enroll in courses based on the topic they expect to learn, some elements of the class will undoubtedly attract them more than others. Allowing some choice within the larger course mandate will challenge students appropriately and motivate them to learn (Rose and Meyer 2002: 74–75).

New digital technologies make it easier than ever to incorporate these UDL principles into postsecondary teaching strategies. While disabled students stand to gain the most from such changes to the traditional curriculum, all students can benefit from a flexible learning program that lets them access course materials by using the means and methods that work best for them.

The following demonstrates in practical ways how to embed UDL principles into instructional goals, methods, materials, and assessments to facilitate the development of more equitable and effective higher education.

Setting expectations: the course syllabus

For our sample psychology course and most other classes, the syllabus usually provides prospective students with the most available detail about the nature and requirements of the course. In addition to information about logistics, core texts, assignments, and resources, the syllabus provides students with information about the instructor's style and expectations. With the exception of required courses, a student may decide whether or not to enroll based on the syllabus alone.

In the past decade, course materials, including syllabi, have been increasingly made available online. However, the online publication of a syllabus is usually presented as an alternate means of distributing print information, and the online version replicates all the limitations of the paper version without utilizing the

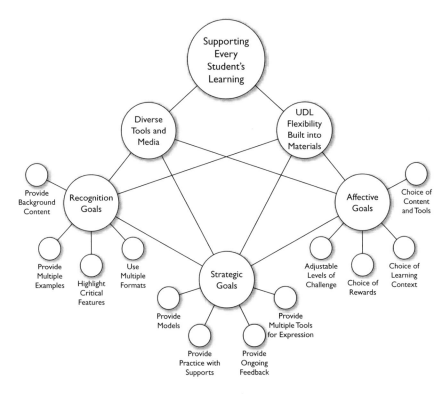

Figure 6.1 Concept map of applied UDL principles

Source: Rose and Meyer, Teaching Every Student website, retrieved online at
http://www.cast.org/teachingeverystudent/ideas/tes/chapter6.cfm

inherent flexibility of the digital medium. In this circumstance, an online syllabus continues to function as a 'flyer' for a course when it could serve as a more inviting portal to both the instructor's style and to the course itself.

Even when institutional or departmental websites are designed to be accessible to disabled students, many syllabi are routinely posted as image-based PDF documents with little attention paid to accessibility concerns. An HTML-based syllabus constructed in accordance with accepted accessibility guidelines (text equivalents for images, consistent use of heading styles, etc.) is navigable by students with physical or sensory impairments and transformable into audio (via synthetic speech) for students with learning or attentional impairments.

Beyond basic accessibility – which is an essential feature of UDL but falls short of its full implementation – HTML-based syllabus designs inherently support multiple media types – text, audio, image, video and interconnectivity via hyper-links – capabilities that can be used to support UDL and re-emphasize flexibility. The transformative nature of HTML can be harnessed to support and enhance students' recognition, strategic, and affective goals.

As referenced in the concept map developed by Rose and Meyer (Figure 6.1), the reinforcement of a students' recognition strategies can be achieved by providing multiple formats (via the accessibility features detailed above) and by supplying additional background content via hyperlinked definitions to unfamiliar vocabulary or connections to associated Web resources that can enhance a student's content awareness. Similarly, some enterprising instructors have hyperlinked class notes to syllabus entries and sequenced the availability of these notes by having them only available from the day of the class onward. This approach not only allows an instructor to highlight the critical features of a lecture or an assignment, but, in many cases, also minimizes the need for human note-takers as a disability accommodation.

To enhance a student's strategic capabilities, an instructor might not only post a listing of assignments and/or assessments, but might augment these entries with examples (or non-examples) of successful submissions. By providing prospective students with clear and unambiguous models of course expectations, the potential for confusion is minimized.

Finally, supporting student persistence in the face of challenging course expectations can also be achieved by increasing student engagement in the learning process. Students who perceive themselves as active participants in their own education demonstrate significantly higher levels of perseverance in the face of challenge. One way to actively involve students is to vary the learning context. In the case of large survey courses like Introduction to Psychology, students might be prompted to complete lab assignments by working in small cooperative groups (4–6 students) independent of the regularly scheduled sections led by faculty assis-tants. By offering both options, an instructor empowers students to choose their optimal way of learning the course material. Clearly indicating these opportunities in the course syllabus can encourage engagement and potentially entice some students to enroll in a course that they might otherwise avoid.

By applying the principles of Universal Design for Learning to the development of a course syllabus, and by transforming the syllabus itself into a portal to the course, instructors can facilitate the active participation of struggling and hesitant learners.

Teaching every student: UDL instructional methods

Flexibility in teaching methodologies, which the UDL framework facilitates, is also essential for teachers to help meet the needs of their diverse students. When taking into account the principles of UDL, a single form of instructional delivery cannot provide the necessary multiple means of representation, expression, and engagement. Still, for courses such as the one described at the beginning of this chapter, the lecture is the most efficient, though not necessarily the most effective, form of instruction for many learners. So how can an instructor address flexibility and multiple representations of the three networks within the constraints of the lecture hall?

An instructor can reinforce a student's recognition strategies by presenting content in multiple formats, i.e. providing an outline or graphic organizer of that day's information. In this situation, the professor could display an organizer with an overhead or slide projector. While delivering the lecture, he or she could visually and orally indicate where in the organizer the current discussion is located. This visual material could also be made available in a handout form (digitally or on paper) to help students follow the lecture and conversation, and organize their notetaking.

Students vary in their ability to process different information, making it essential that teachers use different media and formats during instruction. This might mean showing students text, images, and video in class as well as doing demonstrations and promoting discussion. To help students activate background knowledge, both text-based approaches and image-analysis approaches can be effective (Croll et al. 1986). A teacher could implement both approaches to ensure that students who might struggle with text or images have an effective means to access, recall, and activate new knowledge.

Another way to support student learning with respect to recognition and strategic goals is to supply additional background content. The knowledge students bring to a new situation varies in type and depth, as does their ability to recall and appropriately use knowledge. Individual differences and challenges in these areas can present a barrier to learning. Thus, we need to help fill gaps in students' background knowledge and help activate their knowledge in response to new information. Doing so supports students' diverse recognition abilities and preferences. Another method to individualize instruction in a large classroom setting is to offer multiple examples of key course content. When presenting these examples, a teacher might also highlight the critical features, perhaps using an organizer or visuals to demonstrate meaningful commonalities.

Monitoring every student's learning: universally designed assessment

The evaluation of student performance is essential for effective teaching. Assessments are necessary to measure progress against course goals on both a class-wide and an individual basis and to inform instructional goals, methods, and materials.

When designing assessment, instructors should be encouraged to consider not only efficiency and time but also student diversity and should incorporate multiple means of representation, expression, and engagement into the assessment process rather than taking a one-size-fits-all approach to testing. Not all students may be able to articulate their understanding of the course concepts in the same mode of expression. Just as no single method of instruction will reach the whole range of diverse learners, so too will no single means of assessment demonstrate what each student has learned and achieved. The purpose of the assessment should be to demonstrate the achievement of standardized goals, not to standardize the means for demonstrating those goals.

In most postsecondary educational settings, the issue of accommodations in assessment is unavoidable given the diversity of enrolled students. Assessment accommodations are changes in testing materials or procedures that enable students to be evaluated on their abilities rather than be disadvantaged as a direct result of their impairment. Without accommodations, the assessment may not accurately measure the student's knowledge and skills. Accommodations are a necessary but insufficient solution to barriers and inaccessible testing. Examples of accommodations include administering tests in large print for a student with visual impairment or providing a student who is unable to write with a scribe to record his or her responses.

By adapting the solutions provided by UDL instructionally, we begin developing assessments that are not only accessible but also employ the same technologies that students use in the classroom and in daily life. When applying the principles of UDL to the assessment, the following factors should be considered: flexibility in setting, flexibility in scheduling and timing, and the method of presentation and response.

Assessment is an essential component of education. When professors are able to develop fair and accurate measurements that allow students to demonstrate their knowledge regardless of how they learn and are supported by their institutions in doing so, they help ensure that all of their students, including those who are disabled, are assessed in ways that best represent student performance (Dolan and Hall 2001).

Reaching every student: course materials

In our introductory psychology course, there are a wide range of students with diverse learning needs: students with evident physical and sensory impairments and students with 'hidden' learning and attentional impairments. In addition, there are students who do not fit into such categories but demonstrate wide variation in their background knowledge and recognition abilities, their capacities to strategically express what they know, and their engagement. In what ways can course materials assist in addressing this diversity?

Print instructional materials continue to be the preferred medium in most postsecondary courses. For many students, print is effective, portable, and convenient, but for others it can present significant barriers. Students who cannot see the words or images on a page, cannot hold a book or turn its pages, cannot decode the text, or cannot comprehend its syntax may each require different supports to extract meaning from book-based information.

For many of these students, a more accessible alternative is available. Modern digital materials can present the same content as printed books but in a format that is much more flexible and accessible. For students who cannot see the words or images, the digital version can be produced in braille or an audio format, and can provide descriptions of the images. For students who cannot hold the printed book or turn its pages, the virtual pages of a digital book can be turned with a slight press of a switch. For those who cannot decode the text, any word can be automatically read aloud. For students who lack the background vocabulary in the text, definitions (in English or another language) can be provided with a simple click of the mouse.

The advantage of digital versions is that these and other supports can be accessed by individuals who need them while being made invisible (i.e. non-distracting) for those who don't. Such customizable alternatives substantially reduce the barriers found in traditional texts, minimizing the effects of what are commonly called 'print disabilities'.

While it is true that, at least at the present time, very few students have access to the flexible digital versions that they need, the availability of these resources is steadily increasing. In the United States, curriculum publishers are increasingly inundated with requests for 'e-text' versions of print textbooks and course materials, and a number of states have enacted legislation either requiring publishers to provide these versions or requiring institutions to give preference to publishers who will provide these versions. Simultaneously, many US colleges and universities are taking advantage of economical and powerful desktop technologies to create their own alternate-format materials for disabled students.

Course instructors can help increase the availability of e-text versions of course materials by requesting them from publishers, by patronizing content producers who offer them, or by acquiring core text resources that are augmented with accessible online versions or accompanying CD-ROMs. Each of these strategies can be effective, and the benefits to all concerned are substantial.

With their materials available in a range of formats, students with diverse learning needs – both disabled and non-disabled – will no longer struggle to extract essential content and procedures from media that is ill-suited to their learning needs. Instructors will discover that alternate-format digital versions of print resources can provide them with an increased array of tools for presenting and discussing essential course content. Information available in multiple formats – text, audio, images, and video – will help students connect new material to information they already possess. Similarly, many of these resources offer inter-activity that can expand a student's means for demonstrating competency, and the increased choices available can significantly increase engagement.

Conclusion

It is not enough to improve access to higher education for disabled students. We also need to ensure that such students – indeed, all students – have the support they need to make genuine progress in their studies and to continue on to graduation. Universally designed learning environments and experiences can help achieve this by providing all learners with equal opportunities to succeed.

The development of equitable and effective instructional goals, methods, materials, and assessments using the framework of Universal Design for Learning is especially important during the first two years of postsecondary studies when individualized supports tend to be fewer and students who are especially challenged by traditional approaches to education are more likely to drop out. As this chapter demonstrates, there are numerous practical steps instructors can take, even in less than optimal venues, to improve the learning experience of all of their students and support their educational progress.

References and further reading

Blackorby, J. and Wagner, M. (1996) 'Longitudinal post school outcomes of youth with disabilities: findings from the National Longitudinal Transition Study', *Exceptional Children*, 62: 399–413.

Brown University, 'The Ivy Access Initiative'. Available at: http://www.brown.edu/ Administration/Dean_of_the_College/uid/ (accessed 05/2005).

CAST (2001) *Teacher Training: Recommendations for Change*. Wakefield, MA: NCAC.

Croll, V. J., Idol-Maestas, L., Heal, L. and Pearson, P. D. (1986) *Bridging the Compre-hension Gap with Pictures* (Tech. Report No. 399). Champaign, IL: The Center for the Study of Reading.

Davis, B. G. (1994) 'Computers and multimedia', in B. G. Davis, *Tools for Teaching*. San Francisco, CA: Jossey-Bass, pp. 334–341.

Dolan, R. P. and Hall, T. E. (2001) 'Universal Design for Learning: implications for large-scale assessment', *IDA Perspectives*, 27(4): 22–25.

Frederick, P. J. (1994) 'Classroom discussions', in K. W. Prichard and R. M. Sawyer (eds), *Handbook of College Teaching*. Westport, CT: Greenwood Press, pp. 99–109.

Hodge, B. M. and Preston-Sabin, J. (eds) (1997) *Accommodations – Or Just Good Teaching? Strategies for Teaching College Students with Disabilities*. Westport, CT: Praeger.

Johnson, J. M. and Fox, J. A. (2003) 'Creating curb cuts in the classroom', in J. L. Higbee (ed.), *Curriculum Transformation and Disability: Implementing Universal Design in Higher Education*. Minneapolis, MN: General College, University of Minnesota, Center for Research on Developmental Education and Urban Literacy, pp. 7–17.

National Center for the Study of Postsecondary Educational Supports (2002) *Preparation for and Support of Youth with Disabilities in Postsecondary Education and Employment: Implications for Policy, Priorities and Practice*. Proceedings and briefing book for the National Summit on Postsecondary Education for People with Disabilities. Available at: http://www.ncset.hawaii.edu/summits/july2002/default.htm (accessed 05/2005).

National Council on Disability (2003) *People with Disabilities and Postsecondary Education*. Washington, DC: Lex Frieden. Available at: http://www.ncd.gov/newsroom/publications/2003/education.htm (accessed 05/2005).

Ohio State University, 'The Ohio State University Partnership Grant'. Available at: http://telr.osu.edu/dpg/index.html (accessed 05/2005).

O'Neill, L. (2001) Universal Design for Learning, *Syllabus*, 14(9): 31–32.

Rochester Institute of Technology 'Class Act: Universal Design'. Available at: http://www.rit.edu/~classact/side/universaldesign.html (accessed 05/2005).

Rose, D. H. and Meyer, A. (2002) *Teaching Every Student in the Digital Age: Universal Design for Learning*. Alexandria, VA: Association for Supervision and Curriculum Development, pp. 10–39. Available at: http://www.cast.org/teachingeverystudent/ideas/tes/chapter6.cfm

Ruhl, K. L. and Hall, T. E. (2002) 'Continuum of special education and general education field experiences in the preservice special education program at Penn. State', *Teacher Education and Special Education*, 25(1): 87–91.

Scott, S., Shaw, S. and McGuire, J. (2003) 'Universal design for instruction: a new paradigm for adult instruction in postsecondary education', *Remedial and Special Education*, 24(6): 369–379.

Silver, P., Bourke, A. and Strehorn, K. C. (1998) 'Universal instruction design in higher education: an approach for inclusion', *Equity and Excellence in Education*, 31(2): 47–51.

Stahl, S. and Branaman, J. (2000) 'Automatic accommodations: the potential of online learning for all students', *Student Affairs Online*, 1(1). Available at: http://www.studentaffairs.com/ejournal/Spring_2000/article.3.html (accessed 11.05).

Stodden, R. A., Galloway, L. M. and Stodden, N. J. (2003) 'Secondary school curricula issues: impact on postsecondary students with disabilities', *Exceptional Children*, 70(1): 9–25.

University of Guelph, 'UID Project'. Available at: http://www.tss.uoguelph.ca/uid/index.html (accessed 05/2005).

University of Minnesota (2003) 'Curriculum Transformation and Disability (CTAD)'. Available at: http://www.gen.umn.edu/research/ctad/default.htm (accessed 05/2005).

University of Washington (2005) 'DO-IT: Disabilities, Opportunities, Internetworking, and Technology'. Available at: http://www.washington.edu/doit/ (accessed 05/2005).

US Census Bureau (2000) *2000 Census of Population and Housing*. Washington, DC: US Government Printing Office.

US Department of Education Office of Civil Rights (2004) 'Students with disabilities preparing for postsecondary education: know your rights and responsibilities'. Available at: http://www.ed.gov/about/offices/list/ocr/transition.html (accessed 05/2005).

Waksler, R. (1996) 'Teaching strategies for a barrier free classroom', *Journal on Excellence in College Teaching*, 7(2): 99–111.

Chapter 7

Supporting inclusive practice

Developing an assessment toolkit

Judith Waterfield, Bob West and Melanie Parker

Introduction

The aim of this chapter is to explore the efficacy of inclusive assessment within higher education. The initial catalyst came from a funded project to develop an assessment toolkit which focused on the needs of disabled students. The project identified that, in addition to those hard outcomes associated with the toolkit, the process of moving from current practice concerned with special arrangements, to providing alternative methods of assessment was crucial. To achieve this, the authors (project team) used an action research methodology. According to Lewin (1952, quoted in Carr and Kemmis 1986), action research consists of analysis, fact-finding, conceptualisation of problems, planning and executing action, then more fact-finding and evaluation, representing circles of activities that continually develop and improve on what has gone before. At its simplest level, action research is designed to combine research and practice in order to impact on or improve on that practice. One key aspect of action research is a collaborative and participatory approach, and in the context of the chapter is predicated upon an understanding of the need to engage with disabled people rather than working under the misapprehension that the research is on their behalf . This also reinforces the British Disability Movement's call for disability research to 'be about research with rather than for or on disabled people' (Goodley 1999: 6).

The chapter outlines the current journey undertaken in exploring inclusive assessment and highlights the reasoning behind the shift in approach. It concludes by identifying the main principles that need to be addressed in creating inclusive assessment and offers some practical suggestions on the types of assessment methods, which could be implemented.

Background

This chapter reflects research in progress undertaken through the Staff–Student Partnership for Assessment, Change and Evaluation (SPACE) Project, funded by the Higher Education Funding Council for England (HEFCE) as part of the Improving Provision for Disabled Students funding programme (2003–5). The objective was to create an Alternative Assessment Toolkit, which would include:

- *a critical review* of the generic assessment debate and its relationship to alternative and inclusive assessments;
- *rich case studies* detailing the trialling of alternative and inclusive assessment practice among disabled and non-disabled students;
- *institutional, departmental and individual procedures* to support the process of institutional assessment change and an exploration of the challenges involved or perceived;
- *materials to support the monitoring and evaluation of student and staff experiences* relating to parity of academic standards, quality assurance, meeting students learning styles and the implications for delivery, marking and resourcing.

Underpinning the Assessment Toolkit is an action research methodology that seeks to address current assessment practice and provision for disabled students. The authors work at the Disability ASSIST Service at the University of Plymouth and the experience of working in a student-facing service with a strategic responsibility for embedding access and inclusion at an institutional level, has ensured that the research has been carried out in a collaborative partnership between specialist staff, disabled and non-disabled students, academic staff and staff responsible for university policy.

In the past decade, the UK higher education sector has witnessed an increase in the number of disabled students applying for and studying on a wide range of courses. The Higher Education Statistical Agency (2004) return for 2002/3 indicates approximately 106,000 students, namely 5.39 per cent of the student population have declared impairments, although the statistics conceal the true measure of the population and the percentages in individual institutions and in particular disciplines as it is based on a method of self-disclosure by the individual disabled student.

Until very recently funding programmes aimed at improving policy and provision for disabled students placed a major emphasis upon the development of specialist support services. This may have provided the opportunity for good developmental practice but did not necessarily create sector consistency, or the development of strategic approaches to inclusive practice. The case for inclusiveness was well made by the Beattie Report which sought to 'translate the concept of Inclusiveness into action' (Beattie 1999, item 2.6). Since 2000, disability funding programmes in England have encouraged dialogue and innovation between disability services and academic departments, to support institutional change and academic developments (HEFCE 2002).

In addition, the advent of the UK Disability Discrimination Act (DDA) Part 4 (2002) and, more recently, the Disability Discrimination Act (2005) have placed a legislative imperative upon educational establishments to be proactive and to engage with disabled students as a 'positive duty' to eliminate discriminatory practice. This has provided the sector with an opportunity, as well as a requirement, to address the validity of current practice and to take a more inclusive approach to the teaching, learning and assessment of disabled students while maintaining academic and professionally prescribed standards.

However, there remains a gap between legislation and practice. To date, the higher education system reflects many of society's inequalities where 'participation in education continues to be focused on fitting people into what is already available' (Stuart 2002). As Barton (2003) asserts, 'inclusion is not about assimilation or accommodation of individuals into an essentially unchanged system of practice'. Instead it is about the 'transformation of those deep structural barriers to change'. To achieve this transformation, there is a need to focus on opening up a dialogue, exploring innovative practice and challenging resistance to the removal of those 'deep structural barriers'. The genesis for our research was a concern for equity for disabled students, but we have subsequently pursued its value for the wider diverse student population and the breadth of learning styles encompassed by learners with a range of cultural and educational experiences. Our shift of emphasis was a response to the results from our first-year baseline research that revealed student learning styles and learning experiences that we believed may have transferable lessons for other student groups. To ensure our research was robust and valid, we felt it imperative to explore the assessment experiences of non-disabled students. Contributing to a higher education culture which does not single out one discrete group of students but which seeks to develop procedures which value diversity is fundamental to equality and social inclusion.

Across the UK the extensive use of 'special examination arrangements' for disabled students is reactive practice which is indicative of an assimilation culture; it forces students to adopt a disability identity, which confers on them a medical model and, at a purely practical institutional level, is an *ad hoc* response with resource and equity implications that are neither desirable nor sustainable.

While the fear of litigation against higher education institutions (HEIs) is a driver for change in itself, a progressive society should be able to look towards the university sector as a repository for new thinking, not merely in educational practice but as a leader in social, cultural and political change. This latter point was signalled in the draft guidance for the Disability Discrimination Act (2005) which stated:

> the government's desire for the public sector to act as an exemplar of good practice and contribute in a demonstrable way to a more inclusive society. HEIs in particular having the potential to make a considerable contribution towards achieving these aims.
>
> (Equality Challenge Unit 2004)

The requirement from September 2005 for HE Progress Files to chart the progress of an individual is an additional driver requiring changes to policies and practices. These files will include two elements, namely a transcript recording student achievement, but also a means by which students will monitor, build and reflect upon their personal development in learning. It will require a more coherent backwards linkage between these systems for recording the students' own learning, their skills development and self-awareness and in practice this must be applicable for all students.

Action research and inclusive assessment

In 2002 the stimulus for the current research and partnership came from the South West Academic Network for Disability Support (SWANDS) Project, which combined the expertise and experience of disability officers, academic staff and disabled students from eight HEIs in the region. To ensure validity and applicability, academic representation was sought from the disciplines of Arts, Business, Education, Humanities, Human Science, Science and Technology. The current research partnership represents a deliberate move to 'build in some systematic way on what has gone before . . . to try to pull together more systematically and on a larger scale what research has so far established' (Yates 2004: 23). Across the SWANDS network, debate was at its most vigorous when discussing the possibility of and barriers to inclusive assessment modes, as opposed to special examination arrangements. There was an acute recognition that the current arrangement of thousands of special examination provisions per academic year stretch resources, physical facilities and administration within the sector. There is as yet little research to support the validity of the range of special examination arrangements currently deployed in this way. As Williams and Ceci (1999) argue, there is no 'empirically defensible reason to assert that 150 per cent, 200 per cent, 250 per cent, or any other percent is the magical compensatory threshold' to ensure equity in traditional assessment arrangements.

We considered it imperative that inclusive assessments should be measured tools strategically embedded into course planning and approval, rather than the expediency of 'special arrangements' or the offer of an '*ad hoc*' solution for individual students by individual staff. The UK Quality Assurance Agency for Higher Education (QAA) published a series of Subject Benchmark Statements, many of which contained a range of subject-specific assessment modes commonly found in each subject area. Taken together, these assessment modes form a repertoire of assessment possibilities that may be used in non-cognate subject areas to innovate assessment practice (for further information on Subject Benchmarking Statements, see Chapter 4 by Chapman and Carlisle). The SWANDS project collated those assessment modes, identifying collectively a list of forty-eight methods, which are recorded in the project audit tool for sector usage (Waterfield and West 2002). This was intended to help staff audit their institutions for compliance with the Special Educational Needs and Disabilities Act (2001), and, when considering the issue of assessment, we wished to encourage staff to think about what 'reasonable adjustments' could be made to make assessment more equitable. This innovative work secured additional HEFCE funding for the SPACE partnership project.

The research undertaken by the SPACE partnership involves a longitudinal study, which will follow the same cohort of disabled students and track their assessment experiences and the views of their academic staff throughout their degree studies. In total, there will be three main phases of research activity at the end of each academic year. The aim of the first phase has been to critically examine disabled students' experiences of current assessment methods and the extent to which their potential and performance are developed and reflected by these methods. This has involved an extensive survey, interviews and student focus group meetings. Feedback from over 100 disabled students has been collected and analysed.

The first phase findings are instructive. The quantitative feedback showed an 83 per cent satisfaction rate with 'special arrangements'. However, when the partnership carried out the qualitative elements of its research through student focus groups and one-to-one semi-structured interviews, the feedback was quite different, as Box 7.1 shows.

Box 7.1 Qualitative feedback from the first phase questionnaires from disabled students across the SPACE partnership

The single room allocated in my last exam was completely inappropriate. It was a very hot day and I had to have a window open. Students outside were playing loud music.

There were too many distractions that prevented me from performing well. Students were arriving at different times. The door was in constant use.

We started later and were all put together for extra time and people wanted to know why. I felt a bit stupid. People finished before us and distracted us before they left.

I still feel I struggle to give my answers in any time-constrained situation.

If I could have had a viva or handed in a portfolio I wouldn't have needed a helper.

Exams are dependent upon how well I am on that particular day, not whether I have extra time.

. . . massive time pressure of an exam and pain caused by sitting for long periods.

Feedback from students helped inform our thinking with regard to the discrepancy between the findings of the quantitative and qualitative research. Students perceive and value 'special arrangements' as the institutional recognition of their disability and they completed qualitative evaluations to that effect. However, when given the opportunity to discuss those arrangements more thoroughly through (qualitative) semi-structured interviews and focus groups, it became obvious that the overall experience was less than satisfactory. The students indicated that they were anxious not to criticise a system which had been put in place to 'help' for fear that it would be removed. Furthermore, although quantitative methods of data collection are often very efficient, their weakness lies in requiring participants to 'fit their experiences into a framework' (Sikes *et al.* 2003: 122).

The findings also revealed that although the majority of students had received 'special arrangements' for examinations, only 31 per cent had received them for in-class assessments and only 28 per cent had received them for other types of assessment, such as portfolios and essays. This raises serious questions regarding the consistency and efficacy of special provisions for supporting the assessment of disabled students in higher education. It is also indicative that most 'special arrangements' are focused on examinations. Not addressing the various in-class assessment modes, e.g. e-learning, computer-marked assessments (CMAs) and practicals, etc., when implementing 'special arrangements', could have implications for future module options, progression and degree classification.

These findings confirmed the partnership's belief in the need for change. Simultaneously, work to explore the validity of alternative assessment methods was taking place to support one of the key components of the Assessment Toolkit – the production of rich case studies. However, following student focus group feedback and debate between academics in the partnership and through dissemination activities, the research team shifted emphasis. We started by exploring the validity of *alternative assessments* (examples of which are identified later in this chapter) which we defined as measured tools to assess core learning outcomes while minimising the impact of a disability on a student's performance. Subsequently, we came to consider the applicability, possibility and equity of *inclusive assessments*. We define these as assessment modes suitable for the diverse student population, regardless of disability, learning style or learning experience. This important change of emphasis reflected the recognition that a disabled student may have a particular learning style and learning requirements which need to be addressed, although this emphasis on difference can be counterproductive and excluding. Conversely, an emphasis on providing flexibility and choice for all removes such distinctions and gives all students the appropriate framework of equity to meet their learning potential. We believe that the political and social agenda for inclusion requires us all to reduce discrimination and ghettoisation. We recognise that there may always be a minority of students who will require something particular and individual. However, the majority will be better served by developing more inclusive practice.

The partnership recognises that equity in the context of inclusive assessment cannot be pursued without due consideration being given to the maintenance of academic standards and the need for all students to demonstrate their acquisition of the required learning outcomes of their particular course of study.

In the USA and Australia these issues are also being addressed through the concept of universal design for learning. Critics of traditionalism have pointed to the problems arising from making categorical distinctions between 'disabled' and 'non-disabled' learners and the many differences that exist within these all-encompassing categories. Even accepting the premise that designing assessment for the divergent needs of specific populations increases usability for everyone, universal design is predicated upon the ideal of responding to the individual and their individual learning styles (Rose and Meyer 2000).

Considering this more global approach to the question of inclusivity and universal design, a second phase questionnaire in year two was distributed among equal numbers of disabled and non-disabled students, concentrating on the same discipline areas and year group. The shift in emphasis and broadening of the student catchment for the second phase necessitated the re-drafting of this questionnaire as part of the longitudinal study. The results from this second phase reveal common learning and assessment experiences between disabled and non-disabled students and confirm the appropriateness and relevance of our shift in research focus towards a more inclusive model. This provided a further distancing from the medicalising model of treating disabled students as 'other'. As Christine King, Vice Chancellor, University of Staffordshire, reiterated at the Institute for Learning and Teaching in Higher Education Conference (2004), 'diversity is upon us and we will be changed by it'.

In order to facilitate such change to inclusion we have debated the following three key action questions with academics across the sector in the UK and internationally:

- How can we change assessment policies and current academic practice to remove discrimination and exclusion?
- How can we assess ability and not the effects of disability?
- How can we accommodate the learning styles of a range of learners at assessment?

Responses to these questions from academic staff raised the same broad set of issues (see Box 7.2) that may at first appear to be demoralising to those seeking change through inclusive practice. These issues will need to be addressed if equitable changes to current practice are to be achieved. The statements may be a response by academics to the current diversity of student cohort, increased pressures due to larger class sizes, the dual role of many staff as teacher and researcher, the need to maintain student numbers and perhaps reflects issues that are pertinent to the generic assessment debate, which are being deflected into barriers for change.

Box 7.2 Qualitative feedback from academic staff within the sector

It's a good idea in theory but I think it's the slippery slope to the end of the difference that is HE.

I don't see why we should change – we've done exams for thirty years and not had any students complaining.

I am happy to do it but how do you get a department to change? I don't have the power.

How can we be sure that an inclusive assessment will assess the desired learning outcomes?

There is no way our external examiners will go for this.

It is the professional bodies you need to talk to – we are willing but our hands are tied.

What will happen in the transition between assessment regimes?

However, while there is individual staff practice across the sector to support and develop innovation in assessment practice, there are clearly obligations and responsibilities at institutional, cultural and legislative levels that will confront reluctance whether it resides within the faculty, among examiners, professional bodies or employers. In discussing staff issues in relation to the three questions above and the comments outlined in Box 7.2 we identified a number of recurring themes that seemed to underscore the debate.

Recurring themes

From the SPACE partnership debates and dissemination discussions recurring themes have emerged and are discussed below. The authors believe that these key principles are crucial to assessment change.

- *Changes to current practice have to be embedded at a strategic level.* Comment: The current climate in UK higher education strongly encourages HEIs to develop Mission and Value Statements with attendant Strategic Plans; these include strategies for Learning and Teaching, Assessment, Widening Participation and Personal Development Planning. Changes to course structure will need to be considered at course planning, approval and periodic review stages and policies and procedures will need to reflect the consideration of inclusion.

- *Ensure the assessment of core learning outcomes is a fundamental facet of any assessment regime and therefore not a distinctive feature of inclusive assessments.* Comment: To be equitable and appropriate, any assessment regime must be scrutinised for its efficacy in meeting the needs of a changing student population and for graduate employability.

- *Continuing professional development for staff is essential for dynamic change.* Comment: Staff development should provide a forum where assessment issues can be addressed, where the understanding of diversity and inclusion can be explored and equitable solutions found. Examining the value of assessment modes from other discipline areas that may meet the needs of differing learning styles (visual, auditory, reflective and kinesthetic) is a useful approach, as is the provision of guidance for staff on marking fairly across assessment modes. Faculty staff meetings, Learning and Teaching in Higher Education Certificate courses for new tutors, generic training for new programme managers can all provide a suitable forum for discussion and are vectors for cultural change.

- *Meeting obligations to the professional bodies is a key responsibility of departments for their legitimacy.* Comment: This has consistently been used as an argument against changing assessment practice. The recent amendment to Part 2 of the UK Disability Discrimination Act (2004) to include professional and qualification bodies and employers, has placed a legislative requirement on all parties to find solutions and eliminate discriminatory practice. We are currently seeking policy statements and responses to the idea of more inclusive assessment modes as an alternative to 'special arrangements' from the professional bodies. At the time of writing, the findings have not been finalised.

- *Requesting additional staff time and financial resources to pursue this change in the current climate is unrealistic.* Comment: The current arrangement of thousands of special provisions annually for the assessment of disabled students, which has never been costed, is becoming untenable and demands complicated systems of central and departmental resources being deployed. Of the 100 students surveyed, 71 per cent were in receipt of 'special arrangements', constituting 64 per cent receiving extra time, 15 per cent in small rooms, 9 per cent their own room and 7 per cent with either an amanuensis or a reader. These arrangements already stretch resources. In addition, these arrangements set students apart and they do not address the needs of the broader Widening Participation constituency. Dismantling the costly artifice of 'special arrangements' will free up resources for developing more inclusive approaches to assessing learning outcomes. Inevitably, at the development stage, there will be additional costs but over time this will not continue to escalate as is currently the case. A long-term saving of resources is an opportunity not to be missed, and, from the point of view of social justice, the removal of the distinction between disabled and non-disabled assessment practice is an outcome at the heart of the universal design for learning. Within the UK, Widening Participation funding, the mainstreaming of disability funding and Teaching and Learning development monies are all relevant resources, which can be legitimately utilised to develop inclusive assessment practice.

- *Inclusive assessment might increase the risk of plagiarism.* Comment: Plagiarism is a fact of academic life which is constantly being addressed and which has contributed to the maintenance of traditionalist and positivist approaches to assessment, i.e. unseen examinations (Stefani and Carroll 2001). Although this is a broader debate, it may be argued that attempting to marry assessment methods to the students' preferred learning styles is less likely to result in cheating and more likely to encourage a positive engagement with assessment. The student is more likely to be able to demonstrate their achievement in their own preferred mode and this will reduce student anxiety. Using the risk of plagiarism as a reason not to consider inclusive assessment practice is a smokescreen which prevents the challenging of traditional academic practice and belief in the fairness of the current system. Many of the approaches recommended to prevent plagiarism, e.g. that deadlines for assignments are sited well in advance of the end of term, assignment topics can be diverse and customised by students with staff consent, and intermediate parts of assignments can be submitted for consultation throughout the semester as 'process steps' are germane to inclusive assessment practice (Harris 2004).

The assessment options explored by the partnership

The HEIs within the partnership represent traditional and new universities, and specialist colleges of higher education, each with their own distinctive staff and student profiles, overlaps in course provision, differing assessment cultures and links to professional bodies. This variation provides a rich environment, a cross-fertilisation of discipline practice, and a useful framework for considering new practice.

The starting point for establishing a range of alternative assessment modes that we could evaluate for quality assurance was twofold. One vector for change was the assessment methods alluded to above and derived from QAA Subject Benchmark Statements. The other vector was the preferred assessment methods identified by the students in our first phase survey. Students were asked to identify, from the list of 48 possible assessment methods, their top five preferred modes. Table 7.1 lists the first five preferences and readers will note that unseen examinations do not feature at all!

These methods of assessment preferred by students identified in Table 7.1 correlate with the methods that are currently being deployed in schools and

Table 7.1 Disabled students' preferred methods of assessment (%)

Students' preferred choice of assessment method	% of students identifying assessment mode by preference
Portfolio	26
Coursework with discussion elements	27
Oral examinations	32
Multiple choice	33
Continuous assessment	50

colleges, but which may not be being utilised to any great extent on certain higher education courses. Where they are being used without any other option, they may not represent the optimum choice to meet an individual student's preferred learning style.

Alternative assessments for disabled students

From the preferences outlined in Table 7.1 the following alternative assessments shown in Table 7.2 were developed for disabled students and were carried out for both summative and formative purposes.

These alternative assessments had considerable resource implications and as a result we began to explore the possibility of facilitating assessment methods that could be offered to all students inclusively. The following case studies shown in Table 7.3 involving both formative and summative assessments were offered as an alternative for both disabled and non-disabled students.

Table 7.2 Alternative assessments developed for disabled students

Subject areas	Traditional assessment methods	Alternative assessment methods provided for disabled students	Number of disabled students undertaking the alternative assessment
Illustration	Written dissertation	Video	1
Education	Written assignment	Video portfolio	1
Health and Social Care	Written report	Oral report	1

Table 7.3 Alternative assessments offered to disabled and non-disabled students

Subject areas	Traditional assessment methods	Alternative assessment method offered to all students	Formative/summative purposes
Civil Engineering	Written examination	Oral assessment	Summative
Humanities	Written report	Oral report	Formative

The case study that was developed from the Civil Engineering example in Table 7.3 involved a dyslexic student undertaking the oral examination without any special arrangements, therefore, being subject to the same circumstances as the non-disabled students who had also chosen this option. The dyslexic student achieved an 11 per cent increase in marks compared to her previous exam-based performance in the same module, for which she had received extra time. Similar marked improvements were also recorded against the performance of 8 out of 10 of the non-disabled students who had likewise chosen to undertake the oral assessment. The student feedback was unanimously, to use their words, that 'oral assessment models should be utilised more to explore knowledge'.

However, not all oral assessments facilitated by the SPACE project have been so positively received. The Humanities case study in Table 7.3 provided 26 students (four of which were disabled) with the opportunity of submitting an oral assessment on tape as an alternative to a written report. The case study stimulated much debate among the student group and culminated in a focus group meeting to explore the overall effectiveness of the oral report as an alternative to the written report. Responses were mixed, but the students agreed that it was good to have a choice of possible assessment modes. After reviewing the student feedback and reflecting on the experience of the case study, the module leader felt there was justification for embedding the oral report as an alternative assessment mode and at the time of writing is seeking approval at an institutional level.

Contemporaneously, assessment change was being developed across the partnership. At one of the Arts-based institutions, a design report replaced a conventional essay on a 3D Design course offered across levels. The design report recorded a 30 per cent improvement in student marks and no requests for any special provisions were made or needed. Student feedback similarly recorded the benefits. As one student put it, 'I am dyslexic and the structure helped me understand and work in a better way.' Likewise, a shift away from modes of assessment relying on writing occurred in a case study developed at the University of Plymouth in a Foundation Year Extended Science Module. As a response to increasing student numbers, student feedback and an increasingly diverse student group, an extended essay was replaced by a portfolio as the main method of assessment. Since the portfolio was introduced, marks have improved on the module, there have been fewer instances of students not submitting work on time and no requests for any special provisions have been made for disabled students, who on average make up about 9 per cent of the cohort that has approximately 140 students in total.

These two case studies, representing as they do a change in assessment practice, are in effect *alternative* modes of assessment, essentially replacing one mode with another. However, given our subsequent interest in *inclusive* assessment practice we wished to explore the option of *assessment choice*. The School of Civil Engineering at the University of Plymouth undertook to support this initiative, which has received a further financial and academic commitment from the Learning and Teaching Support Network (LTSN) for Engineering (http://www.engsc.ac.uk). The Behaviour of Structures Module recruits approximately 150 students from the disciplines of Architecture and Construction Education, 10 per cent of whom are disabled. Because of the cross-discipline basis of the module – teaching a numerate subject to non-numerate undergraduates – the module has historically been challenged by student under-achievement. With support from the external examiner and influenced by previous student feedback, the module leader in collaboration with the SPACE Project, provided students with a choice of three assessment options: coursework, portfolio or an end-of-module unseen exam. All three of the assessment choices were utilised by students with the majority opting for coursework, and of particular importance is the fact that no special provisions were requested or required. An overall improvement of 5 per cent in marks has been recorded across the whole group and Box 7.3 contains a cross-section of the student and module leader's feedback.

Box 7.3 Feedback from the module leader and disabled and non-disabled students on being offered a choice of assessment modes on the Behaviour of Structures Module

Module leader   Enabled the students to consolidate their knowledge.

I learnt more about what they knew than I previously did from the examination.

The students have been far less anxious than in previous years and I have had far fewer requests for support.

Students   Enjoyed the choice and good to have a say.

Would like to see this operate in other modules.

Good not to be prescribed learning.

This is a good idea as people have different strengths and weaknesses when it comes to assessments.

By choosing my assessment method it enables me to get the best out of a module by selecting a method that best suits my abilities.

The chance to choose the best assessment is excellent. Not all people are good at exams, so it allows the best choice for each individual.

I would rather have the choice as it helps everyone get the best out of themselves.

As a consequence of pursuing an action research methodology, we have brought the periphery to the centre and located what might at first appear to be a subordinate issue of assessing disabled students at the core of the assessment debate, where its power to illuminate the whole debate is on-going. Our own point of departure, the foundation for our research hypothesis here, was formulated through seeking longitudinal student evaluation of disability service provision at the University of Plymouth and through the SWANDS Network.

One important consequence has been that we have received the views of non-disabled students and these can be read in the context of a social justice perspective, as set out in Box 7.4.

Box 7.4 Feedback on alternative and inclusive assessment from non-disabled students

This is a good idea because every person has their own likes and dislikes, abilities and disabilities.

If the assessment system is changed, I believe all students should partake in order not to alienate those with disabilities.

Everyone doing the same assessment is obviously not fair on people with disabilities.

These statements are echoed in the Disability Discrimination Act (2005) which asserts 'the need to promote equality of opportunity between disabled persons and other persons'.

Conclusion

Action research has proved to be an appropriate methodology for the SPACE Project because it involved 'colleagues and other participants in a shared activity, a process of change'. For us it has provided the impetus to reconsider our approach to the modes of assessment offered to both disabled and non-disabled students. We began determinined to evaluate alternative assessments as a vehicle for equity for disabled students and subsequently recognised the value of inclusive assessments for all. This has been our *modus operandi.*

The project has a further 12 months to run and in that time we will have completed the longitudinal study and developed the Assessment Toolkit for dissemination to the UK higher education sector, which will share the findings of our action research, offer tested examples of inclusive assessment tasks and evaluation tools for use by departments. It will also provide feedback on the discussions relating to questions of parity, quality assurance and the implications for delivery.

Inclusive assessment is a complex and contentious issue, however, by exploring students' assessment experiences and understanding the applicability of assessment practice for measuring learning outcomes, it is possible to begin to move the process forward for equitable change. As the project has developed, the research team has become increasingly aware that inclusive assessment does not have to represent new methods of assessment and increased academic workload, but instead a greater utilisation of existing methods, learning from other disciplines and disabled student experience. As Elton (2000) prosaically states: 'I cannot think of anything more unfair than to treat all students as if they are the same when they are so manifestly not.' Thus, in working to address disability we may appear to have been discussing the periphery when in fact it has led us to examine the central core of university activity. We recognise that there may always remain a small group who will require something different as a response to an individual set of circumstances, a 'special arrangement' or one-off alternative. However, we believe that institutions need to adopt a more inclusive practice where traditional methods of assessment must be examined to better serve disabled students, other non-traditional students and students with a range of learning styles and experiences – in fact, all students.

References and further reading

Barton, L. (2003) 'Inclusive education and teacher education: a basis for hope or a discourse of delusion', professorial lecture, Institute of Education, University of London.

Beattie, R.B. (1999) *The Beattie Committee Report: Implementing Inclusiveness, Realising Potential*. Edinburgh: The Scottish Executive.

Carr, W. and Kemmis, S. (1986) *Becoming Critical*. London: The Falmer Press.

Disability Discrimination Act, Parts II and IIII (2004) Available at: http://www.disability. gov.uk/ dda/new/parts (accessed 07/2005).

Disability Discrimination Act (2005) www.opsi.gov.uk/acts/acts2005/20050013.htm (accessed 07/2005).

Elton, L. (2000) 'Dangers of doing the wrong thing righter', in *Evaluate and Improve*. London: University College London.

Equality Challenge Unit (2004) 'Promoting equality, the public sector duty on disability: suggested first steps for HEI's'. Available at: http://www.ecu.ac.uk/publications/down loads/Briefing Pape.1.pdf (accessed 07/2005).

Goodley, D. (1999) 'Disability researcher template: reflections on grounded subjectivity in ethnographic research', *Qualitative Inquiry*, 5(1): 24–26.

Harris, R. (2004) 'Anti-plagiarism strategies for research papers'. Available at: http:// www.virtualsalt.com (accessed 07/2005).

Higher Education Funding Council for England (2002) *Improving Provision for Disabled Students: Strategy and Invitation to Bid for Funds for 2003-05*. Bristol: HEFCE, 02/21.

Higher Education Statistics Agency (2004) *Students in Higher Education Institutions*. *JSET Journal*, http://jsetunlv.edu/15.1/asseds/rose.html (accessed 07/2005).

Parker, M. (2004) 'In what ways can ethnographic research allow for a critical examination of disability studies in higher education?', unpublished, University of Sheffield.

Rose, D. and Meyer, A. (2000) 'Universal Design for Learning'. Available at: http://jset. unlv.edu/15.1/asseds/rose.html#top_page (accessed 07/2005).

Sikes, P., Nixon, J. and Carr, W. (2003) *The Moral Foundations of Educational Research: Knowledge Inquiry and Values*. Maidenhead: Open University Press.

Stefani, L. and Carroll, J. (2001) *A Briefing on Plagiarism*. LTSN Generic Centre, York, Assessment Series No. 10.

Stuart, M. (2002) *Collaborating for Change?* Leicester: NIACE.

Waterfield, J. and Parker, M. (2004) 'SPACE First Phase Report', unpublished, SPACE Project, University of Plymouth.

Waterfield, J. and West, B. (2002) SENDA 'Compliance in Higher Education', University of Plymouth. Available at: http://www.plymouth.ac.uk/disability

Williams, W. M. and Ceci, S. J. (1999) 'Accommodating learning disabilities can bestow unfair advantages'. Available at: http://chronicle/com/colloquy/99/disabled/background. htm (accessed 07/2005).

Yates, L. (2004) *What Does Good Education Research Look Like?* Maidenhead: Open University Press.

Chapter 8

Learning, teaching and disabled students

Challenging traditional models of support

Bethan O'Neil and Kate Wilson

Introduction

This chapter presents practical measures and a consideration of wider learning and teaching issues to support disabled students. It is contextualised within an innovative context of a consortium of eight small specialist performing and creative arts institutions. In particular, it considers what 'value-added' can be achieved through an alternative model of inter-organisational collaboration for improving provision for disabled students in small/specialist institutions, and what it means when 'inclusivity' does not count growth in student numbers as one of its primary strategic drivers. For specialist institutions 'being inclusive' relates to increasing opportunity and fair access to excellence and specialism and ensuring that when students are on its programmes, retention is good and individual potential is achieved.

This chapter also provides a snapshot of how learning and teaching practice is developing in institutions with small numbers of disabled students. In addition to most individual institutions running base-level provision projects, there is also a pan-consortium learning and teaching project focused on improving provision for disabled students. The particular opportunities and concerns in challenging traditional models of support in the learning and teaching of disabled students are more fully explored against the backdrop of the current legislative and policy framework in the UK, the critical benefits and challenges of developing partnership working, and the opportunity for stimulating cultural and attitudinal change in the shift from integration to inclusion – one made more significant as the particular academic profile of staff in specialist institutions, predominantly comprises professionals employed on hourly or fractional rates.

Small and specialist: the institutional context of disability

In the UK, the Higher Education Funding Council for England (HEFCE) has defined 'specialist' institutions as those that have more than 60 per cent of their provision in no more than two of its 'cost centres', i.e. that the provision offered by the institution falls within no more than two broad subject ranges. They are thus differentiated from general higher education institutions by virtue of their specialist status and the attendant recognition of the range of cost factors associated with their specialist status that has resulted in premium funding. While the above subtitle is 'small and specialist' and well over half of specialist institutions are in arts, it must be noted that not all of those institutions denoted by HEFCE as 'specialist' are small. The University of the Arts (formerly the London Institute), for example, has over 24,000 students, compared to the smallest CADISE partner institution with enrolments of 700 students. CADISE, the Consortium of Arts & Design Institutions in Southern England comprises the Arts Institute at Bournemouth, the Central School of Speech and Drama, the Kent Institute of Art & Design, the Ravensbourne College of Design and Communication, Rose Bruford College, the Surrey Institute of Art & Design, University College, Trinity College of Music and Wimbledon School of Art.

The changes that have impacted on higher education in its move from 'elite' to one approaching 'massification' (Trow 1974) have no less affected higher education colleges and specialist institutions with attendant growth, although in recent years there has been some contraction of part of the sector. Thus, in 2004 of the 170 universities and higher education institutions, a much smaller number of them were specialist institutions as many had been subsumed by their larger neighbours (see Table 8.1).

CADISE was a response to this changing environment and formed in the wake of the Dearing Report (1997) (where *inter alia*, there were calls for increased access for disabled students to higher education and increased learning support provision). It was formed in 1999 to give a representative voice in the arts, design and communication sector, to capture the benefits of collaboration through an enhanced critical mass based on the grounds of 'commonality' and 'complementarity' (collectively some 12,000 students), to meet the unfolding regional agenda and to develop an alternative exportable model of collaborative management for the higher education sector. As Ritterman (2004) has noted when discussing specialist institutions, the role of a specialist institution includes 'finding

Table 8.1 Decline in higher education institutions and specialist institutions in the UK over a 10-year period

	1994	1999	2004
Higher education institutions in the UK	67	60	54
Higher education institutions in England	48*	47	42
Specialist institutions	35*	28	28

Notes: Asterisked figures do not include schools/colleges of the University of London or the medical schools, many of which has been subsequently amalgamated with universities. They do, however, include the music conservatoires.

Source: Adapted from Standing Conference of Principals, SCOP

innovative ways of doing things that matter in ways that also respond to changing agendas'.

In its Heads of Agreement, the formal memorandum of understanding signed by each Chief Executive on behalf of the partner institutions, a number of statements in relation to its commitment to mutually beneficial and collaborative practices, widening participation and excellence in teaching and learning are articulated:

> Whilst recognising and valuing the independent identity and cultures of its partner institutions, CADISE is committed in the regions to increase the diversity of the student population, enhance student choice, widen participation and encourage lifelong learning by developing a coherent framework of regional opportunity and progression

and also '[to] promote the recognition and reputation of individual institutions in delivering excellent learning, teaching, scholarship, research and professional practice' (CADISE Heads of Agreement, May 1999).

The consortium enjoys a successful infrastructure for, and track record of, project management. The opportunity to work collectively on a learning and teaching project, 'Being Inclusive in the Creative and Performing Arts' (project details can be accessed at: www.cadise.ac.uk/learning_teaching/bicpa.htm), while 7 out of 8 partner institutions were at the same time receiving HEFCE funding to establish and enhance their base-level provision, afforded an interesting dynamic in terms of a wider curriculum-based initiative and a real opportunity to effect change and have an impact on curriculum, content, design and delivery. Both projects are two-thirds through with completion of 4 out of 8 case studies on individual 'live' issues in the teaching and learning project and with the opportunity for synergistic development in relation to base-level provision, through a regular CADISE interest group meeting of the Learning Resources Group comprising Welfare and Disability Officers.

The UK policy and legislative framework

In its recently published strategic plan, HEFCE (2005: 11) states in the introduction to its aim in relation to widening participation and fair access that: 'We aim to ensure that all those with the potential to benefit from higher education have the opportunity to do so, whatever their background and whenever they need it.' This, in combination with the further aim to enhance excellence in learning and teaching and ensure that all higher education students benefit from a high-quality learning experience that fully meets their needs and the need of society, places the onus on institutions alone to ensure that there is no discrimination and that reasonable adjustments are made to the curriculum for disabled students. This autonomous obligation of institutions distinguishes the UK from other national systems of higher education. The context of disability provision in specialist institutions has grown in an 'ad hoc' way with limited provision, given the history and uncertainties of resourcing. While financial support that institutions require to implement their 'disability statements' is granted by the intermediate structure of HEFCE, and is directly contingent on the quality and relevance of measures set out in institutional statements, until the Special Educational Needs and Disability Act 2001 came into force, the use of funds earmarked for statements was not subject to any form of control.

However, pockets of best practice and expertise, although developing in a reactive way, have long resided in specialist institutions where individual or small numbers of students have been accepted by individual tutors onto a programme, or as a response to one of the HEFCE initiatives for disabled students. For example, one of the partners was in receipt of the HEFCE SPLD (Dyslexia) special initiative funds (1996–9), the second of four HEFCE rounds of special disability initiative funding. Although the general predisposition of creative and performing arts institutions is to inclusivity, without the push from the Disability Discrimination Act 1995 requiring higher education institutions to include disability statements in their strategies and the incentivisation of the need to comply with it and other legislation, the approach has not been one that could be described as consistent or quantifiable in any coherent way. Indeed, it has been noted in a publication by the OECD on disability in higher education (Ebersold 2003: 93) that in the UK 'colleges and specialised institutions tend to have shorter [disability] statements'.

It should be noted that while the legislative and policy imperative has acted as a key driver, compliance with such requirements has had a more forceful impact in certain areas (for example, admissions) and in the running of the organisation. Progress has been much slower in relation to honing in on change in actual teaching and learning areas. There remains a continuing need, therefore, for the legislation and policy context to be supplemented by practical developments and the creation of resources, particularly given the various modes and learning styles used in the creative and performing arts context.

Teaching and learning in the specialist arts and design institutional context

Creative and Performing Arts education covers a vast subject area and a range of courses which encompass a variety of teaching styles and modes of curriculum delivery, often characterised by learning in workshop, studio, exhibition spaces, stage and auditorium settings, traditional lectures, resource-based learning or in a groupwork collaborative setting. This diversity of approach is fundamental to the delivery of a fluid and personal area of study.

The shift from integration to inclusivity

As institutions move to bring disability issues into the mainstream of their activity, so the need for partnership working between students, support workers and academic staff is highlighted. The shift from integration where disabled students had previously to adapt to existing organisational structures and arrangements, to inclusion where the institution responds and adapts to an individual's requirements, has proved more than a subtle stretch. The development of effective and coherent multi-agency working which results in improved student access is a complex challenge contextualised by a range of factors within specialist higher education institutions.

CADISE institutions have been developing a wider range of welfare provision in recent years, supported by a number of funding initiatives, including the HEFCE strand 1 disability funding, widening participation premium funding and teaching and learning funds. Traditionally, small specialist institutions have tended to operate with a culture that integrates student support within the specialist course or department, with administrators and academic staff providing a wide range of the personal and academic support needed. Consequently, they have tended not to have extensive student support and welfare services operating as central provision, as might commonly be found in larger higher education institutions. However, as funding has tightened, the levels of administrative and support staff in academic departments has reduced in many cases, leaving less time for non-teaching support. At the same time, increased diversity in the student population and the imperative of meeting legislative and quality assurance requirements have led to recognition of the need for institutions to have access to the specialist professionals who can support students with a range of additional learning needs, including disabled students.

The strong culture of integrated support within academic departments brings many benefits and at best can result in academic staff having good awareness of difficulties that a student may be experiencing and a will to be involved in minimising these problems. The tutorial remains central to much teaching in creative subject areas, and this one-to-one interaction, combined with informal teaching and learning in the context of practical problem-based learning, can lead to strong relationships being formed between student and staff members, which in turn can lead to trust and the sharing of personal information. A student perspective gained from one of the case studies illustrates this:

> When I was at school I had a certain amount of help but you were allocated certain times and that was it, . . . and if you had any other problems there was no-one else to see because you were only allocated that time, whereas [at College] the tutors, they are always there to approach, . . . and they're there a lot of the time.
>
> (Design student with dyslexia)

As institutions begin to develop welfare teams of staff, they are challenged to ensure that they build on this culture of integration, rather than replace it with a central provision with the attendant disadvantages. Hence, in many cases within CADISE institutions, specialist welfare staff within higher education institutions, whether Disability Officers or specialist facilitators, such as interpreters for students with hearing impairments, work in close partnership with academic team members, sharing responsibilities to the student.

For example, when a music college partner explored ways to provide fuller access for visually-impaired students to selected modules within its BMus (Hons) programme, the Disability Officer worked closely with the course leader to review and amend the assessment criteria and submission format for the modules. They were able to bring together the specialist subject knowledge of the tutor with the Disability Officer's awareness of the access challenges and successfully amended the module so that it retains the academic standards and is more fully accessible.

Strategies for change

A great deal of effort has been made by all partners in the consortium to ensure that academic staff are aware of their responsibilities to students in the context of disability and equality legislation. The challenge comes in responding appropriately to a particular set of circumstances presented by a student. Because small institutions do not have large numbers of disabled students, a tutor may often find themselves the first to have encountered a particular form of impairment, and thus does not have insights built from previous similar cases. Uncertainty about how to proceed can be acute, with tutors having little confidence that they know what is in the best interests of the students and being anxious to ensure that they work within the institution's regulations and policies. The introduction of specialist Disability Officers and Welfare Officers has had a significant impact in this area by providing a resource to work with both students and academic departments to determine appropriate actions. For example, in another partner institution, the Welfare Officer works closely with the student and the course leader or personal tutor to design and agree a learning plan that takes account of any additional support that a disabled student may need from the point of interview, at induction and throughout the period of study.

Even in relatively small welfare teams, there is often a broad range of staff available to provide different types of support to students. This will include specialist disability facilitators employed to provide specific support to individual students, welfare staff employed by the institution to develop and provide support in a range of welfare areas and academic support staff with roles to assist the development of learning skills and academic tutors. The challenge for institutions is to ensure that the skills and good practice developed by these professionals in their varying roles are brought together to provide coherent, high quality support to those students who need it.

In a number of the case studies on disability, teaching and learning conducted in the collaborative context, a major emerging issue is the way in which this range of support provision is managed within the structure of the higher education institution. Activities, projects and new posts have emerged through a range of initiatives and a range of funding streams, some of which are aligned to widening participation management, others to equal opportunities and others to teaching and learning. Consequently there is a risk, even within small institutions, that academic staff and students are unclear about who to approach on a particular issue and welfare staff themselves may be unaware of initiatives being developed in departments other than their own. One college in the South-East of England has recently developed a 'one-stop-shop' approach to student services on its campus to ensure that the range of services are drawn together for students and are managed within a single managerial unit.

It is equally important for institutions to review their committee structures to ensure that issues relating to disabled students are considered at the appropriate level and are mainstreamed within the institution's development. One of the concerns of welfare staff can be a lack of clarity about how to progress issues at senior levels and many different models exist. At many partner institutions, the terms of reference of the long-standing Equal Opportunities Committee have been extended and, for example, renamed as the Equality and Inclusivity Committee or the Equality and Diversity Committee in order to encompass issues pertaining to widening participation, equal opportunities and disability. These committees have a remit to consider issues, develop policy and take action and to ensure that other major committees concerned with teaching and learning, quality assurance, academic standards, finance, estates, health and safety, and so forth are informed, engaged in debate and responsible for taking action where it falls within their terms of reference. To reflect the significance of the retitled committee, the preferred option is that there is a shift in reporting responsibilities and that it should be through the institution's Academic Board.

In the specialist institutions of CADISE, case study research has explored the professional relationships between students and the various support individuals active within the institution. A number of examples have looked at how the role of a specialist facilitator is practised in the context of studio-based, often practical, activity and the ways in which communication takes place between the three stakeholders. The predominance of practical activity in the study of creative and performing arts often requires that students are physically present in the institution for a high proportion of their time to access specialist resources, to participate in group learning, and to work iteratively with staff through the development of project-based work. As a result of the high attendance expectations and the nature of the practical activity, the amount of contact time between student and tutor is often high compared with more theoretical subject areas and specialist facilitators are very 'close to the action'.

Where students are working on practical projects, often in a studio or workshop environment, the interactions between students and academic staff, are often informal. For example, tutors in a design studio will engage in short reviews of progress with students as they walk around a studio space as well as in more structured tutorials and group critiques. Additionally, students will work closely alongside each other and offer peer support during the development of projects;

they might, for example, discuss their interpretation of the project brief, ask each other's advice, consult on uses of different strategies or materials. Our case studies identified the fact that students with hearing impairment and/or visual impairments can all too easily be excluded from these various informal ways of developing ideas, of reassuring themselves that they are on the right track and reviewing progress in relation to their peers. In some cases students felt unable to fully access these informal discussions.

Teaching staff can adopt strategies to minimise this exclusion, for example, by ensuring they make time early in the project to communicate with the student on an individual basis. They can then be reassured that the student is clear about the brief and has a chance to ask questions. Staff should be encouraged to make sure students with visual and/or hearing impairments are fully involved in group discussions and critiques, inviting comment and ensuring that time is given to listen and respond.

> I suppose, perhaps I'd need to talk with them a bit more because obviously I couldn't write anything down, so I always like to sit with my tutors, to go through it, so that I understand why those things are done, so I get the chance to discuss, I have to be able to talk, so that's an important bit.
>
> (Design student with dyslexia)

In the case of hearing impaired students where verbal communication is limited and needs to be facilitated by a specialist support worker, an in-depth case study demonstrated the risk that tutors and support workers develop their own conversation, again excluding the student (all case studies are to be published as part of the BICPA project on the CADISE website: www.cadise.ac.uk/projects/BICPA). The more this happens, the more likely it is that issues will arise about the extent to which the response to the project is that of the student or the facilitator.

A case study carried out by one partner institute explored this issue through interviews with students, facilitators and academic staff. It demonstrated that facilitators had a well-developed understanding of the boundaries of their role, being clear that it did not extend to advising the student on academic matters. For example, supporting a dyslexic student in essay-writing, the facilitator would advise regarding organisation, structure, clarity of expression, but would not comment on content. However, the case study also revealed that academic staff were concerned about the potential for the boundaries between their role and that of the facilitator to be unclear.

Communication between academic staff and specialist facilitators can be problematic in many ways. In specialist institutions many academic staff are professional practitioners, employed on an hourly-paid basis or on fractional posts; in some cases academic teams can have very small numbers of full-time staff. The facilitators are also not typically employed on a full-time basis and so opportunities to meet can be limited. The Disability Officer often has encouraged academic teams to involve the facilitators in team meetings as a way of sharing expertise, not in discussing individual cases, but in developing each other's awareness of their respective professions.

A further identified barrier to partnership working between academic staff and specialist facilitators has also been a tendency for academic staff to undervalue the professionalism of facilitators. This has improved at the above partner institute as facilitators have increasingly undertaken professional qualifications, which not only demonstrate their skills but which also give them their own experience of higher education level study.

The extent to which students are supported by their facilitators in their higher education level study has emerged in a variety of forms within the case studies. In a case study conducted with a profoundly deaf student, the Disability Officer found herself being asked to wake up the student who had overslept and had not arrived on time to meet his facilitator at the beginning of the day. Similar examples were found elsewhere within the partnership of students who were ill or unable to attend college, asking their interpreter to attend the lecture for them and to take notes of their behalf. In such cases, staff held the view that students should be treated as independent adults and not have their 'hands held' any more than any other student. In a number of cases the specialist facilitators' previous experiences were mainly from working in schools and in further education institutions, as a result, they took time to adjust to the different expectations of a higher education environment and the recognition that as adults students are expected to better manage their own time and resources.

The importance of social relationships in a positive learning experience has been highlighted through the CADISE case studies, again in the case of visually and hearing impaired students. In a number of cases, students have found that their peers experience a barrier to communication and this has led to students with these particular impairments being marginalised socially. Not only has this been an unhappy experience for the students in question, it has naturally impeded their learning as they may be less able as a result to discuss the development of their ideas and work with peers.

In small specialist institutions the number of students with a particular impairment can be very small. In many cases there will be a single student who may also often be the first student with a particular impairment to have joined the college. In such cases it can be very difficult for students to develop and maintain a wider support network. For example, a hearing impaired student who moved from the Midlands to London to study a specialist subject not available in his home area, found himself missing the support of his local deaf group and struggling to access a new group. Additionally, internal support networks for disabled students can be difficult to establish in higher education institutions with small numbers.

However, these case studies have also highlighted various strategies to minimise the impact of these communication difficulties. In one college, disabled students produced leaflets that they distributed around the campus, to raise awareness about disability issues and break down some of the perceived barriers. In another case the college provided basic sign language training for a group of students so that they would have the ability and the confidence to sign with a hearing impaired colleague.

Some preliminary conclusions

The conclusion to be reached within the context of learning, teaching and disabled students from the perspective of specialist institutions, is that partnership and collaborative activity have a part to play both inter-institutionally where new approaches of teamwork between support staff and academics are taking place and intra-institutionally where the sum of institutional experiences can add up to more than the whole. Through sharing experience and expertise in the range of impairments encountered in creative and performing art settings, best practice can be accessed and practical educational resources can be developed that can be tested and embedded in partner institutions to support the curriculum.

As understanding of disability grows among academics, there is a corresponding growth with a student focus to suit individual needs that is becoming mainstreamed. Similarly, within validations of new programmes, induction processes and procedures, learning outcomes and assessment criteria are being developed in such a way that differentiation is built into courses, and is increasingly accepted as a necessary progression by staff. While we are still a long way from the point where every student, regardless of their learning needs, can guarantee inclusion on all curriculum matters, an enhanced willingness has developed through the CADISE 'Being Inclusive in the Creative and Performing Arts' project.

A case study approach in a collaborative context, even on a small scale, has proved an effective way of stimulating change. It has provided time and funding to look closely at a situation and to consider how the learning may be more widely applied within the institution and across the consortium. In some instances, the case studies have led to systemic change, for example, developing more accessible assessment criteria for a single module has led to a full review of the BMus (Hons) programme at the time of validation and the guaranteed interview scheme for disabled applicants in another institution has been adopted as a policy. Additionally, there has been potential to add to development and disseminate through the sector in unanticipated ways, such as a '10 Point ICT Protocol' that is being disseminated by TechDis, a national agency which provides support to both higher and further education institutions in the area of technology and disabled students.

However, it is not suggested that collaboration and partnership on projects for teaching, learning and disabled students are a panacea for all specialist institutions, or that they do not have their challenges. There remains the challenge of ultimately developing the capacity of the partner institutions to design and deliver programmes of study that will enhance choice and provision for disabled students while as a collaborative project sitting outside the strategic planning of the individual institution. There is also the need to ensure a permanent change after the life of the project. Fundamental questions need to be constantly revisited, such as, will the gains from project initiatives survive? Will they be developed further? Which aspects of and how should project gains be embedded and passed on? Who are the academic 'champions' who will 'own' and take forward project gains and will there be a collaborative or institutional focus in future?

It is difficult to evaluate the success of funded initiatives and their impact on the curriculum in isolation as attitudinal and cultural change is not a short-term, but a medium- to long-term strategy. However, investment through initiatives that foster joint consideration aligned to complementarity of the overall subject, the intimate scale of the learning, teaching and research environment and the commitment to excellence and professional currency have provided platforms within the partnership for developing educational tools and resources for the teaching of disabled students, and for the wider reflections and refinements that come from dissemination in the sector. The educational map has changed a great deal in the past two years in relation to disability and the opportunity to collectively share capacity concerns and build capability through collaboration is to be welcomed. What has been achieved in challenging traditional models of support is that staff apprehension over issues of standards in higher education have been successfully managed with champions in the identified projects – work that can be collectively considered and evaluated and that has benefited from an added resource. Costs can still be a big issue for small institutions but confidence is growing institutionally in the possibilities of working with particular students to engage in support for the individual within a reasonable financial framework.

CADISE partner institutions recognise and are committed to extending the opportunity to participate in higher education and to widen participation to previously under-represented groups. The corollary of this has been to ensure that once students have submitted their application, every effort is made to enable them to have an equitable chance of success rather than drop out for lack of support. With statistics showing that there are over 6.5 million disabled people in the UK, and recent statistics published by the NDT (www.natdisteam.ac.uk/resources_statistics_oncourse) indicating that nearly 10 per cent of university students in creative arts and design have an impairment, it is imperative for teaching and learning academic and support staff to work together, so that as numbers increase, barriers to learning are removed and traditional models of support are challenged, in order to better understand and respond to the requirements of individual disabled students.

References and further reading

ADEPTT (Art & Design Enabling Part-time Tutors). Available at: www.adeptt.ac.uk (accessed 07/2005).

Barton, L. (1996) 'Sociology and disability: some emerging issues', in L. Barton (ed.) *Disability and Society: Emerging Issues and Insights.* London: Longman.

Borland, J. and James, S. (1999) 'The learning experiences of students with disabilities in Higher Education: a case study of a UK university', *Disability and Society*, 14(1): 85–101.

CADISE Heads of Agreement (1999) Internal Memorandum of Agreement drafted by CADISE Partners, May 1999, as subsequently amended by later additions to the membership.

Dearing, R. (1997) *Higher Education in the Learning Society*. London: HMSO.

Ebersold, S. (2003) *Disability in Higher Education*. Paris: OECD.

Fink, J., Thompson, J. and Williams, S. and by Wertheimer, A. (2001) *Enhancing the Course Offer (Report of a HEFCE Funded Disability Project at the London Institute, 1997–2000)*. London: The Disability Team at the London Institute.

Fuller, M., Bradley, A. and Healey, M. (2004) 'Incorporating disabled students within an inclusive higher education environment', *Disability and Society* 19 (5): 455–468.

HEFCE (2005) *Strategic Plan 2003–08*. Bristol: HEFCE. Available at: www.hefce.ac.uk/pubs/hefce/2005 (accessed 07/2005).

Holloway, S. (2001) 'The experience of higher education from the perspective of disabled students', *Disability and Society*, 16(4): 597–615.

Hurst, A. (1996) 'Reflecting on researching disability and higher education', in L. Barton (ed.) *Disability and Society: Emerging Issues and Insights*. London: Longman.

Noble, A. and Mullins, G. (2002) *Why Collaborate? Initiatives for Improving Participation and Completion for Students with a Disability in South Australia*. Published in collaboration to Widen Participation, European Access Network, Stoke on Trent: Trentham Books.

Ritterman, J. (2004) 'Scoping the English HE landscape', paper presented at the CADISE Annual Conference, 'The Strategic Merit of Specialist Institutions', Rose Bruford College, April.

Trow, M. (1974) 'Problems in the transition from elite to mass higher education', in *Policies for Higher Education*, from the General Report on the Conference on Future Stuctures of Post-Secondary Education, pp. 55–101. Paris: OECD. Reprinted by the Carnegie Commission on Higher Education in Berkeley, CA.

Chapter 9

Disability and omnicompetence

Facing up to challenges in the training of veterinary practitioners

Anne Tynan

Can disabled people work as veterinary surgeons, doctors and in other similar professions? Patently the answer is yes, since such people already exist, albeit frequently those who have become disabled once they have qualified to practise. This chapter will focus first on two key issues that emerge from recent work exploring this topic, those of 'omnicompetence' (that is, do professionals in these fields need to be competent in all aspects of the role?) and 'fitness to practise'. The second part of the chapter will outline the principal outcomes of a HEFCE-funded project, DIVERSE: the UK Veterinary Medicine Disability Project, which examined these issues and has made recommendations which have transferability across the healthcare and other regulated professions.

There has been considerable debate in recent years about admission of disabled students onto professional courses, largely linked to the issue of perceived requirements for omnicompetence and due to professional conservatism and inertia. As these professions have traditionally been able to recruit the most elite students, there has been a marked reluctance to make any adjustments to admissions policies. Some have also raised concerns about 'wasting' resources, as they perceive it, by providing disabled people with the expensive training needed to become a veterinarian or a doctor. Arguments were similarly made previously about training women for the professions.

This chapter will explore how this issue has been tackled in relation to veterinary education in the UK and explore how transferable are the principles that underpin activities, particularly the issue of limited licensing, whereby an individual's ability to practise is limited to a specific area of work. As in many issues covered in this book, this approach is not only enabling for disabled students, but also for all students studying for these professions and those in related domains. It is argued that the principal barriers are in relation to paradigm shifts and conceptual changes in the thinking of some who train others to work in the medical and veterinary professions, rather than anything to do with inherent capability.

Through work carried out at the Royal Veterinary College, University of London, in 2000–2, it had already been established that, contrary to popular belief, many disabled people were already working successfully as veterinary surgeons in the UK, the United States and Canada (Tynan 2001). In 2001, at least 24 individuals with hearing losses were known to have graduated as veterinarians in the USA, and that figure will clearly have been augmented by now. People with a range of physical impairments, including several amputees and a wheelchair user, have been working effectively as vets for many years. Although more difficult to quantify because of disclosure issues, vets with psychiatric and mental health conditions have also been located in many areas of the profession.

Sir Peter Large, a prominent British disability activist who was himself disabled and was involved in setting up the Association of Disabled Professionals, a networking organisation operated and managed by disabled people, argued that disabled people should 'try to understand how people operate in government, and negotiate and work with anybody who can help' (Large, ADP website). This was his highly successful *modus operandi* for more than four decades and his approach has informed the DIVERSE project's ambitions to encourage disabled students not to be put off by others' perceived barriers to their professional careers.

From the year 2000, the veterinary profession was involved in a concerted effort to try to understand, negotiate and work with the UK qualifications, regulatory and professional bodies. The aim was to assist them to overcome a traditional reluctance in allowing disabled people to train for and to enter regulated professions such as human and veterinary medicine, engineering and law.

This reluctance was largely based on the perception by some that disabled people could not meet the requirements of 'fitness to practise', a term used most frequently within health care but applicable also in other professions. Explanations of this term can be found on the websites of a number of medical schools, a typical example being that of the Queen's University, Belfast, which states:

> The Fitness to Practise procedure applies to courses leading directly into professions for which there are academic, behavioural and health requirements that must be met in order to ensure suitability to practise the profession.
>   The Fitness to Practise procedure exists to protect:
>
> a. the public interest, by safeguarding client well-being; and
> b. student interests, by ensuring that students do not proceed without careful examination into a career for which they may not be suited or for which a regulatory body would not be prepared to register them.
>
> Students may be considered unfit to practise on the grounds of:
>
> (i)   physical or mental health problems;
> (ii) criminal or other serious misconduct; or
> (iii) professionally inappropriate behaviour.
>
> This list is not exhaustive.

Many would argue that only those aspects of fitness to practise which relate to a student's physical or mental abilities to perform are relevant within the scope of this chapter. It is certainly unfortunate (and many believe, unacceptable) that issues of disability are bracketed together with other issues, including criminal or professional misconduct.

Most areas of veterinary practice require specific visual, auditory or physical skills and it is therefore not unreasonable to question how a disabled individual is going to be able to carry out specific procedures. For example, work with large animals such as cows and horses demands both physical dexterity and the ability to work in environments such as stables and farmyards, which is likely to be problematic for some disabled people with mobility impairments. Nevertheless, medical and veterinary schools can reasonably be expected to review curricula to investigate the extent to which omnicompetence is required of all, and whether limited licensing can be used to offer programmes of learning matched to applicants' abilities and learning needs, focusing on capability (what students and professionals can do) rather than taking a deficit approach (what cannot be done).

While there can be legitimate reasons for querying whether disabled students and professionals can practise effectively in all contexts, problems nevertheless remain in relation to the enforcement of fitness to practise procedures. In 2005, Dr Leigh Bissett, the chairman of the British Medical Association (BMA) medical students' committee, explained the issue, perhaps ironically, thus:

> The BMA medical students' office regularly gets calls from prospective students asking whether they should apply to medical school because of a disability. They are unsure of their eligibility under the fitness-to-practise arrangements outlined in school prospectuses. Although I am confident that no school would disallow a disabled student the opportunity to apply for medicine, the lack of any national guidance does not help applicants or medical schools. To complicate matters there have been cases where one medical school has rejected a student on the grounds of disability while another has accepted the same student.
>
> (Bissett 2005)

This approach reflects a compliance approach rather than an inclusive one. Other interventions will therefore be needed in the short term to counteract confusion and lack of experience in translating disability discrimination legislation into practice. These experiences are similar to those of potential applicants to veterinary schools.

Limited licensing and professional competence and omnicompetence

A system of limited licensing, where an individual's ability to practise is limited to a specific area of work, can offer a much wider range of opportunities for disabled people. This is because 'fitness to practise' is more narrowly defined than the current demands that an individual be omnicompetent, that is capable across the full range of professional functions. If, at present, for whatever reason, an individual cannot carry out one or more of the competences within this range, he or she is deemed to be 'unfit for practice'. This is despite the fact that the individual concerned may have excellent skills in all other areas. It also ignores the variety of careers open to veterinary surgeons and other professionals once they qualify which do not require capability in all areas of practice.

Limited licensing, by contrast, focuses on capability. There are signs that professional licensing is moving in this direction, not so much for reasons relating to disability but because of concerns about the overload of the curriculum caused by ongoing developments in all professional fields. As elsewhere noted in this book, curriculum developments designed to accommodate professional needs of disabled students can be seen to benefit the broader student population at large.

In 2001, a consultation paper was published by the Education Strategy Steering Group of the Royal College of Veterinary Surgeons to consider a framework for 2010 and beyond. The paper stated:

> There are few professions where an initial degree confers on the holder an unlimited, life-long licence to practise, and the veterinary profession does need to consider how long it can or should maintain its present position in this respect.

In medicine, the issue of limited licensing and its connection with disabled people has also been explored by staff from several English medical schools. In a report by Roberts *et al.* (2004), detailed research highlighted different societal views of disabled people's inclusion to the study and practice of medicine. The authors state that:

> Disabled doctors felt limited licensing already reflected the reality of their working lives, without this being officially legislated . . . However, disabled doctors and non-disabled medical students did express the view that limited licensing might produce new and empowering opportunities for all doctors.

These issues of fitness to practise, limited licensing and professional competence and omnicompetence are at the heart of discussions on teaching, learning and disability within UK veterinary schools, working in conjunction with the Royal College of Veterinary Surgeons. The work of the DIVERSE project is potentially helpful in providing a possible model for other professional areas, as well as in helping to improve the quality of the teaching and learning of disabled students in the veterinary school context.

The DIVERSE project

The DIVERSE project started by focusing on the stated requirements of the Royal College of Veterinary Surgeons that a new veterinary surgeon must achieve, analysing how this related to disabled people who wished to undertake this training and demonstrating how any difficulties might be overcome. This was established by setting up a 'Competences Matching Exercise' to scrutinise the competences deemed by the Royal College of Veterinary Surgeons to be essential for new veterinary graduates on entry to the profession, described as 'Day One Skills'. Examples include:

> C1.1. Obtain an accurate and relevant history of the individual animal or animal group, and its/their environment.
> C1.2. Handle and restrain an animal safely and humanely, and instruct others in performing these techniques.

Looking at such 'essential competences', the project explored what challenges they might present for disabled people and how any adverse impacts could be offset through the provision of reasonable accommodations or by an individual disabled student's own coping strategies. Alongside this exercise was a second to assess the accessibility of environments in which veterinary students carry out practical placement work, including farms, animal hospitals, small veterinary practices and government laboratories. The project sought to identify barriers provided within each type of environment for disabled veterinary surgeons and to address how these might be overcome.

A collaborative approach

For both practical and strategic reasons, a collaborative steering group on which all six UK veterinary schools were represented was set up to oversee the development of the project. This group also included representatives from one medical and one dental school so that expertise could be contributed from these related areas. Partnerships of this type are indispensable for subject areas leading to a regulated professional qualification. The active and enthusiastic involvement of the Royal College of Veterinary Surgeons, as the registration body for all 6 veterinary schools was invaluable, since it provided reassurance to the individual veterinary schools about the approach taken, created externally a level of credibility in what the project was trying to achieve and provided a high degree of ownership in terms of the recommendations made. This was evident when the General Medical Council (GMC) and the General Dental Council (GDC), who are responsible for the registration of doctors and dentists respectively, accepted the offer to participate in the project steering group. Their active involvement gave enhanced credibility to the project and meant that any issues could be dealt with at any early stage through negotiation. It also meant that the regulatory bodies could balance a positive commitment by the professions to an inclusive approach with faithfulness to their mission to protect the public interest through ensuring fitness to practise.

Mutual understanding

This was not easily achieved but it was the result of sustained hard work to gain the trust and confidence of the professional bodies. This collaborative approach meant that some previously defensive stances were avoided and provided a positive framework from which the professions felt safe to explore concerns and/or to admit to their shortcomings. DIVERSE offered facilitation to remediate some of these shortcomings without constantly criticising the fact that they existed, and this undoubtedly proved to be a decisive factor.

Historically, the General Medical Council, in particular, had acquired the reputation of being unwelcoming towards disabled people who wanted to train to become doctors. The actions of the GMC as recently as 1999, in relation to the case of a 28-year-old disabled woman who was refused entry to medical school, were still the focus of comment 5 years later by Bert Massie, Chairman of the Disability Rights Commission (Disability Rights Commission 2004a):

> Heidi Cox is a wheelchair user and was accepted by Oxford University to study medicine. But because there was no agreement from the GMC that she could qualify – given a range of required learning outcomes, including resuscitation – Oxford could not assure her that she would be able to qualify as a doctor. At a time when we are short of at least 15,000 doctors – and are actively recruiting doctors from the new EU states and elsewhere, according to a survey by the *Financial Times* last week – should we be denying talented young disabled people the chance to become doctors? Heidi Cox's ambition was to become a pathologist. One might wonder how often resuscitation skills are needed in that particular role.

The aim of DIVERSE was to look to the future, building on lessons learned from previous policy and practice across the board. Underpinning this work was the contribution of the DIVERSE VETS, a sub-group within the steering group made up of individual disabled veterinary surgeons. It is essential to involve disabled people at all stages of development work as there is no substitute for their experience and insight with the issues they confront. However, the creation of the DIVERSE VETS group was also a tactical move. Their direct involvement and appearance at meetings left professional regulators no room to refute the fact that disabled people could be effective practitioners: the DIVERSE VETS were living proof that they could be.

This group also included disabled veterinary students. Although the pressures of their studies meant that they could not attend meetings, they were nevertheless able to contribute by means of a series of qualitative interviews conducted during the author's own placements at the other veterinary schools. Such placements were helpful in advertising the project and in enabling the involvement of many individuals around the country. Constant and ongoing dissemination activity of this kind was crucial if the outcomes of the project were going to take root effectively across the country and across the sector. This process was greatly facilitated by the active input of the sector-specific higher education subject centre.

The need for allies: the sector-wide higher education subject centre for Medicine, Dentistry and Veterinary Medicine

The DIVERSE steering group membership was carefully selected to represent the key stakeholders, becoming a powerful force for driving forward the project. However, it was the contribution of one particular organisation represented on the steering group, which acted as a catalyst for changing attitudes and policies throughout the UK.

LTSN-01 is now known as the 'Higher Education Academy Subject Centre for Medicine, Dentistry and Veterinary Medicine' and has a role across the UK to work with the higher education community to improve the student learning experience. The defining contribution via the DIVERSE project of the staff of LTSN-01 was two-fold:

1   To act as a neutral link across the sector, with a highly effective dissemination system via a website, email, newsletters, publications and other resources and events such as workshops and conferences.
2   To provide resources (funding and staff input) for the publication, distribution and dissemination of two Special Reports to support the development of policies being undertaken within the project.

These reports made it possible to explore issues raised by the practical work of DIVERSE in much greater depth.

Pushing the Boat Out: An Introductory Study of Admissions to UK Medical, Dental and Veterinary Schools for Applicants with Disabilities

The initial purpose of this report by Tynan (2003) was to examine the information made available for disabled applicants and students on the websites of all the UK medical, dental and veterinary schools. This was followed by an in-depth examination of all the key policy documents available, including those produced by the professional regulatory bodies. Of particular note was a report by Eversheds Solicitors (2001), *Fitness to Practise in the Medical Profession*, which had examined the issue from a legal perspective.

Reactions to the report confirmed that there had been a widespread assumption that the medical, dental and veterinary professions would somehow be exempt from the requirements of the Disability Discrimination Act. Admissions policies and committees had often made only a token effort to provide for disabled applicants and students, who were frequently treated as if they were a nuisance and a potential danger to patients.

Extensive confidential feedback was also received from disabled people or those working with them. This included young people, their parents, teachers and careers advisors, some of whom decided that the idea of a career in medicine, dentistry or veterinary medicine might now be a distinct possibility and certainly should not be ruled out. People had information on an issue that had hitherto not been in the public domain and therefore could make more informed choices.

The Sequel to Pushing the Boat Out

A subsequent report (Tynan 2004) was published a year later to assess what action had been taken in response to the first report. This second scrutiny of the websites of medical, dental and veterinary schools made it possible to compare the amount and quality of information made available for disabled applicants and students in 2004 with that found in 2003.

More than anything else, this subsequent research demonstrated that the rights of disabled students are often only recognised at the level of each medical, dental or veterinary school if this is perceived to add to the public prestige of that school. The value of the investigative research undertaken by the DIVERSE project was demonstrated when both reports began to be used or quoted as reference material. Endorsements included comments by George Rae, Chairman of the BMA's Equal Opportunities Committee who stated:

> We welcome the publication of the *Sequel*, which highlights some of the key areas that still need to be addressed. The equal opportunities committee will be considering the recommendations in detail at its next meeting in April.

The Department of Health included references to both reports in the 2004 consultation paper 'Sharing the challenge, sharing the benefits: equality and diversity in the medical workforce: Workforce Directorate'.

Examples of the impact of the DIVERSE project at a local level can be demonstrated by 'Selection Procedure and Policy Document (2005 Entry)' of the University of Southampton School of Medicine which explicitly referred to the report, and the report's inclusion among resources provided by University College London Disability Services for its staff. Additionally, the Hull York Medical School is proud to claim on its website that it is cited by DIVERSE as an example of good practice in regard to mainstreaming information relating to disability policies and procedures, demonstrating that the university recognises that the quality of provision made for disabled students contributes positively to the overall quality of an institution.

A professional regulatory labyrinth

It does not make sense to consider professions in isolation from one another and it is even more senseless for anyone wishing to further the rights of disabled people within one professional sector to do so. While professions each have their own distinct characteristics, essential competences and systems of regulation, they also have many common elements, and can present common opportunities or barriers for disabled people. The key to influencing one professional regulatory body, therefore, is to aim to influence all those professions which are in similar or related sectors, so that they can positively influence one another. This thinking led the DIVERSE project team members to recognise the need to be pro-active with regard to the professional and regulatory bodies. There was no point in assuming that they would be able to work it out for themselves. It was not that, in most cases, people were unwilling to be inclusive, but rather that they needed guidance on how to be so.

The UK Inter-Professional Group (UKIPG) was established in 1977 as a forum for the major professional and regulatory bodies in the United Kingdom, covering the healthcare, legal, financial, scientific, engineering and construction professions. This group learned of the work of DIVERSE and held a seminar in February 2005 on the theme 'Assessment of Professional Competence' at which a discussion session entitled 'Disability Rights and Competence Assessment' was led by the DIVERSE team. This was also an opportunity to engage with colleagues in a range of professional fields beyond medicine and veterinary science. It became clear that disabled people across the professions face similar barriers and unhelpful attitudes, and that work towards inclusivity undertaken within the domains of medicine and veterinary science offered pointers for other professional groups to reconsider their own stances towards disabled students. From that event, further consolidation of the views of those working on the DIVERSE project led to a number of recommendations that could help medical and veterinary schools go beyond mere compliance with the current disability legislation in the UK.

Recommendations

These joint recommendations developed from a basic tenet that professional education should not be considered in isolation from professional practice. It is further recommended that:

- Healthcare educators and professional and regulatory bodies should continue to work together to develop effective inclusive policies and procedures in relation to disabled applicants, students and professionals. This holistic approach is essential in addressing the spectrum of needs and situations which present themselves during the full professional cycle.
- The right of disabled people to enter and work in healthcare should be recognised, with regular discussion about how to achieve this end. Such discussion opportunities can be provided by means of events such as conferences, workshops or seminars as well as by the publication of articles, briefings and other resources. Staff development is the key to overcoming discriminatory attitudes, which are usually based on ignorance.

- The establishment and assessment of professional competence standards should not take place in isolation from the consideration of disability issues. This means that professional standards must be worded in such a way as to indicate an inclusive approach towards disabled people. For example, a standard relating to communication skills must take account of the alternative communication methods used by people with hearing or speech impairments.
- Information about the types of reasonable adjustments that can be made for disabled students and for disabled professionals must be shared. Applicants have previously been rejected because it was thought that they would not be able to meet a particular competence, even though professionals with a similar disability have proved that the competence can be met if reasonable adjustments are provided.
- Each medical and dental school should record and monitor the numbers of disabled applicants and students admitted. Although it is probably not appropriate to suggest setting targets, it would nevertheless be useful for medical and veterinary schools to have targeted plans, for example, sending marketing material to organisations of deaf people, in order to encourage more applicants from particular sectors of the community.
- Such schools should consider having an advisory panel of disabled professionals, whose expertise could inform consideration of 'fitness to practise' issues concerning disabled students.
- Individual staff should be informed and creative when considering reasonable adjustments for disabled students. The individual disabled student should also be central to the discussion process, as they may well have developed effective coping strategies for managing various situations.
- Staff should provide candid feedback to their own higher education institutions and to professional regulatory bodies about the validity of individual competence standards when applied to individuals with particular impairments. Despite appropriate risk assessments being carried out, it is not unknown for disabled students to fail, sometimes for reasons directly related to the impact of their impairments, and while students' anonymity must be respected, any generic lessons learned should be noted and shared
- Disabled students and professionals can be very helpful to educators and regulators and should offer guidance derived from experience on how disabled people can meet professional competence standards.
- The actions of disabled students and professionals should be informed by disability legislation. However, it is suggested that they should consider recourse to it as a last resort, instead aiming to work together with medical and veterinary schools to advance inclusivity.

The DIVERSE project has helped the Medical and Veterinary professions to make substantial steps forward towards inclusivity in the training and development of disabled students, but there is no room for complacency. Ongoing work has already begun at a European level, with partnerships being developed between the

DIVERSE project team and colleagues in Germany, Poland and Slovenia, offering opportunities for further sharing of good practice and more detailed work in relation to students with specific impairments, all within the context of European legislation.

References and further reading

The Association of Disabled Professionals (ADP) website. Available at: http://www.adp. org.uk/ (accessed 04/2005).

Bissett, L. (2005) 'Medical school access must be fair', *BMA View*, 2 April, p. 4.

Department of Health (2004) 'Sharing the challenge, sharing the benefits: equality and diversity in the medical workforce: Workforce Directorate'. Available at: http://www. dh.gov.uk/Consultations/ClosedConsultations/ClosedConsultationsArticle/fs/en? CONTENT_ID=4089415andchk=%2BNet5M (accessed 04/2005).

Disability Now (Online) (February 2005) 'Large legacy'. Available at: http://www. disabilitynow.org.uk/people/profiles/prof_feb_2005.htm (accessed 04/2005).

Disability Rights Commission (2004a) 'DRC Speeches. Bert Massie: Does diagnosis matter to service users? Disability and the Health Service, April 2004'. Available at: http: //www.drc-gb.org/newsroom/commissionerspeechdetails.asp?id=45 (accessed 04/2005).

Disability Rights Commission (2004b) 'Code of Practice on Trade Organisations and Qualifications Bodies'. Available at: http://www.drc-gb.org/thelaw/practice.asp (accessed 04/2005).

DIVERSE project website. Available at: http://www.ltsn-01.ac.uk/diverse/index_html/ (accessed 04/2005).

DIVERSE event (November 2004). 'Disabled people entering and working in healthcare practice: time to take stock?' Available at: http://www.ltsn-01.ac.uk/diverse/events/ (accessed 04/2005).

Eversheds Solicitors (2001) 'Fitness to Practise in the Medical Profession': A report to universities UK and the Council of Heads of Medical Schools'. Available at: http ://www.gmc-uk.org/qabme/library/docs/CHMS_Eversheds%20Report%20on%20FtP. doc (accessed 04/2005).

Higher Education Academy Subject Centre for Medicine, Dentistry and Veterinary Medicine (formerly known as LTSN-01) website. Available at: http://www.ltsn-01. ac.uk/ (accessed 04/2005).

Hull York Medical School (2004) 'HYMS website makes the grade', HYMS sheet, the newsletter of the Hull York Medical School, April, p. 4. Available at: http://www. hyms.ac.uk/news/Aprilnews.pdf.pdf (accessed 04/2005).

Macdonald, R. (2004) 'Information for students with disabilities', *Student BMJ*. Available at: http://www.studentbmj.com/issues/04/04/news/139.php (accessed 04/2005).

Roberts, T. E., Butler, A. and Boursicot, K. A. M. (2004) 'Disabled students, disabled doctors – time for a change?', Special Report 4, p. 30. The Higher Education Academy: Medicine, Dentistry and Veterinary Medicine. Available at: http://www.ltsn-01.ac.uk/ docs/roberts_final.pdf (accessed 04/2005).

Royal College of Veterinary Surgeons (2001) 'Veterinary education and training: a framework for 2010 and beyond', p. 4. Available at: http://www.rcvs.org.uk/Templates/ Internal.asp?NodeID=90433 (accessed 04/2005).

Royal College of Veterinary Surgeons (2002) 'Essential competences required of the veterinary surgeon: essential competences required of the new veterinary graduate 'Day One Skills'. Available at: http://www.rcvs.org.uk/shared_asp_files/uploadedfiles/{62C9 103C-3AA6-4D70-9C76-9490BA745E44}_day_one_skills.pdf (accessed 04/2005).

Queen's University, Belfast, Academic Council Office, Reference 2002 AC 129, Reference 2004 AC 299, 'Section N7: Fitness to Practise'. Available at: http://www.qub.ac.uk/aco/quality/pdf/N7.pdf (accessed 04/2005).

Tynan, A. (2001) *At the Portal of the Profession: The Veterinary Profession and People with Disabilities – A North American Perspective.* London: The Royal Veterinary College. Available at: http://www.rvc.ac.uk/RVC_Life/PDFs/AtThePortal.PDF (accessed 04/2005).

Tynan, A. (2003) *Pushing the Boat Out: An Introductory Study of Admissions to UK Medical, Dental and Veterinary Schools for Applicants with Disabilities.* LTSN-01 (the Learning and Teaching Support Network subject centre for Medicine, Dentistry and Veterinary Medicine). Available at: http://www.ltsn-01.ac.uk/resources/features/pushing_the_boat_out (accessed 04/2005).

Tynan, A. (2004) *The Sequel to Pushing the Boat Out.* LTSN-01 (the Learning and Teaching Support Network subject centre for Medicine, Dentistry and Veterinary Medicine). Available at: http://www.ltsn-01.ac.uk/resources/features/pushing_the_boat_out (accessed 04/2005).

UK Inter-Professional Group website. Available at: http://www.ukipg.org.uk/ (accessed 04/2005).

University College London Disability Services (2005) 'Resources – Mainly for Staff: Teaching and Learning'. Available at: http://www.ucl.ac.uk/disability/resources/staff/teaching-learning/ (accessed 04/2005).

University of Southampton School of Medicine (2005) 'Selection Procedure and Policy Document (2005 Entry)'. Available at: http://www.som.soton.ac.uk/prospectus/under grad/pdf/selection_2005.pdf (accessed 04/2005).

Chapter 10

Language issues for deaf students in higher education

Judith Mole and Diane Peacock

The higher education context

Over the past 40 years, the profile of students in British higher education has undergone gradual change which has, nevertheless, resulted in radical effects. Between 1988 and 1993 a major expansion of provision led to increased participation from many students, who either would not have considered or would not previously been perceived as eligible for study at this level. By the mid-1990s, these changes were characterised by the implementation of new legislative and economic frameworks, new academic infrastructures (modularity, unitisation and credit accumulation) and higher expectations for flexibility (access, seamless progression and the promotion of technology supported learning). At the same time the higher education sector witnessed the growth of new disciplines, the decline of traditional disciplines and an increase in interdisciplinary study. In the UK the *Higher Education in the Learning Society* report of the National Committee of Enquiry into Higher Education (Dearing 1997) made further, far-reaching recommendations to enable higher education 'to meet the needs of the United Kingdom over the next 20 years'. Paragraph 29 of the Summary Report highlighted the need to increase participation of those groups 'under-represented in higher education, notably those from socio-economic groups III to V, people with disabilities and specific ethnic minority groups'.

Over this period Deaf British Sign Language (BSL) users have entered higher education and now form a minute, but measurable, group at a small number of UK higher education institutions. (Written in lower case, 'deaf' denotes the medical condition of hearing loss. Upper case 'Deaf' is the political and social term of belonging to the Deaf community. It is used in the same way other nationalities and groups would be spelt with uppercase letters, e.g. Spanish or Muslim. When referring to Deaf people we mean native BSL users, not deaf people whose native language is English (see Ladd and John 1991).

At the same time there have been major legislative changes affecting the education and employment rights of disabled people including the Disability Discrimination Act (1995), the Special Educational Needs and Disability Act (2001) and UK government recognition of BSL as a language in 2003. In tandem with these developments there has been a shift to promote and enact mainstream-ing policies in the compulsory education sector. This has led to an increasing number of Deaf learners being integrated into mainstream schools and further education colleges, with the subsequent closure down of many segregated schools.

Language acquisition

Deaf people, depending on when they became deaf, miss out on learning language through informal immersion by picking up sounds and language around them. For many people who have been profoundly deaf from an early age, their deafness may have a significant effect on their use of English (Conrad 1979; Kurtzer-White 1999; Stern 2001). Particularly critical is the loss of exposure to language as it is used *in situ*, in formal and informal situations, with different intonation and inference. This loss can seriously affect the educational opportunities of Deaf people (Marschark *et al.* in press).

Many Deaf people will use BSL as their first language, not English. British Sign Language is not a signed form of English or a collection of gestures. It is a fully functioning language with its own grammar and syntax, which is very different from the syntax of English. BSL can express the same complex concepts and ideas that any other language can. It is not a 'new' language and is not international or universal. BSL is considered by some to be the natural language of Deaf people, even if it has been learned later in life (Smith 2000).

The majority of Deaf people (90 per cent) come from hearing families; most Deaf children are therefore not raised with BSL as their native language and so miss out on a critical developmental stage of early language learning (Stern 2001). This often leads to Deaf children beginning their schooling with a language deficit, compared with hearing children. Furthermore, Stern suggests that the majority of Deaf 4- or 5-year-olds start compulsory schooling with a vocabulary of around 500 words compared to the 3,000–5,000 words of hearing peers.

A study of English language literacy skills of Deaf people conducted by Conrad (1979) concluded that the average Deaf person left school (at 16 years) with a chronological reading age of between 8¾ and 12½ years. Further research conducted by Gregory, Bishop and Sheldon (1995) and research commissioned by the Department for Education and Employment conducted by Powers, Gregory and Thoutenhoofd (1998) found no significant change in these levels of literacy. According to Smith (2000):

> Deaf children need two languages (BSL and English) for healthy growth and development and participation in society, but far from having a bilin-gual option, many deaf children are in danger of having no true language foundations at all.

Conrad's landmark study caused a change in the thinking on Deaf education and led to the introduction (in some parts of the UK) of alternative educational systems, namely Total Communication (i.e. an educational philosophy which advocates the use of sign and speech simultaneously – this approach usually uses Manually Coded English with signs in English word order which is very different from BSL) and Bilingualism (i.e. an educational philosophy which advocates the use of BSL as the primary language in school which can be used to learn English as a second language), although Oral/Auralism (i.e. an educational philosophy which advocates the use of speech and listening/lip-reading as the preferable communication method for d/Deaf people) is still widely used today.

> BSL is not used for teaching in the majority of schools attended by deaf children, is not a language option in mainstream schools, and there are virtually no Deaf teachers of the deaf (with a very few exceptions). Policies, determined in the main by non-Deaf people, continue to promote speech and lipreading (oral communication), or sign systems that support oral communication but which lack the visual grammar of BSL that gives the unconstrained and natural communication needed for the early development of a first language.
>
> (Smith 2000)

In fact, the Total Communication and Bilingual education systems used for Deaf children in the UK often utilise a hybrid of languages and language systems. In a study of the communication methods used in bilingual education, Swanwick (1996) found that a mixture of languages and language modes were used, including BSL, natural spoken English, Manually Coded English (i.e. a communication system (not a language) which uses signs with English, rather than BSL, word order) and written English.

The mixing of languages and communication modes can be confusing to children who are already disadvantaged in their language acquisition methods and stages. Manually Coded English (or Sign Supported English) is a commonly used communication system in secondary and further education in the UK. However, once students progress to higher education, the majority of interpreters will use BSL, a language many students will have previously used only in a social, rather than educational, context.

In the UK there are no segregated universities for Deaf students. In order for Deaf students to participate in higher education, they are obliged to attend a mainstream institution which uses English as its language of discourse and assessment. The Deaf students who progress to higher education are invariably those who have successfully mastered a higher level of written English and have the communication confidence to benefit from the experience.

Language acquisition in an academic setting

All students, when entering higher education, find themselves joining a community of learners where the use of general academic and discipline-specific language is taken for granted. Successful participation in this community enables students to gain the positive cultural and linguistic experience described by Pinker:

> 'Culture' refers to the process whereby particular kinds of learning contagiously spread from person to person in a community and minds become co-ordinated into shared patterns, just as 'a language' or 'a dialect' refers to the process whereby the different speakers in a community acquire highly similar mental grammars.
>
> (1995: 411)

Since the introduction of modularity, in addition to general academic and discipline-specific language, higher education has spawned numerous hybrid terms that many students struggle to fully comprehend. The following examples are just some of the commonly used terms to describe aspects of assessment: assessment; assessment method; assessment criteria; assessment component; assessment weighting; assessment regulations; continuous assessment; online assessment, in-class assessment; formative assessment; summative assessment; grading; grading criteria; grade point scale; and deferred, referred, mitigation.

Nation (2001: 187–216) in *Learning Vocabulary in Another Language* highlights the significance of 'specialised uses of vocabulary', both in the acquisition and demonstration of student knowledge and in the context of how that might impact on teaching. Much of the literature surveyed by Nation (Campion and Elley 1971; Praninskas 1972; Farrell 1990; Coxhead 1998, 2000) focuses on classifications that distinguish general service words from those used in academic, specialised or technical contexts. Nation (2001: 194) further suggests that new vocabulary learning should be directed not only to the learner gradually encountering commonly used words (as teachers might support by providing a module glossary), but also by teachers finding methods of ensuring students learn to use the new vocabulary.

For many of those students who entered the post-Dearing environment of higher education, being fluent and confident using the spoken and written language conventions of their academic discipline and of university life can be a complex, demanding and daunting prospect but essential if they are to achieve their learning goals and feel part of 'academic culture'.

Nicol (1998: 89), when citing research by Marton *et al.* (1984) and Stefani and Nicol (1997) on the social context of learning, states that:

> Learning is now understood to be 'situated' in academic and disciplinary contexts that influence not only how students construct their subject knowledge but also how they construct interpretations of how they are supposed to learn, what is worth learning and what it means to be a student.

To better understand what it might mean to be a Deaf student in higher education, we first need to explore some characteristics of these 'academic and disciplinary contexts'.

The face-to-face learning environment of higher education includes didactic delivery of content via large-scale lecture, the discursive exchange of ideas and views in a small group discussions and seminars, the instructional model used in laboratory or workshop teaching, and the more informal one-to-one exchange of a tutorial. Depending on the discipline and the level of study, the frequency of use of these settings and their respective delivery modes will vary. During the first year of undergraduate study, being proficient in the oral and written language of the discipline, in as many settings as is required, is a prerequisite to being able to demonstrate the capability to develop the higher-order learning required of finalists and to experience that contagion of learning described by Pinker (1995: 411). Glaser (1999: 94) cites Bartholomae's (1985) view that when undertaking written tasks a university student has:

> [to] invent the university for the occasion . . . He has to learn to speak our language, to speak as we do, to try on the peculiar ways of knowing, selecting, evaluating, reporting, concluding, and arguing that define the discourse of our community.

From a 'situative perspective', Greeno *et al.* (1999: 138–139) in their paper, 'Achievement and the Theories of Knowing and Learning', suggest that: 'Following extended experience in a discipline and membership in a community of people who practise it, we pick up certain practices – ways of perceiving (the self, the discipline, and the world) and of acting.' They then characterise the differences between 'communities of practice' by contrasting the tendency of 'mathematically-minded' people 'to model things mathematically, to symbolize, to analyse', with the thinking and communications modes of writers or artists who 'reflexively translate their experiences' into their own creative practice.

Higher education students need to be able to use language to perform a number of key competencies. These include being able to describe, discuss, reflect, apply conceptual models, analyse, synthesise, problem-solve, evaluate and ascribe meaning and purpose to the wide variety of often very specific concepts and skills that underpin different aspects of their subject disciplines. These competencies have different weightings and applications depending on the discipline. For example, a fine art student might need to use critical, polemical and metaphorical terminology to position their work ideologically. In science, a student studying genetics might draw on conceptual, technical and problem-solving terminology to explain genetic analysis in haploid eukaryote and an engineering student might use analysis, mathematical modelling, symbolic graphical representation to articulate why at some point between t_1 and t_2 the slope of a graph is zero, and the body neither accelerates or decelerates. By doing so, students demonstrate their learning and their community membership to teachers and peers.

Effective communication is achieved through explicit and implicit exchange of meaning but the communication process can easily break down. Shared first language users from different disciplines, when discussing or reading about key concepts in their own discipline, may struggle to understand even moderately complex concepts or processes in the other discipline. Glaser (1999: 94), for example, likens the difficulty students would encounter, having acquired the language of one discipline, to write coherently in another, to being 'not unlike the loss manifested by experts when they are required to operate outside of their disciplines'.

The impact of mediated communication

When a native BSL user enters higher education, they access a complex network of specialised communication, via a third party (the interpreter or note-taker) who may themselves have minimal knowledge of either the subject or the language of higher education (Robbins 1996; Harrington 2001; Winston 2004). A useful analogy when considering the challenges which a Deaf student supported by an inexperienced interpreter (both in terms of their knowledge of BSL and the subject) might face, is to imagine oneself with a good command of conversational French, attempting to simultaneously interpret a university lecture in French on Saussurean linguistics, quantum mechanics or postmodernism, to an English-speaking student who would then be tested in French on their comprehension. It is inevitable that inaccuracies and misunderstandings occur and that Deaf students often struggle to fully achieve their academic potential or become fully integrated into the community of learners (Harrington 2000).

BSL differs from English in many ways. Its grammar and syntax can be said to be more complex than English (Stokoe 1980, cited in Kyle and Woll 1985). Because BSL is a visual-spatial language, most signs are visually motivated (or iconic); items are therefore signed to reflect what they look like/their function (Sutton-Spence and Woll 1999: 164). There are also many abstract signs that have evolved over time and their iconic origin is no longer known. In cases where a BSL user does not know an established sign they will use one of two strategies: fingerspelling or productive lexicon.

Sutton-Spence and Woll (1999) describe fingerspelling as borrowing English into BSL. They describe a variety of common uses for fingerspelling, including proper names, words which currently have no sign equivalent, new concepts and in academic discussion. However, 'Fingerspelling signs are totally unmotivated visually. There is nothing about their form to link them to the referent except convention' (ibid.: 222). It follows that fingerspelling is useful in learning the English spelling of words, but extensive use of fingerspelling can be a barrier to communication when it impedes the clear flow of the overall 'message'.

The established lexicon in BSL is far smaller than the established lexicon in English. This does not mean the language is less rich, in the same way one would not describe French as a poorer language than English, despite the fact that it also has far fewer words. Productive lexicon allows a BSL user to create a new, temporary sign for the purpose of communication. These signs are not arbitrary, they are nearly always visually motivated, and use the established norms and grammar rules such as placement, hand shape, non-manual features, etc. (ibid.: 198). Some of the signs created initially through productive lexicon will become established signs and, as such, are widely used. 'Temporary signs' are a useful tool to facilitate communication, but much time can be wasted negotiating and agreeing these signs, particularly in an interpreting situation where the pace of communication is determined by a third party. Having to negotiate such productive lexicon with a number of interpreters can take up valuable learning time (Robbins 1996).

BSL is very specific in its conveyance of meaning. English, and specifically the English used in education, uses umbrella terms in order to make generalised points or to abstract the meaning of a concept. BSL contains few umbrella terms, and will usually explain a concept, rather have one specific sign. *Force* is signed as TENSION, PULL, PUSH, TWIST, PUSH-DOWN, etc. depending entirely on the context in which the word is used. At present, there are no single commonly accepted signs for terms like *mammal, celestial body* or *fossil fuel*. This does not mean that these terms cannot be conveyed in BSL, but that language communities of Deaf academics have not yet used single signs of these terms frequently enough for them to enter common usage.

Similarly, verbs in BSL can change depending on the context. BSL uses classifiers to demonstrate actions. For example, *to go* is signed differently if it is five or 100 people going; *to pick up something* will change depending on the shape and weight of the object. Interpreters attending a lecture will have to be clear on the *exact* meaning of the lecturer in order to be able to render a full and accurate translation.

In this context, English presents many challenges for foreign language users and interpreters alike. Academic language borrows heavily from standard terminology and uses this as technical vocabulary. For example, *cookie, stress, plate* or *creep* in technical/academic contexts do not mean the same as their commonly used homographs (words which are written the same but have different meanings), and are therefore signed differently. There are also common incidences of the same borrowed words being used in different academic subjects with different meanings. Polysemy (one word having many meanings, e.g. *sound, set*), homophones (two words sounding the same but written differently, e.g. *there* and *their*) and contronyms (the same word having opposite meanings, e.g. *bolted, sanguine*) are all common in English (Bryson 1990: 62).

Interpreters will also be hampered by other features of language which academics deliberately use in teaching and assessment. Academics will use abstract language in order to invite students to think about a topic independently, or to avoid inadvertently giving an answer away. The use of abstract, umbrella and taxonomic terms given above is an example of this. Given that much of BSL is visually motivated, and the interpreters may not know the lecturer's intention, they can accidentally confuse the student.

An academically successful Deaf student said of her experience at university in 2002:

It was a real challenge at times to keep up with other students, as it took longer to absorb academic and [specialist] terminology. Interpreters had to finger-spell a lot of words to me in lectures and it's hard to remember words visually without hearing them and connect them later to words on the page and include them in essays.

Conclusion

This chapter has attempted to illustrate some of the communication and linguistic difficulties facing Deaf people who wish to enter higher education and thereby fulfil their academic potential, alongside hearing people. If we are to increase the participation of the 'under-represented' Deaf community in both higher education and the professions, then a number of key issues need to be addressed.

It is imperative there is an improvement in the written English language competence of d/Deaf students leaving school, including better preparation for those students wishing to progress into further or higher education. Studies have consistently shown that the UK education system, as it is currently organised, is failing Deaf students. The small numbers of Deaf students progressing to higher education often do so despite, not because of, the system they have come through.

More research is needed to develop concise lists of frequently used general academic and technical vocabulary to support undergraduate study. Academics also need to be made much more aware of clear communication principles when working with Deaf learners. This good practice will in turn benefit all learners.

There is a need for age- and education-level appropriate reference materials for both Deaf BSL users and their interpreters. There are few subject-specific BSL/English glossaries, despite the fact that these would enormously benefit Deaf learners. As BSL is not taught at a higher level to Deaf students, colloquial BSL is often used in academic settings. Language communities of Deaf academics are needed to establish subject-specific terms and concepts in BSL, which can be documented as reference materials. Deaf students need to be able to see the same signs from different interpreters and be able to discuss the concepts of their chosen subjects without each time having to establish a temporary productive lexicon with a communication partner.

Interpreters, lip-speakers and note-takers working in UK higher education must have accredited skills in translation/transcription and in the subject in which they are working, or access to accredited professional development to facilitate their increased knowledge of academic subjects, both in English and BSL.

References and further reading

Bryson, B. (1990) *Mother Tongue: The English Language*. London: Penguin Books.
Campion, M. E. and Elley, W. B. (1971) *An Academic Vocabulary List*. Wellington: NZCER.
Conrad, R. (1979) *The Deaf School Child*. London: Harper and Row.

Coxhead, A. (1998) *An Academic Word List*, Occasional Publication Number 18, LALS, Victoria University of Wellington, New Zealand.

Coxhead, A. (2000) 'A new Academic Word List', *TESOL Quarterly*, 34 (2): 213–238.

Dearing, R. (1997) *Higher Education in the Learning Society: Report of the National Committee of Enquiry into Higher Education*. London: HMSO.

Farrell, P. (1990) *Vocabulary in ESP: A Lexical Analysis of the English of Electronics and a Study of Semi-technical Vocabulary*, CLCS Occasional Paper 25. Dublin: Trinity College.

Glaser, R. (1999) 'Expert knowledge and the process of thinking', in R. McCormick and C. Paechter (eds) *Learning and Knowledge*. London: PCP/The Open University.

Greeno, J. G., Pearson, P. D. and Schoenfeld, A. H. (1999) 'Achievement and theories of knowing and learning', in R. McCormick and C. Paechter (eds) *Learning and Knowledge*. London: PCP/The Open University.

Gregory, S., Bishop, J. and Sheldon, L. (1995) *Deaf Young People and Their Families*. Cambridge: Cambridge University Press.

Harrington, F. J. (2000) *Towards a Whole Institution Approach on Disability and Deafness*, report for the HEFCE, Preston: University of Central Lancashire.

Harrington, F. J. (2001) 'The rise, fall and re-invention of the communicator: re-defining roles and responsibilities in educational interpreting', Supporting Deaf People online conference 2001: Direct Learn Services. Available at: http://www.online-conference.net/sdp1/papers_sdp1.htm (accessed 02/2005).

Kurtzer-White, E. (1999) 'The impact of deafness', in D. M. Luterman, *The Young Deaf Child*. Baltimore, MD: York Press Inc.

Kyle, J. and Woll, B. (1985) *Sign Language: The Study of Deaf People and their Language*. Cambridge: Cambridge University Press.

Ladd, P. and John, M. (1991) Unit 9, in *Issues in Deafness*. Milton Keynes: The Open University Press.

Marschark, M., Sapere, P., Convertino, C., Seewagen, R. and Maltzen, H. (2004) 'Comprehension of Sign Language Interpreting: Deciphering a Complex Task Situation', *Sign Language Studies* 4 (4) (Summer 2004).

Marton, F., Hounsell, D. and Entwistle, N. (1984) *The Experience of Learning*. Edinburgh: Scottish Academic Press.

Nation, I. S. P. (2001) *Learning Vocabulary in Another Language*. Cambridge: Cambridge University Press.

Nicol, D. J. (1998) 'Using research on learning to improve teaching practices in higher education', in C. Rust (ed.) *Improving Student Learning: Improving Students as Learners*. Oxford: The Oxford Centre for Staff and Learning Development.

Pinker, S. (1995) *The Language Instinct*. London: Penguin.

Powers, S., Gregory, S. and Thoutenhoofd, E. (1998) *The Educational Achievements of Deaf Children*. London: DfEE, Research Report no. 65.

Praninskas, J. (1972) *American University Word List*, London: Longman.

Robbins, C. (1996) 'Computer technology education and the deaf student: observations of serious nuances of communication'. Available at: http://www.rit.edu/~easi/itd/itdv03n4/article3.htm (accessed 02/2005).

Smith, C. (2000) 'Deafness, BSL and controversies'. Available at: http://www.deafsign.com/ds/index.cfm?scn=articleandarticleID=23 (accessed 04/2005).

Stefani, L. and Nicol, D. J. (1997) 'From teacher to facilitator of collaborative enquiry', in

S. Armstrong, G. Thompson and S. Brown (eds), *Facing up to Radical Changes in Universities and Colleges*. London: Kogan Page.

Stern, A. (2001) 'Deafness and reading', *Literacy Today*, 27, June 2001.

Stokoe, W. C. (1980) 'The study and use of sign language', in R. L. Schiefelbusch (ed.) *Non Speech Language and Communication*. Baltimore, MD: University Park Press.

Sutton-Spence, R. and Woll, B. (1999) *The Linguistics of British Sign Language: An Introduction*. Cambridge: Cambridge University Press.

Swanwick, R. (1996) 'Deaf children's strategies for learning english – how do they do it?', paper presented at Bilingualism and the Education of Deaf Children: Advances in Practice Conference, University of Leeds, June 1996.

Winston E. A. (2004) 'Language myths of an interpreted education', paper presented at Supporting Deaf People online conference 2004: Direct Learn Services. Available at: http://www.online-conference.net/sdp2/presenters_sdp2.htm (accessed 02/2005).

Chapter 11

Creating engaging, accessible multimedia for learning

David Sloan, Sarah Stone and John Stratford

Introduction

The use of multimedia in e-learning resources can undoubtedly enhance the learning experience, and has specific potential for students who may otherwise face significant obstacles to an equitable and effective learning experience as a direct result of their impairment. At the same time, there is a responsibility placed on e-learning developers and multimedia producers to ensure that the resources they create follow best practice in accessible design, and do not introduce new and unnecessary barriers to learning for disabled students.

There are convincing legal and moral reasons for ensuring that learning and teaching experience does not unjustifiably discriminate against an individual on account of an impairment. There are also many challenges – attitudinal, practical and technical – facing teachers and developers who want to use multimedia to enhance the accessibility and the quality of the learning environment. To address this issue, the authors have been involved in a project – Skills for Access – that has adopted an innovative approach towards the development of a web-based multimedia resource aimed at inspiring and encouraging the use of accessible multimedia in e-learning development (http://www.skillsforaccess.org.uk).

This chapter outlines the opportunities and challenges presented by the use of optimally accessible multimedia to support learning and teaching, and outlines an effective strategy for inclusive design and use of multimedia as part of a holistic approach to optimising accessibility of the learning environment. It draws on the authors' experiences in the fields of educational multimedia production and inclusive design, and in developing the Skills for Access resource in particular.

The role of multimedia in teaching and learning

The increasing pervasiveness of information and communication technology (ICT) in the classroom, in the library, in the field and at home offers an opportunity for increased access to education, and can also enhance the delivery of teaching to support multiple learning styles. The effective use of multimedia in e-learning resources has been widely identified as offering significant potential in enhancing the learning environment (Littlejohn 2003). With the increasing power of desktop computing and software, the potential for teachers to create and use multimedia as part of their curriculum design has never been greater.

When we talk about 'multimedia', we mean using one or more of graphics, video, audio and animated content to supplement textual content presented in an e-learning resource. The use of multimedia, sometimes termed 'rich media', presents significant opportunities for the teacher to enhance the learning environment and thus the learning experience of students. This can be achieved through, for example, photographs, video and audio recordings to capture and convey real-world experiences and events, whether past or in real time, or animated, interactive diagrams to demonstrate and simulate concepts and allow real-time interaction to show the effect of change.

Disability, learning and multimedia

For disabled people, the potential of ICT to reduce exclusion by breaking down barriers, resulting in improved access to and quality of education has been well documented. Technology can reduce or overcome barriers resulting from both the nature of the physical learning environment and methods of teaching delivery. Assistive technology of varying types exists to directly support the disabled student by reducing or overcoming the impact of a specific sensory, cognitive or physical impairment.

Moreover, ICT can support independent learning for a disabled student – for example, through the Internet or an institutional intranet or Virtual Learning Environment – providing remote access to information in a variety of formats, including multimedia. This can support multiple learning styles, facilitate communication with teaching staff and peers, and aid flexibility in assessment methods. As an effective way of enhancing the learning environment by presenting information and experiences in a variety of ways, multimedia can be seen as a particularly powerful assistive technology in supporting effective learning: 'In some cases, the best way to enhanced accessibility may be to use more media . . . used in the right way, multimedia is a critical resource for accessibility!' (Slatin and Rush 2002: 359). For example, the use of an animation may vividly convey a particular principle of molecular biology that may be difficult to describe in words, and thus be particularly effective to a student who has difficulty processing textual information. An audio recording of a pivotal speech given during a political crisis may, for a blind student, bring life to words that would otherwise have been read in monotone by a synthetic text-to-speech device.

While the very use of technology such as web content and multimedia can enhance accessibility, the need to ensure that these resources are designed to be as accessible as possible to as many people as possible, regardless of impairment, has for some time been acknowledged as being of vital importance. A number of initiatives have sought to define and disseminate best practice in inclusive design of web content, most notably the Web Accessibility Initiative (WAI) of the

World Wide Web Consortium (W3C). The WAI has developed accessibility guidelines for web content authors – the Web Content Accessibility Guidelines (WCAG) (http://www.w3.org/TR/WCAG10), for developers of web browsers and assistive technologies (The User Agent Accessibility Guidelines (UAAG): http://www. w3.org/TR/UAAG10/) and for developers of website authoring tools (The authoring Tool Accessibility Guidelines (ATAG): http://www.w3.org/TR/ATAG10/).

Within the e-learning community, there has been significant activity in promoting the importance of accessibility in the development of educational resources that can be reused for different purposes in different environments (Brewer and Treviranus 2003). For example, guidelines for the creation of accessible e-learning resources have recently been published (IMS Global Learning Consortium 2002). The complementary Accessibility for Learner Information Package Specification (IMS ACCLIP) and Access for All Metadata Specification offer respectively a framework for storing a learner's specific accessibility preferences and a structured way of describing an e-learning resource's specific accessibility requirements, its customisability and any equivalent alternatives. Both these IMS accessibility specifications are available at http://www.imsglobal.org/accessibility/.

In addition to the World Wide Web, the issue of media accessibility has not gone unnoticed by the broadcasting sector. For example, the Independent Television Commission (ITC), until the end of 2003 the regulatory body for independent television in the UK, has developed guidance for provision of accessibility features for broadcast television (Guidance on subtitling, audio description and signing, available online at http://www.ofcom.org.uk/codes_guidelines/broadcasting/tv/sub_sign_audio/), and the ITC's successor, Ofcom, has assumed a role in promoting accessibility in UK broadcasting. The ITC also commissioned research exploring issues relating to the accessibility of digital television provision, with a focus on the issues faced by older people (Carmichael 1999).

Accessible multimedia: opportunities

Awareness and knowledge of accessible web design have never been higher. To a large extent this is as a result of legislation that exists or is being introduced in many countries across the world, supporting the rights of disabled people not to encounter unjustified discrimination. Increasingly this legislation places responsibilities on both those involved in the provision of educational services and those who create and provide ICT, including web sites, with a resultant increase in the profile of accessibility in web and e-learning design and development.

At the same time, the wider benefits of accessibility and inclusive design have become more apparent. Keates and Clarkson (2004) discuss a number of products, designed with accessibility in mind, that have become commercially successful in areas that might not initially have been anticipated, such as the Ford Focus car and the Big Button telephone from British Telecom (BT). On the web, the parallels of accessible design principles and effective search engine design have been noted by a number of commentators (for example, Olejniczak 2004). Extending this to multimedia, providing accessibility features for a video can make available a rich textual description of the video content that may be a valuable aid to automated cataloguing and searching.

Acknowledgement of accessibility as a core skill in competent web design has become a noticeable trend, led by grassroots movements such as The Web Standards Project (http://www.webstandards.org), publications such as *Designing with Web Standards* (Zeldman 2003) and initiatives like the CSS Zen Garden (http://www.csszengarden.com), a showcase of complex designs using Cascading Style Sheets to present the same HTML web page in wildly different visual styles. In this way, accessibility has been demonstrated to be compatible with creative, visually exciting web content, and has gone a long way in engaging those with a strong background in graphic design and media production community who may previously have been seen as unsympathetic or even hostile to accessibility. As this community increasingly embraces accessibility, so the level of expertise and experimentation grows in accessible design techniques.

Attitudes towards accessibility in the film and broadcasting sectors have also changed. In discussing the lack of accessible television programmes, Carey (2005) noted one argument against expenditure on captioning and audio describing analogue television as being the comparative lack of re-usability of an analogue recording, once the accessible programme had been broadcast. However, the advent of DVD, digital television and associated technologies such as the personal video recorder (PVR) technology, allowing storage onto a hard disk of programmes or sections of programmes for later viewing, is indicative of a trend towards broadcast digital media that is easily stored and available on-demand. This significantly enlarges the size of the audience that can benefit from accessible television, thus raising the cost-benefit.

With web-based multimedia, the reusable aspect is integral. Digital video can be made available online to be accessed at any time, by anybody with the necessary equipment. Given the potential of reusable learning objects, and the frameworks being developed to allow description of accessibility-related information of a specific resource (such as IMS ACCLIP), the cost-benefit of providing accessibility solutions to digital multimedia for e-learning becomes more attractive.

The technology available to provide accessibility features such as captions and audio descriptions of web-based multimedia also gives non-specialists the potential to do it themselves. While a lack of solid research-based guidelines, access to training and limited examples of best practice, along with demands on time, may limit the level and quality of the solutions that can be provided, with free tools available to author accessibility solutions, it is eminently possible for a producer to create and combine features such as captions for deaf and hard of hearing people with a digital media file. Given a choice of no accessibility or rudimentary 'low-budget' accessibility, the latter is surely an improvement, as long as it is undertaken thoughtfully with the educational issues firmly in mind.

Making multimedia accessible: practical solutions

There are a number of key accessibility strategies which can be applied to the production and incorporation of multimedia into e-learning resources. We now provide an overview of these and outline how they may be applied to video, audio and animated content.

It should be noted that implementation can be challenging, given the many variable factors relating to the accessibility of specific media technologies, formats and players, and the relationship of these to browsers and assistive technologies. As technologies evolve, and accessibility support improves, it is expected that these challenges will reduce in complexity.

Providing text alternatives: captions

For multimedia, perhaps the most recognised accessibility solution is captions, which are text alternatives of spoken and important non-spoken sound information, improving the accessibility of video and audio accessible to people who are deaf or hard of hearing. In accessibility circles, the term 'captions' refers to the provision of text equivalents for spoken and non-spoken sound information for deaf people, while the term 'subtitles' refers to the provision of text translations of the spoken word into another language – an accessibility feature for anyone whose first language is not that of the video soundtrack. Confusingly, though, in the UK and Ireland, the broadcasting community uses the word 'subtitles' to refer to both these features, removing the distinction between what are two completely separate accessibility issues. The advent of digital media has made it easier to provide 'closed' captions; that is, captions supplied with the media, but not displayed unless a user requires them.

Captioning a digital video requires three key steps:

1   Generation of an appropriate set of captions. The challenge and skill of captioning are in presenting captions that are readable in the time during which they are displayed, while conveying adequate information to allow full understanding by the reader.
2   Synchronising captions – providing captions with a time-stamp which will allow the media player to display captions at the appropriate time in the media clip.
3   Combination of the caption file with the media clip.

In all cases, the job of creating and combining synchronised captions can be eased by using captioning software, such as the free Media Access Generator (MAGpie) from the National Centre for Accessible Media (http://ncam.wgbh.org/webaccess/magpie/).

For technologies that produce animated web content, such as Macromedia's popular Flash technology, there may also be a need to provide text alternatives to spoken or other audio information. It may be possible to ensure that the animation directly provides a visual equivalent to any audio information, for example, by displaying text as it is spoken, or augmenting sounds with changes in appearance or position of specific components of the movie. Alternatively, software such as MAGpie can be used to generate a caption file for integration into Flash movies.

While providing text captions can aid accessibility for many people who are deaf or hard of hearing, people who use sign language as their first language may have difficulty reading and processing on-screen text. In this case, the ideal solution is to provide on-screen signing. This method has been used to sign television programmes, but generally requires recording a human providing a signed translation, and can thus be very resource-intensive. Investigations have taken place into the use of avatars (animated characters) to provide automated signing, for example the ViSiCAST project (Elliot *et al.* 2000), generated from a text transcript, but the technology remains at an experimental stage.

Audio description

Audio description is the accessibility technique used to make video content accessible to people who cannot see it. While someone who is blind may be able to hear the soundtrack and gain a level of understanding of what is going on, there is a need to describe information not detectable from the media clip's soundtrack alone. Audio descriptions are short recordings of spoken information to explain specific visual events, inserted at the least intrusive points in the main soundtrack.

Again, digital media has made easier the task of providing 'closed' descriptions. Audio descriptions can be created using sound recording software and a microphone for capturing the spoken content; the description files then need to be time-stamped so that the media player can play the appropriate audio description at the appropriate time when playing the media clip.

Unfortunately, popular media technologies for delivering web-based video vary in their support for the provision of additional audio tracks to supplement the main soundtrack. For example, the widely used Windows Media Player from Microsoft has no facility to enable media producers to include additional audio description files in a video clip.

For animated content, the challenge of ensuring that someone relying on screen-reading technology can access and understand the content and functionality of a resource created in, for example, Macromedia Flash or Director/Shockwave, is altogether more complex. There are two principal solutions:

1   If the resource has been developed using Macromedia Flash MX or a more recent version, Flash's own accessibility support can be used to expose text visible in the animation to certain screen readers. (This option is only available when a user has Macromedia's Flash Player 6 or more recent, and a screen reader and browser that support Microsoft's Active Accessibility

(MSAA), a technology for the Windows operating system that supports the exchange of information between software applications and assistive technologies.) Appropriate text alternatives – not normally visible – can also be provided for a specific object or portion of the animation, or even the whole animation itself.

2   Self-voicing animation involves provision of a soundtrack that adequately provides an alternative for all essential visual information contained in the movie, and thus does not require the use of compatible text-to-speech technology on the user's part. In Flash, this requires the recording of appropriate spoken audio to play along with the movie, while Macromedia Director includes a text-to-speech conversion technology which allows the audio output of the descriptive information in text form.

Transcripts

Provision of a text transcript for a video or audio clip is another important accessibility enhancement, and if a transcript already exists as a result of media production, adapting it for accessibility purposes is a relatively straightforward step. Best practice would encourage designers to include not just the spoken word in transcripts, but other key aspects of the action, including non-spoken sound and visual events essential to understanding what has happened.

Transcripts can be a significant first step before work starts on providing captions and audio descriptions, and may be attractive to, for example, a screen reader user who, if short of time, may prefer to listen to the transcript rather than going through the process of navigating to, opening and listening to what may be a long media clip. However, because a transcript is by its nature an alternative to an accessible video, the experience of viewing the content or listening to the soundtrack is lost, and therefore wherever possible, the most equitable accessibility solution is a well-captioned, audio-described media clip.

Keyboard access

To ensure that multimedia can be accessed and controlled by those unable to use a mouse, whether for reasons of visual or physical impairment, and who may rely on an alternative input mechanism such as an eye-operated device, trackball or voice recognition software, keyboard control is essential. For video and audio, access to the media player itself and the ability to control playback and perform tasks such as enabling captions or audio descriptions should all be possible using the keyboard or alternative input device.

Unfortunately, keyboard accessibility of popular media players is inconsistent. Research by WebAIM (undated) on accessible online delivery of multimedia found a general trend whereby if a media clip was played in a 'stand-alone' media player, this was significantly more keyboard accessible than when the clip was directly embedded within the content of a web page.

Interactive animated content may also present challenges to those browsing using the keyboard or other input device. Specific steps must be taken to ensure that objects in a Flash movie, such as buttons, can be activated using the keyboard, and that keyboard access is logical, though some technological limitations may exist (Heins and Regan 2002).

Display customisation

People who experience reading difficulties when viewing on-screen content may need to make adjustments to text size, font type, or text and background colour combinations. Thus, to enhance accessibility of their resources, authors of animated multimedia should program features to enable a degree of display customisation.

Accessible multimedia: the challenges

Despite both the increasing amount of resources – from guidelines to software tools – available to support accessible web and multimedia content creation, and the compelling reasons for creating optimally accessible content, there are a disappointingly low number of examples of effective use of multimedia to support and enhance the learning environment for disabled students. Indeed, this reflects the general lack of accessible multimedia on the web. There are a range of explanations for this situation.

One explanation is that, despite advances in digital technology, accessible multimedia development may still be seen as complex, time-consuming, and not cost-effective. It is true that there is still a demand on expertise, while the addition of accessibility features to a long and complex piece of multimedia may take a significant amount of time. Where production methods do not consider accessibility from an early stage, post-processing tasks, such as creating a transcript from which captions can be created and added, may be more lengthy and costly. Consideration of accessibility issues from the outset is therefore essential to ensuring the most efficient creation of accessible multimedia. While poor accessibility can be as frustrating as no accessibility at all, the difference in experience for a disabled person between the complete absence of any accessibility features and those that do exist may be significant.

A further view is that until recent improvements, many multimedia technologies and formats used for web content contained inherent barriers that prevented access to certain groups of people, most conspicuously blind and visually impaired people – it was simply not thought possible to make certain multimedia resources accessible to these groups. However, arguably as a direct result of increased legislative responsibilities, technologies for creating online multimedia and the tools necessary to play that multimedia content, have made great advances in their support for accessibility features.

However, there is still much work to be done, not only to ensure that multi-media technologies fully support accessibility features such as captions and audio descriptions, keyboard accessibility and assistive technology support, but also to ensure that authoring, associating and reusing existing features such as caption files are made as seamless and efficient as possible.

Beyond these practical challenges, the authors' experiences with practitioners indicate that there are also a number of attitudinal reasons as to why many multimedia developers and teachers have so far failed to fully embrace multimedia as an opportunity to widen access to previously excluded groups of learners.

This seems partly to be an unfortunate result of the presence and nature of legislation promoting the rights of disabled people, which should in theory encourage web and e-learning authors to redesign existing resources to reduce or remove access barriers. Unfortunately, as a reaction to legislation that is often vague in terms of exactly what a developer must do from a technical perspective, anecdotal evidence suggests that some organisations may have been moved to take down websites or refrained from publishing or using certain electronic resources in order to avoid a breach of the law.

For example, the UK Disability Discrimination Act (1995) is widely assumed to apply to web and e-learning content (Sloan 2001). The nature of this legislation, in requiring 'reasonable steps' to be taken, rather than defining in detail what reasonable steps are, means that no technical baseline for legal compliance exists. This situation which may seemingly promote creative solutions to online accessibility problems, appears in reality to cause some unease amongst website developers and providers.

When confronted with a realisation that resources created in good faith may potentially be unlawful and discriminatory and without clear technical guidance on what is required from an accessibility standpoint, e-learning developers and teachers may respond with number of emotions, such as:

- fear of the consequences of breaching, or being accused of breaching, the law;
- embarrassment of inadvertently producing something that is inaccessible to a disabled student. While it is extremely unlikely that a developer would knowingly set out to create an unjustifiably discriminatory resource, there may often be an underestimation of the importance of accessibility to the target audience – and hence a bias towards, for example, preserving a particular visual appearance of a resource at the expense of display flexibility to suit specific needs;
- defensiveness, particularly when an e-learning resource that has been success-fully used to support teaching is subsequently assessed for accessibility and found not to comply with specific guidelines;
- demotivation, as legislative compliance is perceived as an exercise in check-box ticking and following rigid standards, rather than applying creativity to produce individualistic solutions;

- helplessness, as resource developers spend fruitless hours searching for information relating to the specific accessibility problem they are attempting to solve, so they may decide not to proceed with their development.

These reactions to the uncertainty over the legality of e-learning resources with respect to disability discrimination legislation, allied to a misconception as to the true requirements of accessible design, may lead to a reduction in creativity and innovation in use of multimedia and e-learning. Worse still, there may be a withdrawal of existing e-learning resources, and rejection of potentially useful digital material, and a curtailment of current and future development, all on supposed 'accessibility' grounds.

Thus, the immediate impact of legislation, instead of encouraging accessible design, may be a deterioration in the quality of the learning environment, as institutions and individuals are less inclined to use e-learning resources that were previously seen as highly effective. Ironically, people with specific learning difficulties may be particularly affected by a withdrawal or reduction in use of engaging multimedia and, since multimedia has an important role to play in widening access to educational experiences, it would seem logical to conclude that legislation should encourage rather than discourage its use.

It is critical therefore to encourage multimedia producers to embrace and adopt accessibility in their work. On the one hand, there is a need to ensure accessibility advice is not presented in a hectoring or unsympathetic way, but acknowledges the ideals, objectives and competing pressures of those involved in media and e-learning production. For example, Clark (2002) offers accessibility advice in a way that is strongly sympathetic to the web design community, while resources such as Skills for Access have been designed to provide advice and support on accessible multimedia creation in a way designed to be pragmatically applied in the media production and educational environments.

What is also required is the promotion of a holistic approach to the use of multimedia in e-learning, that supports the most appropriate and practical way of ensuring accessibility, by considering the context of the multimedia resource within the learning environment.

A holistic approach to accessibility of multimedia in e-learning

Wherever legislation does not lay down specific technical requirements, but rather supports the rights of disabled students in receiving equitable access to education, there is freedom to be creative in using multimedia and e-learning as a way of providing reasonable adjustments to ensure these educational experiences are accessible.

Multimedia e-learning may therefore actively play a part in enhancing accessibility for many disabled students, even though it may not be technically possible to make a particular resource, or its learning outcome, universally accessible.

So it is eminently possible that a specific multimedia e-learning resource may not be accessible to students with a particular impairment – for example, visual impairment – but significantly enhances accessibility for students with other access needs. In such instances, a goal of universal accessibility for that particular resource may simply not be possible, yet the introduction of multimedia in learning could be a reasonable adjustment to an existing accessibility barrier in the physical learning environment.

Accessibility should therefore not be considered in 'micro' terms, on a resource-by-resource basis, but at a broader level. In other words, there is a need to undertake a review process in terms of the overall accessibility of a mode of assessment, or of a module or even a whole course. What is essential is a requirement to assess the impact on the overall learning experience of any accessibility barriers affecting a disabled student's ability to use a specific multimedia learning resource. In some cases, the 'reasonable adjustment' needed to overcome the shortcoming is provision of the information in an equivalent alternative electronic format; yet in other cases, the adjustment may not even be a technical solution. For example, a reasonable adjustment for students with visual impairments may be the provision of a tactile model of a concept presented in a complex multimedia animation.

Approaches to accessibility of multimedia in e-learning can thus be viewed from two perspectives:

* Multimedia developers should strive to use techniques of best practice, relevant standards, guidelines, and features of multimedia technology to optimise the accessibility of the multimedia content they are creating for the target audience.
* On a wider scale, developers should bear in mind that the use of multimedia itself is an enabler, in that for certain groups, it is a way of making accessible information, experiences and concepts that, delivered in a traditional way, may have previously been extremely difficult, if not impossible to access. A trade-off may be that the resource by its nature excludes some people, and this is likely to be acceptable so long as the excluded group is supported in another way.

It is increasingly apparent that an effective way of viewing e-learning accessibility in general, and multimedia in particular, is to take a holistic approach (Kelly *et al.* 2004). This requires being aware of the context in which a specific resource is used, its intended aims and ultimately provides guidance on the most appropriate approach to ensuring accessibility. Therefore, in order to approach the issue of accessibility effectively in relation to a specific multimedia learning resource, certain objectives of good design should be established, summarised in Box 11.1.

Box 11.1   Establishing context of use in order to implement an appropriate accessibility strategy: key questions

- What are the aims of this piece of multimedia? What are the pedagogic goals? How does the resource fit in with the rest of the learning environment?
- Will all students be require to use it? Is its use compulsory for completion of a course? Will it be used in assessment?
- Where is the resource intended to be used – a controlled environment such as a laboratory or classroom, or could it potentially be used anywhere? In other words, what assumptions can you make about the browsing and access technology available to intended users (and their knowledge of that technology)?
- What are the potential barriers to using the multimedia resource for its intended purpose? What levels of sensory or motor abilities are required? How might specific learning difficulties or other cognitive impairments affect the ability to use the resource?
- What alternatives already exist and what alternatives can be reasonably created? To help answer this question, think how the subject or topic was previously taught.
- What is the best way that the information can be presented or learning objectives reached such that:

  - as many as possible of the intended audience can achieve the intended learning objectives using the multimedia resource?
  - those affected by unavoidable accessibility barriers can achieve the same objectives in a way best suited to them?

Addressing these questions clearly and honestly makes the job of planning accessible design much easier, and ensures the resource developer is fully aware of what needs to be made optimally accessible and how. This knowledge will also help to determine how multimedia can best be used to achieve the desired end goals. In many cases making the multimedia resource optimally accessible is undoubtedly the best way to proceed, but for other situations, following checkpoints and guidelines without considering the context of the resource may lead to an unsatisfactory solution for all.

This should not mean that futile attempts are made to reach a non-existent level of universal accessibility; nor does it mean the resource should be removed. Taking a user-centred, context-sensitive approach in this way encourages the provision of information and functionality in the best ways possible and through the most appropriate media, given the circumstances for which the resource is being designed.

This approach is absolutely not an endorsement of the segregation of disabled students by providing an alternative, less acceptable resource on account of their impairment. Rather, it advocates using the power of multimedia to enhance the accessibility of a learning environment to its full capacity – treating multimedia itself as an assistive technology – while being aware of any accessibility consequences of using a resource, and taking steps to minimise any adverse impact on access.

Conclusion

Multimedia offers significant potential in supporting and enhancing the accessibility of learning to many groups, and should not be seen as something to avoid for fear of discrimination. The tools and resources available to support the development of accessible multimedia are increasing in number and quality. But for multimedia to be used to its full potential, designers need to view accessibility as a professional challenge with the understanding that in meeting the challenge they are opening opportunities for all students to engage with their designs.

At the same time, teachers and developers need to see multimedia and accessibility in the context of the wider curriculum and learning outcomes. Accessibility of multimedia in e-learning involves first of all thinking about intended learning outcomes, how multimedia can support the widest possible access to these outcomes, and then considering how remaining access needs may best be met. Wherever possible, this should be through applying inclusive design principles, but acknowledging provision of alternatives may in some cases be the most appropriate option.

References and further reading

Brewer, J. and Treviranus, J. (2003) 'Developing and reusing accessible content and applications', in A. Littlejohn (ed.) *Reusing Online Resources: A Sustainable Approach to E-Learning*. London: Kogan Page, pp. 119–128.

Carey, K. (2005) 'The case for a European Centre for Accessible Media', presentation given to NESTA Seminar, 19 Feb. Available at: http://www.nesta.org.uk/assets/pdf/case-for-ecam-nesta-seminar.pdf (accessed 02/2005).

Carmichael, A. (1999) *Style Guide for the Design of Interactive Television Services for Elderly Viewers*. Independent Television Commission, Kings Worthy Court, Winchester. Available at: http://www.computing.dundee.ac.uk/staff/acarmichael/Carmichael_Design StyleGuide.pdf (accessed 02/2005).

Clark, J. (2002) *Building Accessible Websites*. Indianapolis, IN: New Riders.

Disability Rights Commission (2004) 'The Web – access and inclusion for disabled people: a formal investigation conducted by the Disability Rights Commission'. Available at: http://www.drc-gb.org/publicationsandreports/report.asp (accessed 02/2005).

Elliot, R., Glauert, J., Kennaway, J. and Marshall, I. (2000) 'The development of language processing support for the ViSiCAST project', in *Proceedings of ASSETS 2000 – The Fourth International ACM Conference on Assistive Technologies*. New York: ACM Press, pp. 101–108.

Heins, J. and Regan, B. (2002) 'Building Standards – conformant Accessible Learning Objects with Flash MX – a Macromedia White Paper'. Available at: http://download. macromedia.com/pub/solutions/downloads/accessibility/fl_learning_obj.pdf (accessed 02/2005).

IMS Global Learning Consortium (2002) 'IMS Guidelines for Developing Accessible Learning Applications, version 1.0'. Available at: http://ncam.wgbh.org/salt/guidelines/ (accessed 02/2005).

Keates, S. and Clarkson, J. (2004) *Countering Design Exclusion: An Introduction to Inclusive Design*. London: Springer, pp. 11–15.

Kelly, B., Phipps, L. and Swift, E. (2004) 'Developing a holistic approach for e-learning accessibility', *Canadian Journal of Learning and Technology*, 30(3). Available at: http://www.cjlt.c/content/vol30.3/kelly.html.

Littlejohn, A. (2003) *Reusing Online Resources: A Sustainable Approach to E-Learning.* London: Kogan Page.

Olejniczak, B. (2004) 'Optimising your chances with web accessibility', *Digital Web Magazine*. Available at: http://digital-web.com/articles/optimizing_your_chances_with _accessibility/ (accessed 02/2005).

Slatin, J. and Rush, S. (2002) *Maximum Accessibility*. Boston, MA: Addison-Wesley.

Sloan, M. (2001) 'Web accessibility and the DDA', in A. Paliwala and J. Moreton (eds) *The Journal of Information, Law and Technology (JILT)*, 2001(2). Available at: http:// elj.warwick.ac.uk/jilt/01-2/sloan.html (accessed 02/2005).

WebAIM (undated) 'Media Player accessibility'. Available at: http://www.webaim. org/techniques/captions/mediaplayers/ (accessed 02/2005).

Zeldman, J. (2003) *Designing with Web Standards*. Indianapolis, IN: New Riders.

Chapter 12

Enhancing disabled students' learning through virtual learning environments

Barbara Newland, Victoria Boyd and Juliette Pavey

Introduction

Virtual learning environments (VLEs) offer huge potential to support effective and enjoyable learning by disabled students in higher education; however, they can also be problematic if appropriate adjustments are not made. This chapter explores how learning can be enabled and enhanced using VLEs and provides practical guidance on effective implementation.

There has been rapidly increasing use of VLEs in education throughout the world over the past few years. The leading commercial providers of VLE software, Blackboard and WebCT, state that their products are available in over 50 and 70 countries worldwide respectively (Blackboard 2005; WebCT 2005). Within the UK, 86 per cent of all Higher Education Institutions (HEIs) had a VLE in place by 2003 (Browne and Jenkins 2003). Over 77 per cent use either Blackboard or WebCT while nearly 23 per cent use a VLE that has been developed in-house. Some HEIs may use both a commercial and in-house solution as 50 per cent of institutions use more than one VLE.

One of the reasons for the increasing use of VLEs is the movement towards a more blended approach to learning, where a combination of face-to-face and online learning is used. Blended learning is part of a flexible approach to learning which Collis defines as 'learner choice in different aspects of learning' (Collis and Moonen 2001). Many students require a flexible approach to learning for a variety of reasons including work and/or family commitments while studying or as a result of impairment. Combining flexibility and inclusivity can impact greatly on students' experience, particularly disabled students (Grimaldi and Goette 1999; Pearson and Koppi 2003). Online learning can also remove physical barriers to learning and encourage many forms of participation (Salmon 2000).

The term VLE refers to an environment in which 'online' interactions of various kinds take place between learners and tutors (JISC 2005) and can also be referred to as a LMS (Learning Management System). VLEs act as central support mechanism bringing together learning resources, communication and assessment tools through a personalised portal. The portal can provide links to courses being studied and may be extended to encompass the wider learning environment. This may include links to other communities and societies, bringing together the varying elements of a student's higher education experience in a central repository. VLEs offer a variety of communication tools including announcements, asynchronous and synchronous discussions and email. Asynchronous discussions usually consist of forums and threads to which participants can respond at any time from any place. Synchronous discussion, sometimes referred to as 'virtual chat' closely resembles actual, real-time conversation and can incorporate a series of tools such as whiteboard space for annotations. Assessment through a VLE can include online quizzes, electronically submitted essays or descriptions of an assignment. Benefits include improved feedback structure, convenience, flexibility and a balance of assessment methods (Bull 1999).

It is important to distinguish between the use of commercial and in-house VLEs in relation to accessibility. Commercial companies are highly committed to ensuring their products are accessible in compliance with international legislation such as the 2001 Special Educational Needs and Disability Act (SENDA) in the UK, Section 508 (a 1998 amendment to the 1973 Rehabilitation Act) in the USA and the Disability Services Act in Australia. Specifications making the WWW accessible are driven by the WAI (Web Accessibility Initiative), part of the W3C (WWW Consortium), whose 'commitment to lead the Web to its full potential includes promoting a high degree of usability for people with disabilities' (WAI 2005).

The developers of in-house VLEs can be equally committed to ensuring the accessibility of their products, but each one needs to be considered separately in relation to this issue. Previous studies have focused on the accessibility of the functionality of the software (Cowork 2002; Smith 2002). Therefore, this chapter does not address the technological viewpoint to the same extent, but instead focuses on the attainment of pedagogical objectives. It evaluates the implementation of a range of e-tivities, which Salmon (2002) defines as 'frameworks for online active and interactive learning'. This chapter describes and evaluates the work of the Accessibility in Learning Environments and Related Technologies (ALERT) project, which examined how the VLE could be adapted to ensure a valuable learning experience for disabled students.

ALERT was a two-year project between the University of Durham and Bournemouth University, funded through the Higher Education Funding Council for England (HEFCE) initiative for 'Improving provision for disabled students' (HEFCE 2002). The project has produced a series of guidelines on the use of a VLE to support and enhance disabled students' learning for academics, learning technologists and disability support staff (http://www.dur.ac.uk/alert/guidelines. htm).

Methodology

The ALERT guidelines draw directly on the experience of disabled students and academic staff. Fourteen case studies were identified in various academic disciplines involving students with a wide variety of impairments (see Table 12.1).

Table 12.1 Distribution of ALERT case studies by subject, impairment and focus

Academic discipline	Impairment	E-tivity
Anthropology	Cerebral Palsy	Animation
Computing Science	Dyslexia	General Usage
Economics	Dyspraxia	Online Discussion
Geography	Hearing Impairment	Online Quizzes
Geology	ME	Role Play
Law	Spinal Problems	Use of Media
Mathematics	Visual Impairment	
Medicine	Wrist Problems	
Sociology		

Some of the case studies were given the specific focus of an e-tivity including online discussions, online quizzes and role play. All case studies were collected over the academic year 2003/4.

The Learning Technology Team (LTT) at the University of Durham identified areas of extensive and/or innovative use of the VLE and the Durham University Service for Students with Disabilities (DUSSD) contacted disabled students in these areas. DUSSD recruited the students by appending a call for participants in the specific disciplines to their weekly email newsletter. The students who responded were briefed on the objectives and rationale of the project and a time was arranged for a face-to-face interview. At this point, staff teaching on the students' modules were also contacted and asked to provide a complementary perspective on the student experience.

At the recommendation of DUSSD, student interviews were broken into two 45-minute sessions, in order to minimise respondent fatigue. The interviews were semi-structured, the first being mainly based on multiple choice and closed response questions. The second allowed students to be more discursive and to adopt a more qualitative approach. With the student's consent, audio recordings of the interviews were made in order that transcriptions of the interview could be produced for later analysis.

The questions in the first interview were predominantly about computer usage, confidence and skills. A number of the questions were aligned with the annual Communications and Information Technology (CandIT) audit conducted by the LTT at the University of Durham, with all students as they enter and leave the university (Pavey 2003). This enabled a comparison of responses from those students with a declared impairment to the results from the audit, which provided a richer context for the interpretation. In the second interview, students were invited to speak more openly about their learning styles and preferences, allowing an insight into what effect, if any, the student perceived their impairment had on their approach to learning.

For this research it was vital to ensure anonymity and confidentiality. At the beginning of each interview the students and interviewer signed a confidentiality agreement, in line with the University of Durham Ethics Committee policy. All student data was anonymised and each case study was given a unique identifier. Comments by participants on the guidelines were taken into consideration before their final publication.

All student participants were aged between 17 and 25 and were studying full-time at the University of Durham. Some 70 per cent of the respondents had used a computer for over 10 years and 80 per cent said that they were either 'confident' or 'very confident' computer users. These statistics are very typical of those for all students at the university, the majority of whom are full-time, 17–25-year-old students.

The data collected from the interviews were extremely rich as the students were very open and eager to talk about their use of the VLE and learning preferences. A book voucher was offered as an incentive for the students to attend the interview sessions and to thank them for their time. Only one interview could not take place due to lack of co-operation, and several of the interviews had to be re-scheduled due to unforeseen circumstances, holidays and exams.

The academic staff concerned were also asked to participate in a semi-structured interview. Their first interview was replaced by a short online form which they could complete in their own time, consisting of multiple choice questions and closed questions. These questions were similar to those used in student interviews and asked about computer usage, IT facilities available to them and how much time they spent developing an online module. Subsequently, the academics took part in a face-to-face session, which lasted about 30 minutes, and gave them the opportunity to talk qualitatively about their experiences and support of disabled students. The same anonymity and confidentiality applied to staff participants. The VLE was also used as an information repository for staff and students relating to various aspects of the interview process and developments with the study.

For this study, e-tivities were identified as animation, online discussion, online quizzes, role play, use of media and general usage (Table 12.1) and were those elements or frameworks which were thought to be utilised across departments with a large number of students. Animations are used in a variety of modules often when information is procedural in nature or where it may be difficult to observe in the real world. Good computer animations have the potential to overcome some barriers to learning for some students, and, used correctly, are potentially a powerful tool for learning (Birkeland 1998). Online discussion refers to asynchronous communication either between tutor and student and student and student that extends interactions and learning beyond face-to-face, classroom time. Online quizzes are utilised in courses mainly for self-assessment purposes and for reinforcing learning.

The use of the VLE to support role play, although limited, is utilised within some courses at the University of Durham. The benefits of role play to students are many, in particular for researching a problem, having exposure to real-world scenarios, simulating the decision-making process, appreciating the views of others and working as part of a team (Pavey and Donoghue 2003). The use of media refers to any inclusion of video or audio within courses; the use of video in particular is becoming a more widely used medium to support learning. The term general usage, although not an e-tivity as such, refers to any other utilization of the environment not covered by the other frameworks. More specifically, it relates to how varying use can impact on student learning, such as consistency across modules.

Guidelines on using a VLE were developed from themes identified through analysing the interview transcripts using qualitative data analysis software. These guidelines include:

- provision of lecture support materials;
- use of synchronous discussion tools;
- use of asynchronous discussion tools;
- use of online assessment;
- holistic approach.

Each guideline is divided into pedagogical, practical and strategic sections and provides recommendations, discussion and action points with quotes from participating students and staff. For the purpose of this chapter, examples of the guidelines will be highlighted under each of the section headings.

Pedagogical recommendations

To highlight some of the pedagogical recommendations of the ALERT guidelines, the provision of learning support materials through a VLE, including Word documents, PowerPoint presentations, web resources and multimedia, is discussed. Advance provision of lecture support materials before a face-to-face session helps support all students (Doyle and Robson 2002), not just those who are disabled. Remote access to digital resources gives students the ability to customise materials to be more usable in light of their individual needs, and provides a structured set of notes which can be annotated in class and re-used for revision.

Having uniform, pre-prepared materials in a lecture provides students with a reference point for intangible concepts and new vocabulary and terminology, and allows them to listen more carefully. Giving students more time to pay attention and placing less emphasis on note-taking promote understanding and encourage deep learning, where students transform the learning material in the process of making sense of it (Marton *et al.* 1984). For students with slow reading speeds or dexterity problems, having pre-prepared notes is invaluable in enabling them to work at a comfortable pace:

> before lectures I can print out the notes, I can follow because I'm not copying down, so I can follow what the lecturer's saying, I can then annotate my notes . . . while concentrating on what he or she is saying.
>
> (ALERT student)

> I guess the fact that students have a more organised . . . have their course materials provided digitally, it gives them the opportunity to enhance the documents that are provided in whatever way they need to for whatever disability they have.
>
> (ALERT staff)

Academics are often concerned that students will not attend lectures if lecture notes are available online. However, recent research has found that only 1 per cent of students stop attending lectures for this reason (Newland 2003).

Many disabled students, including those with dyslexia, dyspraxia and writing problems, have to rely on peers to either take or duplicate notes, imposing secondary learning on them. In using another student's notes, either for annotation or revision, students are working with materials which have already been subject to one level of interpretation by the students who have taken the notes, rather than receiving the originals verbatim. Having pre-prepared lecture support materials provides an equal starting point for all students (Newland *et al.* 2005).

This also impacts upon levels of confidence and independence among disabled students, as they are offered a greater sense of self-determination and ownership of materials. Interactive technology has been proved to improve independence and motivation (Hardy 1999) and to raise self-esteem, developing problem solving and communication skills (Strack 1995). 'If I knew that my lecture resources were going to be online before the lecture, that would be the best thing that could happen for me, cos then I could just print them off and annotate them' (ALERT student).

Providing students with a repository of structured, developmental notes also acts as an effective revision tool. Alerting students to the central location of all course materials in the VLE gives them a highly visible and organised accessible resource, which offers what the constructivist school refers to as 'scaffolding', where explicit links between old and new learning are made (Cottrell 2001). Such material is at the core of constructive alignment (Biggs 1999), which states that students build meaning from their experiences, which are then aligned with explicit knowledge in their education:

> when you read back through my notes you can tell which lecture notes came up before and which ones didn't because the other ones are so much more disorganised compared to the ones which have been done beforehand.
>
> (ALERT student)

Practical recommendations

An illustration of ALERT's practical recommendations are provided through the guideline on VLE-based assessment. Key elements in promoting effective assessment are its fitness for purpose and ability to accommodate a diversity of student needs and preferences.

VLEs are equipped with various features which allow the introduction of flexible, reusable and customisable learning activities. Many disabled students need alternative assessment formats (Teachability 2000) and the adaptability of VLE-delivered resources can help with this. A popular use of the interactive capabilities offered by a VLE is the use of automated assessment through quizzes, which provide a valuable and engaging way of tracking progress, giving feedback and helping students to increase their understanding. High quality feedback is instrumental in encouraging understanding (Ramsden 1992) and the VLE as an adaptive environment has the potential to encourage high level learning (Laurillard 1996).

'Online assessment' is often taken to refer to quizzes, but by making details and descriptions of assessment available through the VLE, students gain a clearer picture of what is expected of them. This can also be advantageous in terms of having access to resources for revision purposes in one central repository:

> Those assignments are set at the beginning of the year, and they don't really change . . . so I think they should just be put on there at the beginning of the year, like, 'You're gonna have to do three formative essays, three summative essays, they'll count for this, they're due around this date'.
>
> (ALERT student)

Involving students in VLE-based assessment tasks presents the opportunity for different types of activity and accommodates a variety of different learning styles (Becta, TechDis and JISC 2003). For students with concentration or memory problems, changing learning activity can provide a break from text-based learning and help with varying stimulus and levels of engagement:

> It could be useful for a break from everything else and also it could guide your work . . . you know where you're falling down, cos it can tell you what you're getting wrong and then you can build on that.
>
> (ALERT student)

Online quizzes are a flexible and convenient method of enabling students with concentration, cognition, memory or dexterity problems to complete assessments at their own pace in their own environment. Students' individual ability to complete tasks must be taken into account (Wiles 2002), and by giving students the independence to complete at their own convenience, the pressure of peer competition and time restraints can be removed:

> We have done like, some multiple choice tests and things on the computer . . . I think it's great because you can do it . . . you can do it wherever you feel comfortable, whenever it fits in with your time.
>
> (ALERT student)

Using online assessment . . . just as a formative thing would be quite useful, and the feedback I got off students this year was they did quite like having that and they could go off and do it in their own time.

(ALERT staff)

Strategic recommendations

Departmental and institutional agreement on appropriate use of a VLE is vital in promoting consistency, applicability and innovation. To illustrate how communities of practice (Wenger 1998) shape and improve provision for disabled students, we will discuss the use of asynchronous communication tools.

A considered and collaborative approach to using a VLE and its e-tivity capabilities is vital in making the best possible provision for all students. A balanced programme can be developed through a departmental strategy on the use of features such as discussion boards and quizzes. This allows students to participate fully without being overloaded with tasks such as being required to actively participate in several discussion boards simultaneously, which can be time-consuming and lower the quality of the debate: 'We will only run discussion forums in one first year, second year, and third year course . . . the core courses, and try and kind of build up that, you know the more fruitful use of discussion forums' (ALERT staff).

The role of the tutor is crucial to the success of online discussion; they can facilitate interaction by informing, guiding and encouraging. Tutor support is especially important for disabled students, who use communication and feedback to gauge progress and identify areas in which they may need more focus. By agreeing at a departmental or institutional level how this support can be assured and standardised, more definite and diverse provision for all students can be made: 'if the opportunity was there and it was encouraged it would be much more useful' (ALERT student).

VLE recommendations

The ALERT guidelines also include VLE recommendations to help staff to implement the pedagogical, practical and strategic suggestions. Some examples are:

- Put all materials in the VLE at the beginning of a course with timed release.
- Provide the opportunity for online socialisation in discussion prior to academic debate to enable students to become familiar and confident with using the technology.
- Supplement VLE-based quiz activity with additional support, e.g. dedicated discussion areas to raise issues.
- Make it clear to students the importance of writing meaningful subject headings in threads.

Discussion and action points

The ALERT guidelines conclude with reflective discussion points aimed at encouraging members of staff to consider their own practice and the rationale they employ in making decisions with regard to the VLE. Furthermore, it is anticipated that members of staff will collaborate with their peers in reflecting on practice, and, as a result of this, evaluate both departmental and institutional policy. By providing action points, the guidelines encourage a pro-active approach to adapting practice, and offer 'next stage' considerations that will help staff to decide the logical progression in improving provision.

An example of the discussion questions is provided below from the guideline relating to the provision of lecture support materials:

- Pedagogical

  - Why do you think making learning support materials available in advance of a lecture helps disabled students' learning?

- Practical

  - When do you make your learning support materials available through the VLE? What is your reasoning behind this?

- Strategic

  - Do you work with colleagues in producing learning support materials?

Conclusion

It is imperative that VLEs are used in such a way as to enhance learning by enabling a more inclusive curriculum which will support all students. The pedagogical, practical and strategic recommendations in the ALERT guidelines provide advice for academics, learning support staff and disability practitioners on ways of achieving this. Clearly some of the recommendations discussed will require strategic planning at institutional and/or departmental levels. However, many others can be implemented quickly and easily and illustrate that minor changes can have a far-reaching impact in supporting disabled students' learning through VLEs.

References and further reading

Becta, TechDis and JISC (2003) 'Alternative assessment, inclusive learning and teaching', *ILT for Disabled Learners*. Essex: Becta and JISC TechDis Service.

Biggs, J. (1999) *Teaching for Quality Learning at University*. Buckingham: SRHE and the Open University Press.

Birkeland, K. (1998) Available at: http://www.wsu.edu/NIS/Universe/animation.html (accessed 06/05).

Blackboard (2005) Available at: http://www.blackboard.com/about/newsletters/Summer 2004_vol1a.html (accessed 06/05).

Browne, T. and Jenkins, M. (2003) *VLE Surveys: A Longitudinal Perspective between March 2001 and March 2003 for Higher Education in the United Kingdom*. Oxford: UCISA. Available at: http://www.ucisa.ac.uk/groups/tlig/vle/vle2003.doc.

Bull, J. (1999) 'Computer-assisted assessment: impact on higher education institutions', *Journal of Educational Technology and Society*, 2(3): 123–126.

Collis, B. and Moonen, J. (2001) *Flexible Learning in a Digital World*. London: Kogan Page.

Cottrell, S. (2001) *Teaching Study Skills and Supported Learning*. New York: Palgrave.

Cowork (2002) Available at: http://techdis.ac.uk/archive/cowork/development/materials (accessed 06/05).

Doyle, C. and Robson, K. (2002) in Ball, S. and Campy, D. (eds) *Accessible Curricula: Good Practice for All*. Cardiff: UWIC Press.

Grimaldi, C. and Goette, T. (1999) 'The internet and the independence of individuals with disabilities', *Internet Research: Electronic Networking Applications and Policy*, 9(4): 272–280.

Hardy, C. (1999) 'Raising self-esteem', in M. Blamires (ed.) *Enabling Technology for Inclusion*. London: Paul Chapman Publishing Ltd.

Higher Education Funding Council for England (2002) 'Improving provision for disabled students', *Strategy and Invitation to Bid for Funds for 2003–05*. Bristol: HEFCE, 02/21

JISC (2005) Available at: http://www.jisc.ac.uk (accessed 06/05).

Laurillard, D. (1996) *Rethinking University Teaching*. London: Routledge.

Marton, F., Hounsell, D. and Entwistle, N. (1984) *The Experience of Learning*. Edinburgh: Scottish Academic Press.

Newland, B. (2003) 'Evaluating the impact of a VLE on learning and teaching', in P. Kommers and G. Richards (eds) *Proceedings of EDMEDIA World Conference on Educational Multimedia, Hypermedia and Telecommunications*. Chesapeake, VA: AACE, pp. 601–603.

Newland, B., Pavey, J. and Boyd, V. (2005) 'Influencing inclusive practice: the role of VLEs', in Rust, C. (ed.) *Improving Student Learning: Diversity and Inclusivity: Proceedings of the 12th Improving Student Learning Symposium*. Oxford: Oxford Brookes University, pp. 225–233.

Pavey, J. (2003) 'A C&IT skills audit of staff and students', in P. Martin (ed.) *Information and IT Literacy: Enabling Learning in the 21st Century*. London: Facet Publishing.

Pavey, J. and Donoghue, D. (2003) 'The use of role play and VLEs in teaching Environmental Management', *Planet*, 10: 7–10.

Pearson, E. and Koppi, A. (2003) 'Developing inclusive practices: evaluation of a staff development course in accessibility', *Australian Journal of Educational Technology*, 19(3): 275–292.

Ramsden, P. (1992) *Learning to Teach in Higher Education*. London: Routledge.

Salmon, G. (2000) *E-moderating: The Key Teaching and Learning Online*. London: Kogan Page.

Salmon, G. (2002) *E-tivities: The Key to Active Online Learning*. London: Kogan Page.

Smith, S. (2002) 'Dyslexia and virtual learning environment interfaces', in L. Phipps, A. Sutherland and J. Seale (eds) *Access All Areas: Disability, Technology and Learning*. London: JISC TechDis Service and ALT.

Strack, G. (1995) 'Curriculum constraints and opportunities', in B. Tagg (ed.) *Developing a Whole School IT Policy*. London: Pitmans.

Teachability (2000) *Creating an Accessible Curriculum for Students with Disabilities*. Glasgow: University of Strathclyde.

WAI (2005) Available at: http://www.w3.org/WAI/about.html

WebCT (2005) Available at: http://www.webct.com/success

Wenger, E. (1998) *Communities of Practice: Learning, Meaning and Identity*. Cambridge: Cambridge University Press.

Wiles, K. (2002) 'Accessibility and computer-based assessment: a whole new set of issues?', in L. Phipps, A. Sutherland and J. Seale (eds) *Access All Areas: Disability, Technology and Learning*. London: JISC TechDis Service and ALT.

Chapter 13

Disability and mainstreaming continuing professional development in higher education

Alan Hurst

Introduction

This chapter is based on the experiences of running a Higher Education Funding Council for England-funded special initiative project. The ultimate outcome is the production of a handbook which mainstream staff responsible for training and continuing professional development can use in their programmes working alongside specialist staff from their organisation's disability services but without having to rely too much on them. The project involved devising and delivering sessions free of charge with a small number of interested partner institutions, working with staff both from learning and teaching development and specialist disability services. Following feedback and evaluation, it was planned for these colleagues to organise and deliver sessions themselves where I acted as observer and contributed to further critical reflection which was used when compiling the final version of the handbook. A final stage involved dissemination at a number of regional events prior to circulating the handbook.

The need for this resource has assumed greater significance in the early years of the twenty-first century. The implementation of the Special Educational Needs and Disability Act 2001 (SENDA – effectively Part 4 of the Disability Discrimination Act 1995) made it imperative that all staff working in higher education know of their responsibilities if they are to avoid putting themselves and their employing institution 'at risk' in relation to the law. Consequently, there is a responsibility to provide appropriate training. Academic staff in particular need to know about challenges to inclusive learning for students with a range of impairments and how these might be addressed. While the specialist knowledge of staff working in disability services means that they have a part to play, in keeping with what might be seen as a genuinely inclusive institution, the major responsibility must rest with mainstream staff and learning development/human resources. Currently many might feel unprepared and ill-equipped to tackle this. The handbook which is the outcome of the project tries to address this. However, what should be borne in mind throughout is that what is being promoted is good professional practice in the classroom and throughout the institution generally, and is not specific to disabled learners.

More details will be given later about the tasks and exercises which have been tested in the sector and which are included in the handbook. Before this, there are a number of key questions to be considered in relation to disability and its inclusion in mainstream staff training and development.

What are we doing?

This question intends to prompt thinking about the terms used and their implications. This is an important consideration when devising publicity for sessions/programmes to attract participants. For example, there is disability awareness, disability awareness training, and disability equality training. The first of these implies a general effort to sensitise people to what it might mean for someone with an impairment to participate in higher education and in society. The second suggests that participants will be given specific instructions on what to do and how to behave when meeting a person with a particular impairment. The third contains a focus on treating disabled people equally. All have weaknesses. Thus, awareness might mean knowing but not acting. Training suggests ensuring particular actions occur irrespective of context and individual. Equality, with its inference on treating everybody in the same way, ignores the old adage that equal treatment for all is unfair to some. While not in common parlance, it might be preferable to promote the notion of 'disability education' since this recognises not only that people have knowledge but that they can build on and adapt that knowledge to meet different situations. Perhaps the concept of disability education might embrace all aspects and would be congruent with views on professional development expressed by others (e.g. Craft 2000) who suggest that it is really an attempt to change culture. It might also be more appropriate to consider 'equity' rather than 'equality' since the heart of the matter is about securing fairness for everyone. In Australia, higher education institutions devise equity plans which are used by the federal government to allocate widening participation funding.

Who is involved?

There are two dimensions to this question. The first of these refers to who should deliver the sessions. It should be clear from what has been said already that it is seen as a mainstream responsibility involving staff routinely and closely involved in training. This is especially true in relation to the professional development of teaching and learning support staff since what is really being promoted is good classroom practice. Given that there might be scope for some input of a specialist kind, ideally sessions should include a partnership of mainstreamers and specialists. One matter which is often raised is whether only disabled people themselves are well placed to conduct the sessions. Undoubtedly because of their personal experiences, they can have an important perspective. However, what they might lack is an appropriately detailed knowledge of excellent learning, teaching and assessment practices and the general higher education context. Occasionally too individual and personal perspectives can get in the way of objectivity and detachment. It would be dangerous also to assume that those involved do not themselves have impairments which are hidden and which they have chosen not to disclose.

One approach that has sometimes been considered useful is the involvement and participation of disabled students. If they are willing and have the confidence to participate in discussions on disability issues and if the atmosphere in the sessions is supportive, students being questioned by staff can lead to the latter gaining useful insights.

The second dimension is about who should be the target for the sessions. There is an argument to be made for suggesting that disability education should be compulsory for all staff. This stance may stem from wishing to avoid the threat of legal challenges under disability discrimination law which might be more difficult to defend if attendance remains voluntary. During the project, a variety of approaches was adopted. Some institutions issued an open invitation to all staff; some identified particular units such as schools and departments and faculties; some organised sessions around a particular theme such as assessment; some included sessions within existing training programmes, particularly those directed towards new and untrained staff. Only in the last case could an element of compulsion be detected. At many other sessions, it came as no surprise to find that those present were 'the converted' and were already committed strongly to developing and improving their knowledge in relation to disabled students. The concept of 'compulsion' to some extent goes against the traditional culture of higher education where staff have been allowed to base their actions on their own professional judgements. Certainly, presenting sessions at which attendance has been made compulsory with many participants reluctant to attend and resistant to whatever is on offer is an unenviable challenge. On the other hand, some staff do face compulsory professional development, for example, in relation to Health and Safety and Equal Opportunities. In terms of the successful embedding of practice, perhaps the best answer is to ensure its inclusion in programmes directed to all new staff and which all must attend. One potential strategy to use when trying to attract existing staff is to offer some form of incentive. For example, some institutions use certificates of attendance, the gradual acquisition of which can count towards salary increments or promotion opportunities. Another powerful way of bringing about institutional changes is to organise sessions for senior managers of the institution. These then set an example for all staff – after all, if busy people like senior managers can attend, why not everyone else? It can also be very useful in terms of persuading this group to reaffirm or enhance their commitment to high quality policy and provision for disabled students.

When is the optimum time for sessions and how long should they be?

This is another challenging question. One could argue that it might be preferable to undertake some development prior to staff encountering disabled students, on the grounds that they can be prepared before prejudices, stereotyping and expectations appear – an additional reason to include disability in induction and training of new staff. In contrast, if sessions takes place once staff have some experience of teaching, some of the content included in sessions can make use of previous experience of working with a range of students, including those who are disabled. Knowing a little of the background, experiences and any emerging concerns of staff involved is helpful to those responsible for organising and delivering the sessions.

It seems appropriate here also to consider the thorny issue of time allocated to sessions. This is a real conundrum. When sessions have been organised to take half a day, in their evaluations many staff have said that they would have preferred more time. On the other hand, publicising sessions as taking a full day sometimes meets with the response that staff cannot afford so much time. To return to the point made in the previous section, the matter could be resolved if decisions were made about its voluntary/compulsory status.

Sometimes sessions are requested by colleagues anticipating future events. Perhaps the best example of this is when institutions are preparing for a UK Quality Assurance Agency's Institutional Audit when questions might be asked about the extent to which the various parts of the QAA Code of Practice are being implemented (see Chapter 4 by Chapman and Carlisle for further discussion of the QAA). Equally significant might be when course validation and periodic review/ evaluations are due to take place. Preparations for such events could include sessions on how the needs of a diverse range of students are addressed, another form of continuing professional development.

How are the sessions to be delivered?

In line with the underlying philosophy of this chapter, sessions should be based upon principles associated with effective learning for all. First and foremost, they should be participative, with those present being as actively involved as possible for as much of the time as possible. Given that people learn in different ways, there should be a variety of approach used in the sessions, for example, by using some visual materials in video or DVD format (taking care to consider their accessibility for all participants). The varied approaches also contribute to retaining interest. To secure and retain attention, the content should be perceived to be relevant. In this case, working with a clearly identified group of staff is helpful when planning the sessions. Last but not least, the range of activities should provide an enjoyable experience – learning can be fun. The cartoons of John Callahan, for example, use humour to stimulate thinking about disability on a range of points, some of which might indicate matters which are felt to be sensitive (Callahan 1998).

By implementing these principles, participants will have plenty of opportunities to interact with each other and with the presenters. It is this spontaneity and vibrancy that is of crucial importance. In the past few years a number of opportunities for training and continuing professional development in relation to disability issues have been made available online. Despite their undoubted quality and despite their fulfilling a useful role, undertaking them as a solitary exercise is not as successful as collective sessions. At best, they are a supplement to rather than a substitute for face-to-face interaction and the liveliness and challenges these provide for both participant and presenter.

One approach to sessions widely used in the past was to include simulations of impairment. For example, materials were made available to simulate a range of visual and auditory impairments or workshop presenters borrowed wheelchairs for use by the participants. The approach was the subject of a paper by French (1992) where, as an individual with an impairment, she was very critical of simulations. She argued that such opportunities cannot represent the totality and permanence of having an impairment and hence they can be accused of trivialising disability. Since then, others have also suggested that the impact of simulations as learning experiences is questionable (Gosen and Washbush 2004).

Having accepted their views, the sessions organised as part of this project have deliberately avoided simulations despite evidence from sessions delivered many years ago that they had an impact on the learners.

What do sessions cover and what strategies are used?

An overview of the kinds of exercises and tasks which have been used successfully during the project now follows. It is not possible to give step-by-step directions about how they can be used; these will be included in the handbook being produced as a result of the project. Also, it should be noted that creating a programme for a session from these exercises cannot be prescriptive; each session's plan will depend on the nature of the group with whom one is working. Some staff might be new to the context and have no knowledge or prior experience, some might seek a general overview rather than a specific focus, some might be from a clearly identified part of an institution and want a session with their unique situation in mind, for example, work placements.

To open a session it is always useful to try to get the participants actively involved as soon as possible and to use tasks which can be run in a direct and lively style. Thus, if working with staff with little or no experience of disability, it is possible to use pictures/images to evoke responses, and this could lead later into a consideration of images used by the higher education institutions (HEIs) in their publicity. Another task could involve allocating particular social identities/roles to participants (e.g. teacher, shopkeeper, bus driver, etc.) but ensuring that in whatever size of group has been created, one person has no role. This can be used to prompt a discussion about feelings of difference, stigma, being left out, etc.

If appropriate, an exercise might be used to sensitise participants to the use of language and terminology. This too could lead on to an exploration of the language environment of the institution. Perhaps the fundamental point to convey and one which should lay the basis for everything that follows is to introduce models of disability, since this is crucial to the need to make 'reasonable adjustments' required by law. One approach is to use the work of Mike Oliver and ask partic- ipants to rewrite the set of questions used by the Office of Population Census and Surveys and which are rooted in an individual/medical/deficit model into a form which demonstrates the application of the social model (Oliver 1990). This approach could also be adapted to use the categories devised and used on many official application forms such as those used by the UK Universities and Colleges Admissions Service (UCAS).

This could form a useful and logical link to the next focus, namely students. Using a short word-association exercise, asking participants to respond to two different trigger words (e.g. 'student' and 'disabled student') often identifies hidden concerns of staff who often feel that they are open-minded. Moving on to detail about disabled students, using a list of factual statements which participants are asked to identify as 'true' or 'false' can prompt discussion on many items. For example, the statement 'Students must disclose their disability on the UCAS application form' can lead to a debate on issues around disclosure. The list of statements can be as short or as long as required. Depending on the nature of the participants and the time available, they could be asked to write their own statements and also to provide detailed reasons for their inclusion and for the responses they aim to elicit.

Another useful strategy to focus on students is to provide case studies. These can be of 'real' students or they can be fictitious, created to prompt participants to think about specific issues. Two examples illustrate this: the case history of a Deaf student seeking a place on a Film and Media course may well prompt think- ing about whether coverage of soundtracks in the syllabus is a core requirement and if so what 'reasonable adjustments' might be made. Second, the case of a blind student who has a seeing dog and who would like to study a modern foreign language may well raise questions about the overseas placement, its status as a core requirement and the implications of taking the dog. Cases can be devised to encompass the particular requirements of students with a range of impairments. Depending on the group, it may be more appropriate to use more complex examples. Again, the groups could be asked to devise their own cases and to justify their content.

Having explored the situation from a student perspective, there is a need to address institutional aspects. If one is working with a group of academic staff, the focus might be on inclusive learning and teaching. A lively start might be made by using an ideas inventory to collect suggestions about the barriers academic staff are likely to raise if asked to include disabled students in their classes. This could form a useful preliminary to the approach offered by the Teachability project in Scotland (SHEFC 2000).

Teachability began in the 1990s involving HEIs in the West of Scotland and, because of its success, was extended to include all Scottish higher education providers. The original focus was a book containing a series of questions guiding staff to think about the extent to which their modules/courses/programme were inclusive and met the needs of students with a range of impairments. More recently, this has been updated, revised and reissued as a series of shorter theme-based booklets on topics such as creating accessible information, lectures, tutorials and seminars, placements, assessment and e-learning. The aim of the materials produced was to prompt staff to reflect on and review their current practices and so the starting point is to ask the extent to which they consider that their courses are accessible. A series of additional questions concerns whether more accessibility is possible and how this might be accomplished. In order to facilitate thinking, it has proved useful to ask staff to identify the core requirements of their course. All of these stages can form the basis for exercises and tasks. The ultimate aim of the original project working with Scottish HEIs was to persuade course teams/departments to provide a written report which provides an audit of existing practice. (For further details about inclusive learning and teaching, see Hurst 2005.)

Returning to workshop activities, if time permits, sometimes a subsequent session can be arranged in which staff can discuss these written reports, perhaps as groups from the same section, perhaps with groups from other sections. During the life of the HEFCE project on which this chapter is based, the production of Teachability-style reports has sometimes been undertaken in connection with quality assurance procedures, both internal to the institution and also when external bodies have been involved. These regular events can be used as a stimulus to action in terms of staff training and development.

Additionally, other existing resources can also be used as the core for exercises/ tasks working with academic staff, for instance the series of checklists devised by Waterfield and West (SWANDS 2002). As a short, sharp task to reinvigorate a flagging group, participants can be asked to list as many forms of academic assessment as they can think of in a restricted timed interval (e.g. two minutes). This can then be compared to the list taken from the SWANDS document (which lists over forty) and can prompt discussion about assessment and distinctions between modified and alternative formats. The HEFCE-funded National Disability Team have also published a series of checklists relating to a wide range of issues concerning higher education and disability, and they too offer possibilities.

Some staff at workshops might have concerns about particular disability issues. For example, many staff are keen to find out more about dyslexia. To start this, one might use an ideas inventory to collect views on what participants consider dyslexia to be. This might be followed up by discussion of definitions drawn from those with expertise in dyslexia and their implications for teaching. Some authorities, when writing about schools, have seen dyslexia as a different way of learning rather than a learning difficulty, an approach which is very much in accord with the social model of disability (Neanon 2002). Based on another school-focused source, additionally in another workshop exercise participants could then be asked to identify what a dyslexia-friendly higher education environment might look like (Mackay 2001).

If participants are from a range of backgrounds and include both teaching and non-teaching staff, it might be appropriate to approach inclusion in a different way. Starting from the principle that a genuinely inclusive institution involves everyone knowing both their rights and their responsibilities, one exercise to demonstrate this is to identify who should take what action at particular stages of a student's passage through higher education. This can be represented by a chart with roles listed across the horizontal axis and stages of progression in the vertical axis starting with initial enquiry and ending with graduation. A relevant anecdotal starting point could be the repetition of a frequently found experience when a call is made to the specialist disability services and the speaker begins, 'Hello, I've got one of your students here . . .'. The use of 'your' indicates where responsibility is seen to lie.

Another focus for tasks and exercises relates to quality assurance and the evaluation of policy and provision. At a simple level, participants could be given a list of the features identified by the HEFCE as constituting base level provision and asked to comment on how they view their own institution (HEFCE 1999). Another strategy is to list aspects of policy and provision associated with quality and ask that they be ranked in order of priority. Finally and more demandingly, certainly in terms of time, participants might be asked to devise their own evaluation tool, comparisons with what is available already (for example, the National Disability Team checklists) could then be made.

Finally, a word about workshop resources is needed. This is connected to my earlier point, namely the importance of variety of approach and of stimulus. There is a range of material available which can be used in disability education. Much is available free of charge. For example, the video *Talk* produced by the Disability Rights Commission is useful for setting the social context of disability in the United Kingdom. However, using the version that is captioned, signed and has a voice over alongside the version without these features allows a demonstration of what inclusive practice might look like when using visual materials and how this could circumvent issues such as disclosure, reasonable adjustments and anticipatory duties. It could also prompt a discussion of barriers which are intrinsic to the subject, barriers which are created as a result of decisions taken about how to deliver the course, and barriers which arise inadvertently.

Also free of charge are promotional videos produced by many HEIs both in the UK and overseas. The ways in which these can be used are many and varied and depend on the imagination of the organiser and the needs of the participants, but can prompt rich discussions about how HEIs promote themselves to students, including those who are disabled. Other useful audio-visual resources are available for purchase. A good example of this is the DVD *Making the Case*, produced by the Learning and Skills Council in 2003, which explores issues stemming from the implementation of the UK SENDA legislation. The DVD format plus the accompanying guidance notes present considerable flexibility in how this might be used to promote discussion on related issues. Finally, one should not forget the possibilities offered by stories and features which are reported on television and radio and in the press, which can be accessed and used within workshop sessions. Their immediacy is often useful at the start of sessions – and of course they are usable normally free or at minimal cost for educational purposes.

Conclusion

The implementation of the SENDA legislation prompted increased activity in the UK in relation to professional education and development. However, in many instances this can be viewed more as a reaction to avoiding legal disputes and maintaining the status quo rather than as an opportunity to implement a routine, rigorous strategy aimed at changing the culture. A major question remains about whether such exposure to disability and inclusive practices should be compulsory. The public sector duty proposed by the Disability Discrimination Act 2005, which will take effect from December 2006 (ECU 2004), requires that HEIs consult with disabled students and potential students to identify and monitor their participation, retention and progress. It is important that all HEIs show how they meet this new duty. For example, they might be pushed into a position where disability education has to be made compulsory. While this might look like progress, caution is needed. The frontispiece to a book on disability rights in the USA asserts that 'A law cannot guarantee what a culture will not give' (Johnson 2003). It is precisely because it is attempting to change cultures in many HEIs that effective disability education constitutes such a major challenge.

Acknowledgements

Sincere thanks to colleagues for constructive feedback after attending sessions and to postgraduate students, Mary Cullen and Rob Peace, for permission to use ideas taken from their writing.

References and further reading

Callahan, J. (1998) *Will the Real John Callahan Please Stand Up?* New York: William Morrow and Co.

Craft, A. (2000) *Continuing Professional Development: A Practical Guide for Teachers and Schools.* 2nd edn. London: RoutledgeFalmer.

Equality Challenge Unit (ECU) (2004) *Promoting Equality: The Public Sector Duty on Disability: Suggested First Steps for HEI.* London: ECU.

French, S. (1992) 'Simulation exercises in disability awareness training', *Disability and Society*, 7: 257–266.

Gosen, J. and Washbush, J. (2004) 'A review of scholarship on assessing experiential learning effectiveness', *Simulation and Gaming*, 35(2): 270–293.

Higher Education Funding Council for England (HECE) (1999) *Guidance on Base Level Provision for Disabled Students in Higher Education Institutions*. Bristol: HEFCE.

Hurst, A. (2005) 'Inclusive learning in higher education', in P. Hartley, A. Woods and M. Pill (eds) *Enhancing Teaching in Higher Education*. Abingdon: Routledge.

Johnson, M. (2003) *Make Them Go Away: Clint Eastwood, Christopher Reeve and the Case Against Disability Rights*. Louisville, KY: The Avocado Press.

Mackay, N. (2001) 'Dyslexia-friendly schools', in L. Peer and G. Reid (eds) *Successful Inclusion in the Secondary School*. London: David Fulton.

Neanon, C. (2002) *How to Identify and Support Children with Dyslexia in the Primary School*. Cambridge: Learning Development Aids (LDA).

Oliver, M. (1990) *The Politics of Disablement*. London: Macmillan.

Scottish Higher Education Funding Council (SHEFC) (2000) *Teachability: Creating an Accessible Curriculum for Students with Disabilities*. Edinburgh: SHEFC.

South West Academic Network for Disability Support (SWANDS) (2002) *SENDA Compliance in Higher Education : An Audit and Guidance Tool for Accessible Practice within the Framework of Teaching and Learning*. Plymouth: University of Plymouth.

Resources

Disability Rights Commission *Talk* video. Available at: www.drc-gb.org.uk (accessed 07/05).

Learning and Skills Council *Making the Case*, DVD and CD. Available via Skill at http://www.skill.org.uk (accessed 07/05).

National Disability Team (NDT) checklists. Available at: http://www.natdisteam.ac.uk/resources_briefings_ndtchecklists.html (accessed 07/05).

Chapter 14

Supporting disabled students on placement

Benedict Fell and Jane Wray

Introduction

Students on a wide variety of courses across the UK undertake placements as part of their learning and the benefits of doing so are considerable. In professional training courses such as social work, nursing, medicine and teaching, placements are a mandatory component of courses and are inextricably linked to successful completion and the subsequent award of 'professional status'. For disabled students, adjustments may need to be made so that they can demonstrate their competence and gain maximum benefit from the placement opportunity.

In this chapter, we both consider the legislative drivers that particularly apply in the UK for increasing equality of opportunity for disabled people, the benefits of placements and give some practical advice on how disabled students can be supported on placement. Our experience suggests that successful placement outcomes for disabled students can be enhanced by effective planning, communication and negotiation between the involved parties. We use the illustrative example of Hannah throughout as a means of highlighting the support in action. Hannah is a fictitious name and is loosely based on a case that we have come across during our work supporting disabled students about to go on, and during, their placement. We introduce Hannah below before looking at how support for her placement was arranged and put in place later in the chapter.

Box 14.1 Hannah Jackson, 2nd year BA Youth and Community Studies

Hannah was a second-year Youth and Community Studies student with mental health difficulties. She had experienced agoraphobia and acute anxiety for a number of years which she had managed well in the three years preceding her arrival at university. When she became particularly worried or stressed she would experience anxiety attacks and this affected her blood pressure. While attending university a range of support had been put in place, and with the exception of one occasion when she had needed to leave a lecture, she had successfully completed her first semester. She was about to undergo her first placement with a children's centre. Like most students, she was particularly worried about how she would manage with this new and demanding experience.

The value of placement learning

The importance of 'learning by doing' has been re-iterated at different stages within higher education. The Dearing Report (1997) was commissioned to look at the future of higher education in the UK. This report, *Higher Education in the Learning Society*, noted:

> All the evidence that we have reviewed endorses the value of some exposure of the student to the wider world as part of a programme of study. This may be achieved through work experience, involvement in student union activities, or work in community or voluntary settings.
>
> (Sect 9.26, p. 135)

More recently, a government White Paper, *The Future of Higher Education* (DfES 2003), has fuelled the drive for more work-based learning: 'We believe that the economy needs more work-focused degrees – those, like our new foundation degrees, that offer, specific, job-related skills' (Section 5.9). It is clear, therefore, that the government in the UK increasingly recognises the value of placement learning. 'Work-focused', 'work-based', 'work-linked', 'work-experience', 'work-related' are often terms that are used interchangeably in the UK context. Seagreaves *et al.* (1996, cited in Lewis 2003) suggested that linking learning to the requirements of people's jobs has three strands:

1 *Learning for work* – this strand is linked directly to the acquirement of employability skills within the curriculum.
2 *Learning at work* – this strand relates to an individual's activities undertaken at work.
3 *Learning through work* – this strand relates to the recognition and accreditation of learning achieved in the workplace.

Without seeking a conclusive definition of 'work-based learning', it is clear that it is a period of time encompassing activities based on the work undertaken within the context of that workplace. 'Placements', periods where a student effectively 'does the job' are the primary vehicle through which this learning takes place. Placements vary in type and name including:

- work experience at secondary school;
- field trips;
- years abroad;
- Modern Apprenticeships;
- Entry to Employment (E2E);
- voluntary work;
- vacation placements;
- course-related projects at an employer's premises;
- work shadowing;
- internships.

(Skill 2003)

Fell and Kuit noted that placements 'have a long history in higher education, particularly in the former polytechnics where an 'industrial year' was an integral part of a sandwich degree' (2003: 214). They also cite Davies who observed that 'the benefits of supervised work experience are unique, identifiable and not achievable by other means' (1990, cited in Fell and Kuit 2003: 216).

Placements vary in length and setting and may be paid or unpaid. A particular advantage of evaluating placement learning is that many of the issues faced by disabled students in higher education are magnified in this form of teaching and learning (Healey *et al.* 2001). Burgstahler noted the positive outcomes of place-ment learning for disabled students:

> Attitudinal barriers and accommodation issues are compounded by the fact that college graduates with disabilities often have had few previous work experiences. Participating in work-based learning experiences has been recog-nised as a contributor to positive employment outcomes for all students, including those with disabilities.
>
> (2001: 3)

The value of work experience and placements in facilitating access to the employment of disabled students has been identified by Skill (2003). Skill: National Bureau for Students with Disabilities is a UK charity that promotes opportunities for disabled people in learning and employment. Its guide, *Into Work Experience: Positive Experiences of Disabled People* (2003), lists a number of opportunities inherent in placement learning. It suggests placements can do the following:

- improve and strengthen your skills and knowledge;
- develop interpersonal skills;
- teach 'employability' skills;
- find out how your disability affects you;
- demonstrate to employers what you, as a disabled person, can do and so encourage them to be more pro-active about employing disabled people;

- explore career options by 'trying out' different areas of work;
- gain practical experience of securing a job;
- add aspects of your experience to your CV;
- maybe earn some money.

(ibid.: 5–6)

Burghstahler also identified the advantages for employers:

> For employers, providing work-based learning opportunities to students allows them to help prepare workers for the next generation and also test the job skills of potential future employees. When a participant has a disability, employers also gain practice in working with an individual to create a work environment that maximises productivity.

(2001: 3)

An additional benefit is that a work placement can often allow disabled students to 'test out' the world of work to examine the impact of their impairment within particular employment settings and discover what adjustments would be required when they enter that environment as employees.

Legislative drivers

The UK education sector has witnessed a wide range of legal imperatives that have a bearing on disabled students undertaking placements. The Quality Assurance Agency (QAA) has responsibility to safeguard the public in setting standards for higher education qualifications and continue the management of quality within HEIs (www.qaa.ac.uk). It has produced two documents relevant to an examination of the learning of disabled students on placements. Its *Code of Practice for the Assurance of Academic Quality and Standards in Higher Education – Section 3: Students with Disabilities* (QAA 1999), contains 24 principles ('precepts'): '11. Institutions should ensure that, wherever possible, disabled students have access to academic and vocational placements including field trips and study abroad.'

The QAA's (2001) *Code of Practice for the Assurance of Academic Quality and Standards in Higher Education. Section 9: Placement Learning* also contains principles of good practice in arranging placements. However, although this code does not address disabled students *per se*, it does call for institutions to check a provider's ability to support students: 'The criteria to be used when approving placements should address placement providers' ability to support students on placement.'

Under Part 4 of the Disability Discrimination Act 1995 (as amended by the Special Educational Need and Disability Act 2001), placements fall under the definition of 'student services', defined as 'any services that an institution provides or offers to provide wholly or mainly for students attending or undertaking courses' (DRC 2002: Section 3.11). HEIs have a responsibility not to discriminate against students. This discrimination can occur in two ways:

1   When a responsible body treats a disabled person less favourably for a reason relating to their disability than it would treat a non-disabled person.

Example 1

A HEI has good relations with an internationally known locally-based business. The Business School at the HEI sends students there. However, placements are at a premium and the placement provider only takes one student per year. Two students have registered a particular interest in going to this business for their placement as they specialise in an area that holds both of their interest. One student has dyslexia and the other is non-disabled. The Business School decides to send the non-disabled student as it feels this student will 'cope' better and might reflect better on the institution. This is likely to be unlawful. (This example is fictitious and does not refer to actual events.)

---

2   When it fails to make a reasonable adjustment when a disabled student is placed, or is likely to be placed, at a substantial disadvantage in comparison with a non-disabled person.

Example 2

A disabled student with dyslexia is placed with a company. The firm have not yet introduced computers or other modern technology into its office. The student asks that he be allowed to bring his laptop into the office as it has specialist software that he needs. This request is denied as it is felt that it would cause resentment among the permanent staff members. This is likely to be unlawful. (This example is fictitious and does not refer to actual events.)

Prior to October 2004, the locus for provision of learning and duty to avoid discrimination was firmly located within the HEI. However, new amendments to Part 2 of the Disability Discrimination Act (DDA) 1995 have subsequently given placement providers new responsibilities. The Disability Rights Commission (DRC) was set up as an independent body to work towards equality for all disabled people in the UK. They have recently published a document *Code of Practice: Employment and Occupation* (2004) that makes explicit the responsibility placed on placement providers:

The Act says that it is unlawful for a 'placement provider' to discriminate against a disabled person who is seeking or undertaking a work placement:

- in the arrangements he makes for determining who should be offered a work placement
- in the terms on which he affords him access to any work placement or any facilities concerned with such placement
- by refusing or deliberately omitting to afford him such access
- by terminating his placement
- by subjecting him to any detriment during the placement.

(DRC 2004: Section 9.42)

The Code also goes on to stress the importance of HEIs and placement providers working together:

It would be reasonable to expect the sending organisation and the placement provider to co-operate to ensure that appropriate adjustments are identified and made. It is good practice for a placement provider to ask a disabled person about reasonable adjustments before the placement begins, and to allow him to visit the workplace in advance to see how his needs can be addressed. Once a particular adjustment has been identified, it would be reasonable for the sending organisation and the placement provider to discuss its implementation in the light of their respective obligations under the Act.

(DRC 2004: Section 9.50)

It can be argued that the twin drivers to increase opportunities for work-based learning and the widening participation initiatives in higher education will inevitably have an impact on disabled students studying for further and higher education qualifications.

The Professional Education and Disability Support Project (PEdDS): implementing a framework, the social work model

The PEdDS Project (www.hull.ac.uk/pedds), funded as part of the Higher Education Funding Council for England's disability funding programme (HEFCE 2002), aimed to explore the experiences and opinions of disabled social work students and support staff regarding the barriers and opportunities for placement learning (see Wray *et al.* 2005a). Social work was seen as an appropriate discipline to focus the study, given its long association with anti-oppressive and inclusive philosophy. One hundred semi-structured interviews were undertaken with disabled social work students (n = 50) and support staff comprising disability support staff (n = 12), practice assessors/teachers (n = 25) and placement coordinators in HEIs (n = 13). From the research undertaken, the following key themes were identified as essential for effective support and have influenced the construction of a working framework for the support of disabled students on placement, irrespective of study programme:

- a shared responsibility for support between HEI, student, disability support service and placement agency;
- the need for adequate pre-placement planning;
- reasonable adjustments to be negotiated and put in place prior to the placement commencing;
- a need for clarity about disclosure and, in particular, whether a disclosure to the programme constitutes a disclosure to the placement agency;
- communication and negotiation to be enhanced between all parties at all stages, including pre-enrolment;
- the contribution that disabled students can make to placement agencies (and the profession) needs to and should be valued.

As can be seen from the above list, none of the issues are particularly restricted to social work and their consideration will constitute good practice in most placement-based disciplines. These messages were refined to develop a framework of support for disabled social work students at the University of Hull. Although each discipline and the requirements of the programme and qualifications body will inevitably differ (especially in their impact on a disabled student), the framework presented is, we believe, transferable across different disciplines. (More detailed recommendations for placement support can be found in Wray *et al.* 2005b.)

The framework – key stages in placement support for disabled students

The framework outlines the responsibilities and lines of communication at different stages during the student's placement.

Stage 1

- Consideration of a student's needs while on placement should form part of the initial assessment of need.
- Prior to the assessment of need taking place, the disability service will discus with the student issues relating to general practice learning and support.
- The disability service will discuss the benefits and potential disadvantages of disclosure, what information will be disclosed and to whom, and establish the student's consent to this information being passed.

Stage 2

- The department confirms the placement and dates for the student.
- Disability services then discuss the assessment of need (Access Report) with the student and what reasonable adjustments might be appropriate.
- These reasonable adjustments are communicated to the department.

- The department checks with its accreditation body (for example, the GSCC – General Social Care Council) to ensure that academic standards and/or professional issues will not be compromised. Qualifications bodies, such as the GSCC, have to set competence standards which are objectively justifiable and adjustments should be made to these standards wherever possible (Skill 2004).

Stage 3

- The department and the student communicate provisional reasonable adjustments with the placement provider agency and practice assessor/teacher and these are negotiated for the duration of the placement.
- Any resource implications are identified and, if necessary, referred back to the disability service. Negotiation will then take place about who is responsible for providing and funding adjustments, bearing in mind the joint responsibility enshrined in the *Disability Discrimination Act 1995 Code of Practice: Employment and Occupation* (DRC 2004).
- During this discussion, any health and safety issues are discussed openly.
- The practice assessor/teacher identifies any additional training and/or support needed and informs the line manager/team of outcomes.
- The department confirms reasonable adjustments and these are written into the practice learning agreement which includes:
  - key contacts for disability services, placement co-ordinator and identified tutor responsible for co-ordinating disability issues in the department;
  - training/support for practice assessor/teacher given by department and disability service where possible;
  - relevant page copied to disability services for information.

Stage 4

- Placement provider implements reasonable adjustments.
- The department reviews reasonable adjustments within a specified timescale in placement with practice assessor/teacher and the student.
- The practice assessor/teacher reviews reasonable adjustments with their placement team and line manager.
- The practice assessor/teacher informs department if more support is needed or if difficulties arise.
- The student informs the practice assessor/teacher if more support is needed or if difficulties arise.
- The department discusses support/difficulties with practice assessor/teacher – issues are referred back to disability services if further advice is needed.
- Disability service contacts student if advocacy/support is needed.

Box 14.2 Putting PEdDS into practice: how reasonable adjustments were made for Hannah

Hannah met with the Placement Support Adviser at the university. Together, they identified that Hannah had a number of different learning support needs in practice. She felt that she became very tense in new and/or unusual situations and that this might result in anxiety attacks. She was aware that she would have to meet people she didn't know and would have to work within new environments. She did not want to be seen as 'not able to cope' and wanted to perform well in practice. She was especially concerned that she might experience an anxiety attack when she was with children. She could recognise that an attack was coming on and usually found that going for a walk and taking ten minutes 'time out' was usually sufficient for her to manage her anxiety. Stress often exacerbated her condition and she needed to take regular breaks throughout the day to prevent this building up. Hannah and the Placement Support Adviser discussed the following possible adjustments to enable her to successfully complete her learning outcomes.

A pre-placement visit enabled Hannah to familiarise herself with the physical environment and be introduced to key members of staff including her practice assessor/teacher. A member of disability support staff also came on this visit to provide additional support to Hannah to negotiate her adjustments.

In consultation with Hannah's practice teacher, a system was set up for Hannah to have accompanied first visits to a community centre with a gradual reduction in support over time to allow her to complete visits independently as the placement progressed.

Hannah was given the opportunity to take regular breaks throughout the day in agreement with her practice assessor/teacher and in accordance with the schedule of activities/workload asked of her (e.g. coffee break/lunch).

Adjustments were agreed to be reviewed at the end of the third week of the placement by the practice assessor/teacher and Hannah – the member of disability support staff who attended initially also offered to be involved in this process.

Hannah took responsibility for communicating any needs and concerns to her practice assessor/teacher. However, it was also agreed that it might be necessary for support arrangements to be adjusted slightly to meet the requirements of the placement learning experience (for example, a break might not be possible as scheduled if something urgent needed attending to with one of her cases).

All of the above adjustments were agreed between the department and the placement to ensure that they did not compromise any academic/ professional standards.

Conclusion

Placements are a vital tool of learning for all students and access to them should be made as easy as possible. PEdDS research (Wray *et al.* 2005a) has shown that despite significant progress being made and goodwill engendered to enable disabled students to participate in higher education, there is still room for improvement. The framework we have presented shows how support can be established and planned in advance in a series of practical steps. As highlighted by the example of Hannah, simple yet effective communication and negotiation can enable disabled students to gain maximum benefit from a placement opportunity. As we have recommended elsewhere (Wray *et al.* 2005b), it is important that departments and agencies are planning ahead and anticipating the needs of disabled students before they go on placement. Indeed, one way to do this might be to have a priority system for placing disabled students before their non-disabled peers. Advance planning can prevent a possible 'crisis' for the student and the placement. In assessing the cost of making adjustments, the cost of failing to make adjustments for that student must also be addressed. Adjustments need not mean huge financial outlays. Employment research has shown that almost half of all adjustments cost less than £50 (DfEE 1998). Many adjustments have no cost implication at all. For example, students on placement who participated in the PEdDS study noted the following adjustments as being beneficial to them during their placement:

- lowering shelf heights in a placement office for students with 'reach' difficulties;
- having an office on the ground floor of the placement building so stairs do not have to be negotiated for students with mobility requirements;
- taking a laptop into the placement and having the necessary paperwork used on the placement on a proforma so that they can be typed and printed off;
- allowing a student, for example, with diabetes, to take regular breaks throughout the day to eat.

As more courses and employers recognise the value of placement learning, it is clear that appropriate support for disabled students will become a factor for departments and HEIs sending students on placement. We have presented the steps taken within our own HEI to address this issue and believe that they have wider applicability across the sector, regardless of the discipline involved. Disabled students deserve equality of opportunity – it is up to the higher education sector as a whole to implement plans to ensure disabled students are successfully included in the placement learning experience. The raft of legislation imposing responsibilities on education and placement providers means that failure to do so is no longer an option.

References and further reading

Burgstahler, S. (2001) 'Work-based learning and students with disabilities: one step toward high-skill, high-pay careers', *American Rehabilitation*, 26(1): 2–8.

Dearing, R. (1997) *Higher Education in the Learning Society: Report of the National Committee of Inquiry into Higher Education*. London: HMSO.

Department for Education and Employment (1998) *Research Brief No.56: Integrating Disabled Employees*. London: DfEE.

Department for Education and Skills (2003) The Future of Higher Education. London: DfES. Available at: http://www.dfes.gov.uk/hegateway (accessed 07/05).

Disability Rights Commission (2002) *Disability Discrimination Act 1995 Part 4: Code of Practice for Providers of Post-16 Education and Related Services*. Norwich: The Stationery Office. Available at: http://www.drc.gov.uk/thelaw/practice.asp (accessed 07/05).

Disability Rights Commission (2004) *Disability Discrimination Act 1995 Code of Practice: Employment and Occupation*. Norwich: The Stationery Office. Available at: http://www.drc.gov.uk/thelaw/practice.asp (accessed 07/05).

Fell, A. and Kuit, J. A. (2003) 'Placement learning and the Code of Practice', *Active Learning in Higher Education*, 4(3): 214–225.

French, D. (2002) *Mapping Resources Related to the Teaching and Learning of Disabled Students*. Bristol: HEFCE.

Healey, M., Jenkins, A., Leach, J. and Roberts, C. (2001) *Issues in Providing Learning Support for Disabled Students Undertaking Fieldwork and Related Activities*. Gloucester: The Geography Discipline Network. Available at: http://www2.glos.ac.uk/gdn/disabil/overview/index.htm (accessed 07/05).

Higher Education Funding Council for England (HEFCE) (2002) *02/21 Improving Provision for Disabled Students: HEFCE Strategy and Invitation to Bid for Funds 2003/05*. Bristol: HEFCE. Available at: http://www.hefce.ac.uk/pubs/hefce/2002/02%5F21.htm (accessed 07/05).

Lewis, D. (2003) *Towards a University of Hull Work-Related Learning Strategy*. Hull: University of Hull.

Quality Assurance Agency (1999) *Code of Practice for the Assurance of Academic Quality and Standards in Higher Education. Section 3: Students with Disabilities*. Gloucester: QAA. Available at: http://www.qaa.ac.uk/public/COP/COPswd/contents.htm (accessed 07/05).

Quality Assurance Agency (2001) *Code of Practice for the Assurance of Academic Quality and Standards in Higher Education. Section 9: Placement Learning*. Gloucester: QAA. Available at: http://www.qaa.ac.uk/public/Cop/COPplacementFinal/contents.htm (accessed 07/05).

Skill: National Bureau of Students with Disabilities (2003) *Into Work Experience: Positive Experiences of Disabled People*. London: Skill.

Skill: National Bureau of Students with Disabilities (2004) *A Guide to the Disability Discrimination Act 1995: For Institutions of Further and Higher Education.* London: Skill.

Wray, J., Fell, B., Stanley, N., Manthorpe, J. and Coyne, E. (2005a) *The PEdDS Project: Disabled Social Work Students and Placements.* Hull: The University of Hull. Available at: http://www.hull.ac.uk/pedds (accessed 07/05).

Wray, J., Fell, B., Stanley, N., Manthorpe, J. and Coyne, E. (2005b) *PEdDS Best Practice Guide: Disabled Social Work Students and Placements.* Hull: The University of Hull. Available at: http://www.hull.ac.uk/pedds (accessed 07/05).

Chapter 15

Equal to the task

Disability issues in postgraduate research study

Val Farrar

In theory research study with a physical-mobility impairment should be easier than undergraduate study . . . However, and it's a big however, in practice it is much, much harder. Research study is a lonely, isolating and anxious experience at the best of times. Doing it with an impairment multiplies those factors.
(PhD student)

Premia is a three-year national project based at the University of Newcastle upon Tyne and funded by the Higher Education Funding Council of England (HEFCE) to improve provision for disabled postgraduate research students (http://www. premia.ac.uk). To place the project in context, the proportion of disabled students at undergraduate level has been steadily rising in the past five years and in the UK that growth is beginning to be reflected in the numbers of disabled students entering research education. There is now less than 1 per cent difference (Figure 15.1).

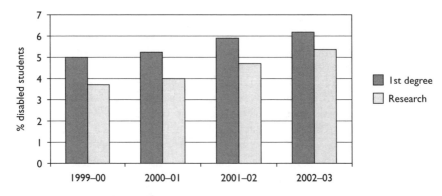

Figure 15.1 Percentage of disabled UK first-year students by level of study

Source: HESA Student Record
Note: Reproduced by permission of the Higher Education Statistics Agency Ltd.

There has been little questioning in the past about whether the research community is accessible to all. It is easy to make the assumption that a disabled student who has made it through to doctoral study will come fully equipped with the confidence, learning management strategies and adaptive technology acquired through previous study to tackle the next stage of education. From that perspective, it may appear unnecessary and possibly detrimental to the independence of a research student to make any adjustments to existing policies and practice from admissions and induction to completion of thesis, viva and career planning.

The Premia team worked with disabled research students to identify the issues and to design online resources available nationally to staff and students to address those issues. We sent questionnaires and talked with disabled researchers from a wide range of universities higher education institutions and academic disciplines about their experiences from pre-entry through to transition to employment. What all of them said was that the issues are different and that their previous education had not necessarily prepared them for the new set of coping strategies they would need.

In this chapter we will examine the research environment from the perspective of disabled students and explore some of the strategies which might be employed to create parity of experience. Why is the research experience different? When do issues arise? What are the key issues? What issues do institutions and their staff need to consider?

Why is the research experience different?

Roles

We started by mapping the student life cycle and the personnel who intervene at key points. The interventions are made by different people – graduate school administrators, those giving telephone advice to prospective applicants, principal investigators, research managers and research supervisors, dedicated careers advisers, external examiners for thesis and viva. Many of these staff are involved in a way that is different from any involvement they may have with undergraduates. The context of research education redefines relationships and activities. The research supervisor has a very different role from a personal tutor or lecturer. The external examiner at a viva relates to the candidate differently from the assessor of course work or internal examination. The selector of a doctoral student is interacting during an interview at another level from the undergraduate admissions tutor analysing the personal statement of a potential student. The personnel, and the nature of their involvement with students, are different.

When do the issues arise?

Disabled research students identified barriers which had been inadvertently erected at pre-entry points through to assessment and transition to employment. Some also spoke very honestly about their perception of self and the attitude of others:

I worry about it more so now. Then I didn't have this extra problem and I was extremely coherent and the only thing that worried me was the wheel-chair. But now I feel that people see someone sitting in a wheelchair and I have this slurred speech. And these people think to themselves, 'Well, this person can't be anything.' It's not written across my head – Bachelor of Science and Master of Philosophy. It's a chair and someone who speaks with an impediment.

(Research student)

Disclosure can be more difficult at this level of study. The stakes are higher, the personal investment of time, energy and intellect is vast and the expectations of student and academic staff can be huge:

I feel that asking for extra help, time, or simply recognition of the fact that I am not the same as a healthy student and really could do with a little more help and understanding is asking too much. I don't want to annoy my tutors or get on the wrong side of them by admitting that I am struggling with anything.

(Research student who has ME (Myalgic Encephalopathy))

What are the issues?

Access to information

The complexity of postgraduate qualifications, the routes into them, the timing of applications and funding mechanisms can create confusion for all potential research applicants. Disabled graduates have the same need for clear, unambiguous information but additionally they want timely, concise and accessible information about funding of support requirements and methods of applying for that funding.

Funding of support requirements

There are a range of funding sources for research study and for disability-related support. Some disabled students may find that the funding source available to them is not sufficient to meet their support requirements, or that an assessment of their requirements cannot take place before they start and so support is not in place at the outset. A HEFCE report (2005) identifies differences in financial support as having a significant impact on the rate of PhD completion. Yet routinely some disabled research students are unable to access essential support at the beginning of their course to participate fully in induction, early research skills training and sometimes their own research programme.

Impact of research

Concentration

All research students need to be independent learners able with the ability to manage a challenging workload. Self-reliance, the ability to remain intellectually committed and creative over an extended period are vital ingredients. The student requires high levels of energy and concentration to reach their goal. Being reliant almost entirely on one's own resources can be formidable for some disabled students:

> One of the challenges with the MA (by research) is that I tend not to have something else to change over to. This has meant that I am not able to take a break from planning and analysing my material . . . I get tired faster and my overall working speed is significantly slower.
>
> (Research student who has ME)

Being an independent traveller within the research community presents particular challenges for those whose impairment creates organisational difficulties. However, we would not expect to set off on a journey to a new destination without a map.

Planning and organisation

> I was aware of the flexibility of the course and was excited by the freedom it allowed me to explore my areas of interest. However, in light of my organisational difficulties, I found it problematical to know whether the way I was approaching the course was correct or realistic and was inclined to believe I was doing it wrong. This is possibly an issue of lack of academic confidence due in part to dyslexia which could have been easily removed by some form of reassurance from my tutor that I was achieving the goals set.
>
> (Research student with moderate dyslexia)

To provide a compass or a map to new research students does not mean they cannot complete the journey independently. Some students described highly inventive solutions they and their supervisors had designed to plan the research, often using other media and visual maps. It is clear that when partnerships are formed between student and supervisor, there is less dependence, greater understanding and appreciation of alternative approaches to learning and more confident, original work.

Reading

The sheer volume of reading which research demands can pose problems, particularly for dyslexic students, but also for students who use adaptive software or whose impairment means that they are unable to sit for long periods in one position:

> It took a while for my supervisor to realise just how slowly I could read. This is accentuated by the subject-specific notation which includes a significant number of sub- and super-scripts, symbols etc. These are both difficult to read, even using access technology, and completely impossible for an OCR (scan and read back) system, my preferred method of reading, to handle. Diagrams were also difficult to access, as these were often three-dimensional plots which took a good deal of time to study for the important detailed information that they include.
>
> (Research student who is blind)

Dyslexic students spoke of the difficulties in browsing and selecting relevant data, and others' assumptions about the speed at which all could read and process the printed word. They also talked about their fear that, in the highly literate research community, reading difficulties would be viewed as a deficit and a reflection of intelligence. Lateral thinking, the ability to see the big picture and make links between disparate concepts are valued within research. They are also qualities that dyslexic students have to offer. One research student talked about being 'free of the shackles of literacy'. Understanding of the students' issues with reading can lead supervisors to enable the student to prioritise reading, identify key texts, maximise their use of adaptive software and release their other gifts within their research.

The language of research

The language of research is the currency we use to exchange ideas and construct theory with colleagues and students. It is integral to the research process. Many students find difficulty in the acquisition and confident usage of this accepted language. Ownership of the terminology seems to be a key to crossing the threshold of, and being welcomed into, the research community. Without the word, the concept is not understood. But new students may not yet know the concept, so the word cannot be known.

That paradox exists for many learners. If disability is added to the equation, then the exchange of complex terminology can be a real hindrance to understanding, to the growth of an equal academic partnership between research supervisors and disabled students and to clear, unambiguous communication between teacher and learner. For research students with dyslexia and D/deaf students, the terminology of research can present a real barrier to progress. Unfamiliar words, or words which have not been specifically introduced to the student, cannot be lip-read:

> Discussions with my supervisor have been difficult because of the huge amount of technical and superior language he uses. This is probably a problem

for any PhD student who is starting work in a new field and doesn't understand all the technical terms, but for a deaf student with a more limited vocabulary, it can be a huge barrier to their understanding of the project.

(Deaf research student)

There is a need to find ways of making research language more accessible and attainable. General and subject glossaries with plain English definitions are one tool for creating a linguistic framework within which the student can be at ease. Tutorials with a focus on general research terms and subject-specific language and in the early phase of the research cycle can accelerate learning and dismantle language barriers. We need to check out with students that they understand terms we are using and make it clear that they can ask us with confidence to explain what we mean.

Extended writing

In the end, the primary method of assessment will be the thesis. All research students need to be able to construct a complex document, expressing ideas and themes with clarity, insight and originality. Yet for some students this is a challenge that has potential pitfalls. For many pre-lingual deaf students (those born deaf) British Sign Language is their first language and they may have linguistic difficulties, most obviously shown in their written English. BSL is a visual language and one with its own grammar and syntax that is very different to spoken English. (For further discussion, see Chapter 10 by Mole and Peacock.) Dyslexic students may be able to use assistive software to aid their written work. As one dyslexic doctoral student said, 'The computer is my wheelchair.' But all these issues mean that some students with language problems need deep wells from which to draw additional energy, time and resourcefulness.

Helping students to plan their thesis, assisting them to work to realistic deadlines based on an understanding of what tasks are difficult for them and what will demand additional time, breaking the whole into manageable chunks become part of the role of research supervisors. The thesis is a formidable task for all research students but can be made achievable for those with additional issues through judicious support:

Having accepted mentally that this is a good student, but an unconventional one, then the rest seems to be, 'Right, how do we get through this and around this and enable him to achieve his potential?'

(Research supervisor)

The whole research environment

In his (2001) book *Demystifying Postgraduate Research*, Jonathan Grix describes the stages of research and says that early in the process:

> None of the reflection and analysis . . . takes place in a vacuum with you hunched over a pile of books: rather there is a need for exposure and exchange of ideas not only with your supervisor but also with your peers and friends.

The exchange of ideas, methods and knowledge in informal settings like the base room for a research team, the coffee lounge and the bar is an accepted and vital element of the research culture. Several disabled students found themselves excluded from this academic network by physical barriers: a blind student became distanced from other researchers because of a lack of funding for adaptive equipment when he started; a deaf student could not join in the discussions over coffee because lip reading was impossible sitting around a long rectangular table; a student with mental health difficulties whose office was on a different floor from the rest of the team found social interaction increasingly difficult. Access to the whole research environment is essential for all students if they are to benefit from the motivation, stimulation and excitement of the research community. That whole curriculum involves social as well as formal learning opportunities:

> A social event, welcoming new postgraduates to the department, was held a couple of weeks into term in the evening. As this was late Autumn, the dark nights were already well upon us and my condition includes night blindness.
>
> (Research student who is blind)

It is possible to move lectures to accessible venues. But we sometimes omit to think through the impact on disabled students' learning when planning induction events and organising space for research teams.

Access to conferences

A component of the research experience is attendance at national and international conferences. While some disabled students have access to support, and funding for that support, to attend and give papers at conferences, others struggle with the sheer logistics of attendance. A full-time student who had just attended their first conference in the third year of their research said:

> While my fellow postgraduates write a paper and jump on a train or aeroplane, I have to arrange funding for and find a non-medical helper willing to come; find and book accessible, often expensive, accommodation; find and arrange an accessible way to get there and ensure that the conference itself will be accessible. Underlying all that is an increasing and rising feeling of dread. At any point something could step in my way and the efforts of the previous weeks could pour themselves down the drain.
>
> (Research student with mobility impairment)

The research supervisor, disability adviser and/or learning support tutor can provide assistance in negotiating and planning conference attendance. Like much of the suggested support, it needs to be in partnership with the student: a fair distribution of the additional tasks which arise for a disabled student. If a student's creative energies are used up by organising support, those are energies which would be better invested in their research.

Access to fieldwork

In supervision, planning of research methods will be a major feature. Supervisors will need to check out with some disabled research students what will be difficult and what is achievable:

> For months I tried to execute a schedule of fieldwork which I repeatedly argued was not feasible . . . It was a very difficult time and has deeply affected my relationship with people who should be my mentors and guides.
>
> (Research student with mobility impairment)

To avoid wasted resources and relationships, it is a good idea to take a cue from the students. They are the people who understand fully the boundaries and nature of their impairment. What they may need, however, is help to identify the new emphases and activities integral to research programmes. Early meetings with students will address research methods and the student can be encouraged to raise any disability issues within that context. As a research supervisor commented about one of their doctoral students, 'We need him to . . . feel that he has the right to say, "Actually I wouldn't find that easy."'

Anticipating the issues

One of the themes which links many of the students' responses is early identi-fication by staff of the issues and then relevant action or advocacy:

> As I continue on this postgraduate research journey, it is becoming clearer and clearer just how competitive the academic arena is. There is a pressure to prove that you are efficient, capable and independent. This doesn't sit easily with being a disabled researcher. Although . . . I am more than capable at the academic and teaching part, I do need support and if that isn't in place, I am not efficient. I am made incapable . . . There is a very tacit pressure not to admit this. To stay strong. To put on a mask and pretend that all is well. It's a big issue for me that I have to negotiate on a daily basis. I think supervisors can play a very important part in reducing these effects by keeping their students informed of everything and being good at pastoral support.
>
> (Research student with mobility impairment)

Students spoke about times when anticipatory action or advocacy would have been or had been effective: taking notes for supervisory sessions when the student would find that difficult; making an introductory phone call to an academic contact on behalf of a student with emotional difficulties; arranging furniture in advance of a team meeting where a deaf student who lip reads is going to be attending; supporting an application for accommodation with Internet connection when the student has a mobility impairment. Sometimes there is hesitancy about intervening when the whole research ethos is about the growth of intellectual independence. However, if a disabled research student can be assisted to access that independence by timely support, advice, guidance or information, then it is an enabling intervention, not a disabling action.

Doctoral student as teacher

One element of the research experience is teaching. But teaching can be a remote possibility for some students. Classes may be held in inaccessible rooms; deaf students who lip read may have to contend with questions which they cannot interpret because of inadequate lighting; deaf students may be expected to work in seminars where their students do not know how to work with a BSL/English interpreter; support may be essential to a student with manual dexterity difficulties in managing visual aids; blind students may need coaching in handling communications and equipment; dyslexic students will have to develop strategies for assessing students' work. Disabled researchers talked about the coping mechanisms they have honed to manage their teaching roles. But not all will be able to circumvent difficult situations:

> Teaching is difficult. I love taking seminars but I dread having to write something up for the students. How could they respect me as a teacher if they see that I cannot write down key words and concepts?
>
> (Research student with dyslexia)

> If I was to try and teach undergraduates here, I think I would struggle. I have taken the CCTV into a seminar and it's OK except I've got a fairly massive time delay so the students would be sitting for longer than they would expect to for me to find out what I'm going to say.
>
> (Research student who is blind)

Usually postgraduate students are offered opportunities to develop their presentation and teaching skills. Those who are responsible for generic skills development need to make their sessions inclusive; in a non-threatening way they can encourage students to identify any potential problems in the teaching situation and work with them to find inventive measures to address the issues.

Assessment

The most common way of assessing research students' work is by thesis or dissertation and then an oral defence of their work, known in the UK as a viva. External examiners are at the heart of this process and the viva will usually be the first occasion that the student and examiner meet. The viva presents the unique opportunity to talk in detail, and at length, about their research, methodology, literature review and findings. For students with written language difficulties it may be viewed as a chance to excel in their preferred medium. For others it is a formidable obstacle: a student with short-term memory difficulties; a Deaf student working through a BSL/English interpreter; a deaf student who lip reads; a blind student who cannot pick up visual clues; a student with a speech impairment.

  The key factors to the success of a viva for these students are their own preparation and the awareness of the examiners of the student's disability-related issues. Like all students, a disabled candidate needs to be able to enter the viva with all the strategies and confidence in place to succeed. External examiners and those who organise the viva need to be able confidently to make reasonable adjustments so that the process is inclusive and accessible.

Institutional considerations

What feedback do we have from disabled research students on their experience of the processes and practices? Do we take serious account of that feedback, both formal and informal, when reviewing provision and practice? Are we willing to tackle the issues they raise or do we become defensive and erect our own barriers to change? Are we reactive to crises rather than reflective in our practice? Is individual student need at the centre of what we do? Do administrative procedures reflect the needs of a diverse student population? Are we ever inclined to see reasonable adjustments to the research environment as an erosion of academic standards? Is our own research degree experience revisited in our dealings with research students – do we view them as academic apprentices who must go through what we endured to gain access to academia? In the end, how far are we willing to go as institutions and research organisations in the adjustments to the issues raised by disabled research students?

Addressing the issues

Awareness of disability issues and good practice amongst those who promote, interview, inform, induct, support, supervise and assess disabled research students will go a long way to enabling students to tackle more tangible barriers:

> Everyone within the department with whom I have contact has been very welcoming, accepting and respectful, and for the first time in my academic career I have felt included on an equal basis which has been fantastic.

> (Student who is blind)

The Premia team has designed online staff resources and student materials which aim to address the issues identified by students in the research phase. They are aimed at all those who intervene in the research student's life. Users can enter the resources by their role and choose relevant options. They will not provide definitive answers to all questions, but we hope that they will give insight into disability issues in the context of research, allow staff to explore reasonable adjustments to policy and practice, suggest ways of making research education more accessible and encourage disabled graduates to enter, and succeed in, the research community.

Acknowledgements

Thanks are due to all the students who willingly and openly shared their time and experiences. We agreed that their names and institutions would remain anonymous but the project would not have been possible without their generosity and insight. Also thanks to Dr Stan Taylor and Dr Jo Whaley for wise words on content and structure.

References and further reading

Farrar, V. (2004) *Access to Research: Institutional Issues for Disabled Postgraduate Research Students*. Newcastle upon Tyne: University of Newcastle. Available at: http://www.ncl.ac.uk/disability-services/postgradresearch (accessed 06/05).

Farrar, V. and Warin, P. (2005) *Resources: Premia – Making Research Education Accessible*. Newcastle upon Tyne: University of Newcastle upon Tyne. Available at: www.premia.ac.uk (accessed 06/05).

Grix, J. (2001) *Demystifying Postgraduate Research: From MA to PhD*. Birmingham: The University of Birmingham Press.

Higher Education Funding Council for England (2005) *PhD Research Degrees: Entry and Completion*. Issues paper 2005/02. Bristol: Higher Education Funding Council for England.

Chapter 16

Conclusion

A manifesto for mainstreaming inclusive practice

As a conclusion to this book, we draw upon a meeting at the National Disability Team conference in Watford at the end of April 2005, at which the majority of chapter authors were present. During a brainstorming session, we explored ideas to form the basis of a manifesto for mainstreaming inclusive practice in higher education, with further inputs gathered from authors not present.

We believe that if we are to achieve inclusive practice in higher education, and move away from *ad hoc* arrangements which treat disabled students as special cases deserving of special treatment, we need to do the following:

- Stop adopting practices which predominantly focus on adjustments and start thinking about inclusive curriculum and assessment design which offer all students choices that align with their abilities. All students are likely to benefit from the flexibility in time, mode and place that is often seen as the basis of making reasonable adjustments.
- Engage disabled students in the debate that goes into curriculum design, so that inclusive practices are informed by authentic voices.
- Think inclusively when designing assessment instruments, so that alternatives are built in at the outset which enable disabled students to have an equivalent assessment experience. There are more innovative and effective alternatives to simply allowing extra time or assessing students in separate rooms, which are likely to benefit all students, not just those who are disabled.
- Ensure that standards are maintained in terms of the quality, scale and scope of work expected. We do nobody any favours if we accept lower standards of achievement from disabled students than we expect from their peers.
- Build credibility by creating a rigorous and evidence-based pedagogy that convinces both disability practitioners and those within the academic community that inclusive practice is not only right but also highly effective, and that effective pedagogy for disabled students is effective pedagogy for all students.
- Actively engage in research into inclusive learning and teaching, reading and using the literature available, adopting action learning approaches, monitoring

the successes of our initiatives, fine tuning our practices and disseminating widely what we find to work well.

- Embed disability matters into the curriculum for all students, so that disability awareness is mainstreamed and fellow students engage in inclusive practices themselves, for example, in group work and peer assessment.
- Balance the need for subject-specific materials and case studies with generic approaches that draw out principles and processes that can transfer to other contexts, subjects, programmes and across the range of impairments.
- Recognise that the same kind of issues and challenges are often faced across an institution. All too frequently within and between HEIs, the 'silo mentality' means there is rarely effective sharing of simple and subtle solutions to common issues.
- Undertake strategic thinking and strategic action. Only by demonstrating joined-up thinking will we increase effectiveness and make a genuine impact on mainstream higher education.
- Harness the sense of social justice, equality and fairness that motivates most higher education practitioners, by providing them with practical resources and guidance that make it straightforward to be inclusive.
- Maintain a focus on learning that sees learning from a learner's point of view, releasing the power of the student voice to make their higher education experiences transformative.
- Recognise that disabled students, like other students, are consumers of higher education, often paying significant amounts in fees and that they are increasingly likely to use their power as consumers to make their feelings heard if inclusive practice is absent.
- Recognise also that there is a good business case to be made for actively recruiting as students disabled people who, up until now, have been disadvantaged by non-inclusive practices.
- Look for synergies between different types of disability practitioners and make use of constructive partnerships between staff in a range of roles across HEIs to act as catalysts for change.
- Recognise the fuzzy and complex nature of concepts of 'disabled' and 'disabled student/learner', which makes inclusivity challenging on occasions.
- Use technologies in support of inclusive practice effectively. While they can make a positive difference to disabled students, they can also present extra barriers to learning where they have been thoughtlessly designed.
- Promote pragmatic and engaging academic/staff development to raise awareness of inclusive practice.
- Capture and effectively disseminate good professional practice. Projects associated with disability often make use of 'soft funding', with staff employed on short-term contracts leading to consequential loss of collective learning as projects terminate.
- Continue to reflect regularly on our practice to ensure continuous improvement and learning from the experiences of others.

- Recognise the considerable achievements to date in improving inclusive practice, not least those fostered by the National Disability Team in the UK, while acknowledging the importance of avoiding complacency and continuously striving to create an equality of opportunity for all learners.

Index